IMAGES
of America

STORY CITY

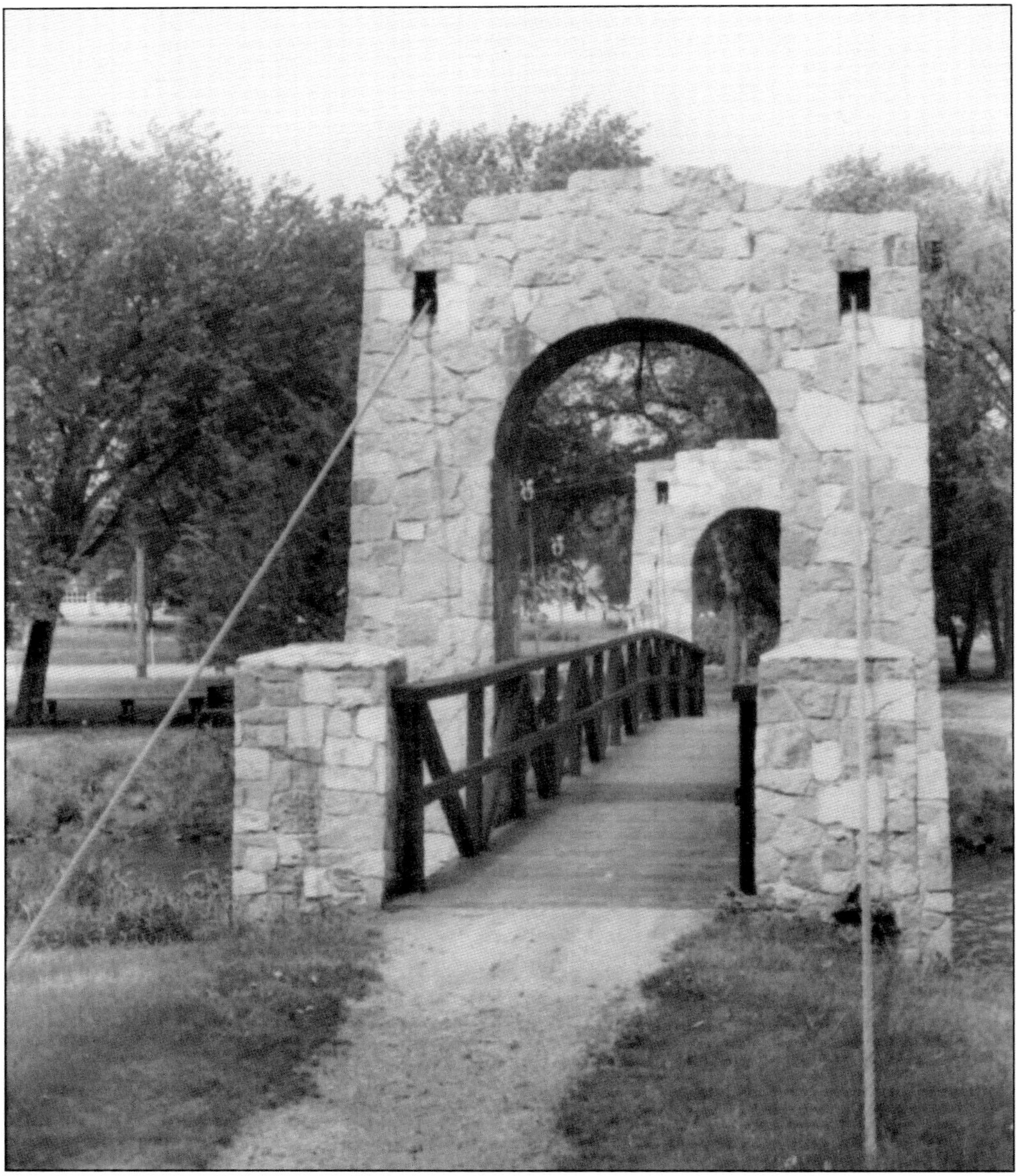

Constructed in 1936 as a Works Progress Administration project, the swinging bridge in South Park is one of the many historic jewels in Story City. The surrounding area consists of beautiful picnic grounds popular with local residents and tourists alike. (Courtesy Story City Historical Society.)

On the Cover: Following an early spring blizzard, Story City residents dig through a snowdrift blocking a road into town on March 23, 1923. Pictured in no definite order are O.L. Ose, John Lee, Ben Holm, Sande, Lester Swenson, Ed Charlson, Ding Larson, Tom Matson, Chris Lebness, Chris Johnson, Bert Egenes, Otis Sevde, Fritchoff Larson, and Bill Petersen. (Courtesy Story City Historical Society.)

IMAGES of America

STORY CITY

Darrek D. Orwig

ARCADIA PUBLISHING

ISBN 978-0-7385-9396-8

Published by Arcadia Publishing
Charleston, South Carolina

Printed in the United States of America

Library of Congress Control Number: 2012935509

For all general information, please contact Arcadia Publishing:
Telephone 843-853-2070
Fax 843-853-0044
E-mail sales@arcadiapublishing.com
For customer service and orders:
Toll-Free 1-888-313-2665

Visit us on the Internet at www.arcadiapublishing.com

To those who sailed from distant shores and traversed Iowa prairies, whose hard work under adversity provided a foundation for Story City to grow and prosper.

Contents

ACKNOWLEDGMENTS

As director of the Story City Historical Society, I have been exceptionally impressed with the quality efforts undertaken to preserve the community's rich heritage for future generations. Early historians such as Nehemias Tjernagle documented many pioneer experiences in the late 19th century as those who settled the tall prairie began passing into the ages. His work of recording this early history paints for us today a very vivid portrait of what life was like for those who took enormous risks to establish new lives along the muddy banks of the Skunk River.

Paul Olson, an editor of the *Story City Herald*, documented early life in Story City, publishing a number of locally produced works using contemporary photographs and historical accounts. His efforts provide researchers of various levels with a wonderful snapshot of what life was like in the Story City area. In 1976, Jil Ose continued this tradition of recording Story City history, including not just historical material but also contemporary work that could be of use to future historians.

In recent years, Peter Harstad and Margaret Harstad Matze have brought many pioneer stories from the Story City area to life. Their talented works have shared the tales of Norwegian immigrants who transformed the rich prairie sod into productive farmland that today is part of our nation's breadbasket.

On top of the remarkable efforts to preserve Story City's history through writing, efforts have also been made through the curating of tangible artifacts and by presentations of community history at the Story City Historical Society. The photographs used in this work are from the Story City Historical Society's collection, graciously donated by those with ties to the community's history. With hard work provided by historical society volunteers, board members, and board presidents, the Story City Historical Society today is a progressive community museum system. My hope is that this book will complement their efforts.

All images appear courtesy of the Story City Historical Society.

Introduction

On foot and horseback along with heavily packed wagons, the first pioneers to the Story City area arrived in the 1850s. Wading through the tall prairie grass and scattered timber along the muddy banks of the Skunk River, they decided to settle on a tract of land with seemingly unlimited potential. The soil was rich and dark, waves of prairie grass flowed all the way to the horizon, a lazy river meandered through a valley with ample hardwoods, and the tide of a westward bound civilization was fast approaching at their heels. With the vast natural resources available, early pioneers began transforming the prairie landscape into productive farmland. Although living close to nature and working the earth while surrounded by family was appealing, it was far from easy.

When one visits a pioneer cemetery in the Story City area, it is easy to see the cost of transforming the prairie into the breadbasket of the world. An abundance of small gravestones mark child burials, a large fieldstone denotes the final resting place of a family burned alive in a prairie fire, and the grave markers of a number of women next to a single man show the health difficulties pioneer women experienced.

Despite the hardships of life on the frontier, the people of the Story City area persevered, and the population continued to expand. One of the key factors to this growth was Scandinavian immigrants arriving from Norway, Denmark, and Sweden. These new pioneers began arriving in the late 1850s, just as tensions started to reach a boiling point over the issue of slavery.

In 1860, an election was held in the Story City area at the still-standing Sheldall Schoolhouse. Lincoln won in a landslide and, following the secession of the Confederate states, Story City area men answered their nation's call and served in a number of different Union regiments. Their wartime experiences helped shape their outlook on the nation and had a major influence on the development of the community.

Following the Civil War, the prairie continued to be heavily settled as people were able to gain access to Story County through the railroad and mechanized horse-drawn machinery made homesteading on the frontier much easier. As other communities began sprouting up around the county, Story City was required to take steps to ensure the community would survive.

Through a great deal of effort, Story City received its first railroad in 1878, and as a result, the community was required to change the center of town from the pioneer community of Fairview to along where the current Main Street district exists today. In 1881, the town of Story City was incorporated and merged with the Fairview settlement. The railroad attracted farm commodities from around the area and the community continued to grow and expand. Later, in 1886, another railroad line entered Story City from Marshalltown.

The end of the 19th century saw additional growth in the community due to new waves of immigrants. At one point, newspapers in a number of different languages served the community. In addition to immigrants, the population continued to swell with newcomers arriving from different parts of the country.

In the early 20th century, there were many additions to the community's Main Street district, consisting of brick commercial buildings that today have been rehabilitated into residential units, service-focused businesses, offices, and antique stores. The historical ambiance adds to the attraction of the vibrant Main Street, drawing significant heritage-related tourism.

The year 1913 was important for the community of Story City as it saw additional economic growth in the community and it was when the well-known carousel was built. Today, this carousel has been restored and is operational throughout the summer months as a tangible way for visitors to enjoy a glimpse of historical entertainment.

Story City has always promoted tourism and entertainment. The Story City band was a popular attraction in the community, playing in a variety of venues over a number of years. Additionally, Lake Comar, a manmade lake south of town, turned Story City into a summer resort community for a few decades in the early 20th century.

The years following World War I saw additional growth in the area, as the community paved the mud streets, gas stations replaced livery stables, and electric lights replaced the kerosene lanterns along Broad Street. These improvements slowed when the Great Depression struck, and although Story City was somewhat insulated from the depths of suffering in other parts of the country, there are still tangible reminders of this period. The suspension bridge in the South Park was constructed as a Works Progress Administration project in the 1930s. This footbridge has become part of the community's identity and is featured on stationery from the chamber of commerce office.

After the attack on Pearl Harbor, many Story City residents served in the armed forces in World War II. Copies of the *Story City Herald* from the era have survived and the front-page news includes stories of men missing in action, wounded, or killed in such faraway places as the jungles of the Pacific, the mountains of Italy, and the snowy forests of France. Next to these articles are pieces about the home front, where those unable to serve in the military were engaging in scrap drives, Red Cross knitting, and wartime rationing. The sacrifices and sense of togetherness displayed in the community are well documented and are an inspiration for future generations.

Today, Story City has a vibrant economy with a strong manufacturing element along Interstate 35, just to the east of town. The appreciation for history in the community led to the progressive development of a local historical society, which has grown to four exhibit buildings in its few decades of operation. Heritage tourism remains strong as visitors ride the 1913 carousel, shop at the variety of antique stores, and take in the beautiful architecture of the historic commercial district and the shade tree–lined residential neighborhoods throughout the city.

Story City is a unique central Iowa community with a rich heritage. As many small communities fade away in rural Iowa, Story City continues to maintain a strong presence due to its values of hard work, thrift, progress, and higher education. In 100 years, I have no doubt that there will be future history books written about Story City and how it has maintained its place on the former prairie landscape.

One

The Pioneer Period

In 1853, Lafayette Township of Story County was organized and pioneer settlers began making the trek across the tall grass prairie of central Iowa to make their new home along the wooded banks of the Skunk River. In 1855, the town of Fairview was incorporated, consisting of roughly 13 acres on high ground above the timbered river bottom.

With a few small log buildings, including a blacksmith shop for repairing wagons and agricultural equipment, Fairview began attracting other pioneers who could acquire the unimproved rich prairie soil for $1.25 per acre. A small steam-powered sawmill was temporarily set up on the banks of the river, providing native lumber for early building projects. As the community grew in popularity, the post office determined that there was already a Fairview, Iowa, and eventually the community changed its name to Story City.

The potential of quality land at a good price caught the eye of Norwegian immigrants living in Lisbon, Illinois. After a brief visit by a party led by Torkel Henryson, a number of acres were purchased and Scandinavian immigrants began arriving in the community. The financial panic of 1857 slowed down the stream of new settlers arriving in the area to a trickle, but in the years that followed, the number of pioneers increased.

During the Civil War, men from Story City answered the president's call for volunteers. A large number of men enlisted, with the greatest numbers being in the 23rd and 32nd Iowa Infantry Regiments. Upon their return after the end of the war, these former soldiers played a large role in organizing and developing the community.

In the years that followed the Civil War, the necessity of a railroad was impressed among community leaders and, after great efforts to secure one, a line was built to Story City in 1878. This development had a crucial impact on the viability of the pioneer community, and with new economic growth along Broad Street, Story City was incorporated into a city in 1881.

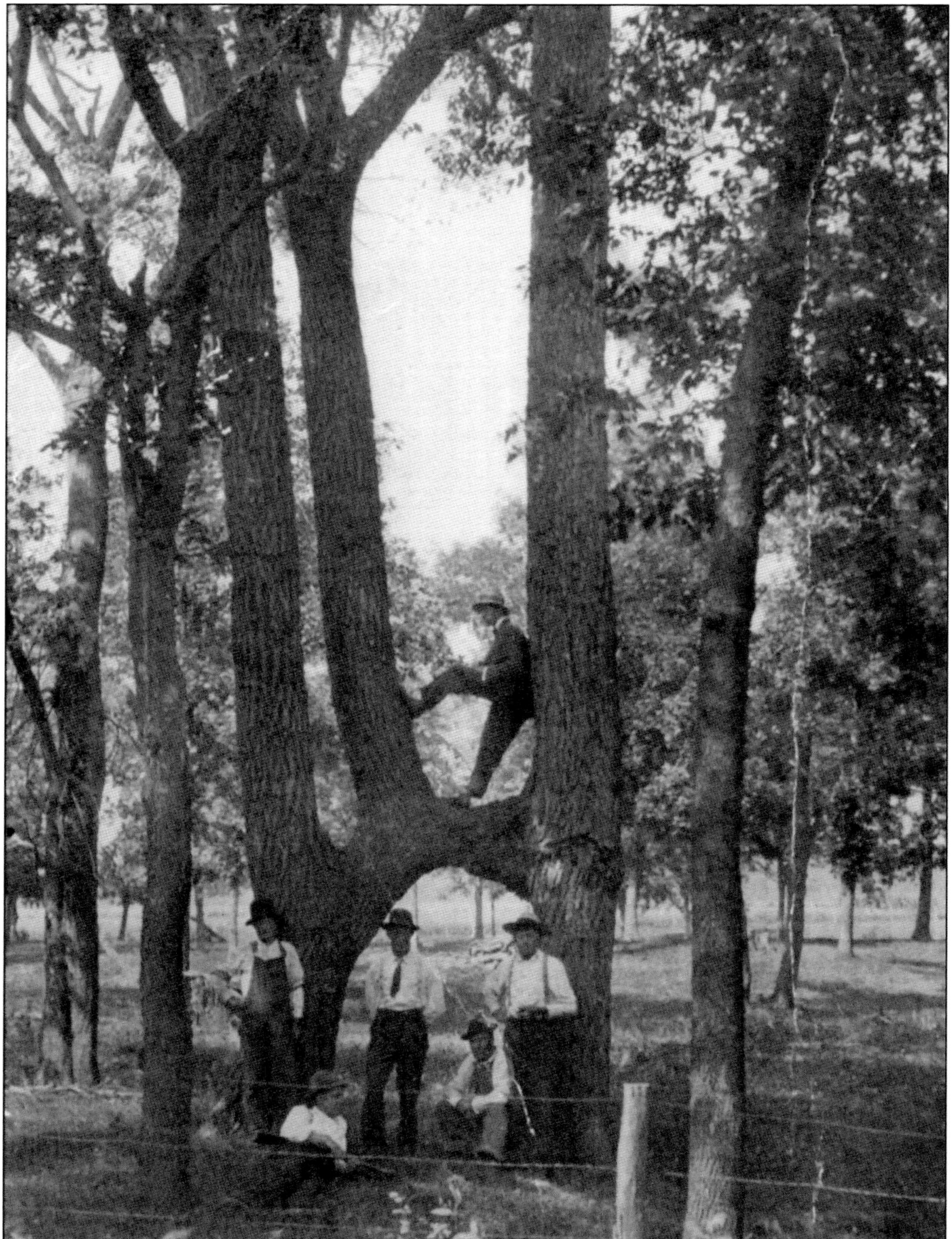

The "H" Tree was a landmark along the Skunk River south of Story City. Early pioneers were fascinated with this unusual elm tree and it drew attention across central Iowa. Scholars have determined that the unique tree was probably the result of a sapling altered by Native Americans for the marking of a river ford, quite possibly by the Johnny Green band of Prairie Pottawattamie, who migrated to the Story City area in the early 19th century.

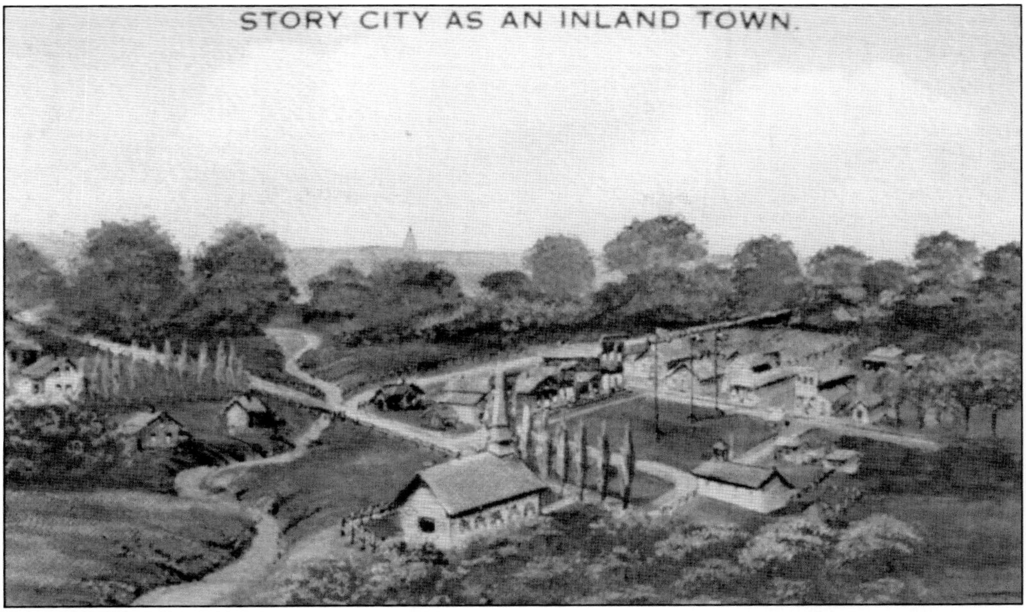

This artist's rendition of the first pioneer community in Story City, Fairview, was likely based on an illustration in the 1875 Andreas Atlas of Iowa. Fairview was established in 1855 across the street from what is now the Story City Historical Society, near the current high school. Consisting of log buildings and simple frame homes of locally produced lumber, Fairview continued to grow through the early settlement period. In 1881, Story City was incorporated on Broad Street to be closer to the railroad and the name was changed from Fairview because another town in Iowa already had the name. As a result, many businesses moved to Broad Street, where today's Main Street business district still is.

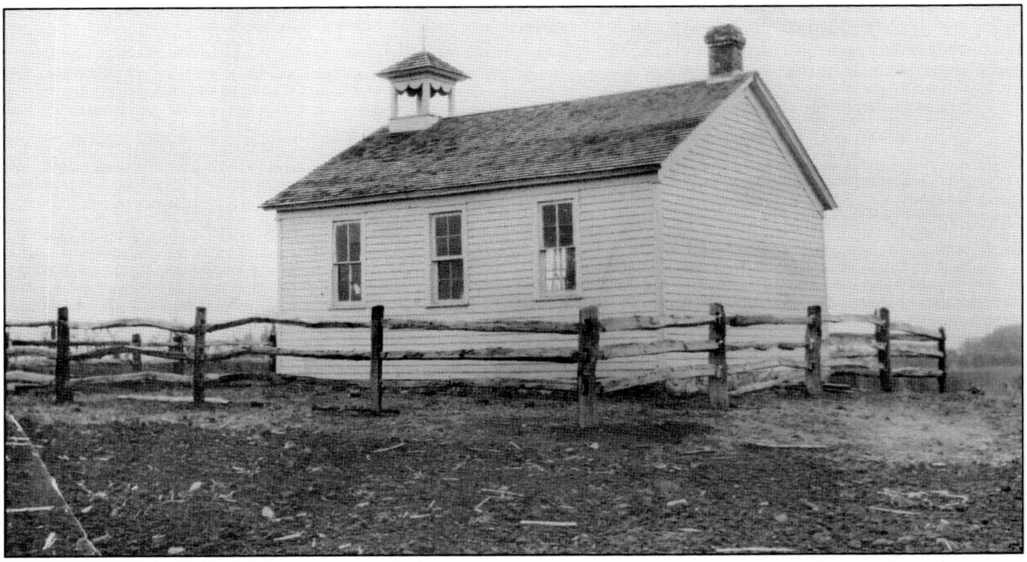

An early school, church, and polling location, the Sheldall Schoolhouse was a vital community building in the pioneer period. Built in 1860 just north of Story City by Lars Sheldall, much of the lumber was from trees harvested locally along the Skunk River. The school was used for educational purposes until the 1880s, when it was converted into a practice room for the Riverside Cornet Band. It was later used as a dwelling and was moved to a few different area locations.

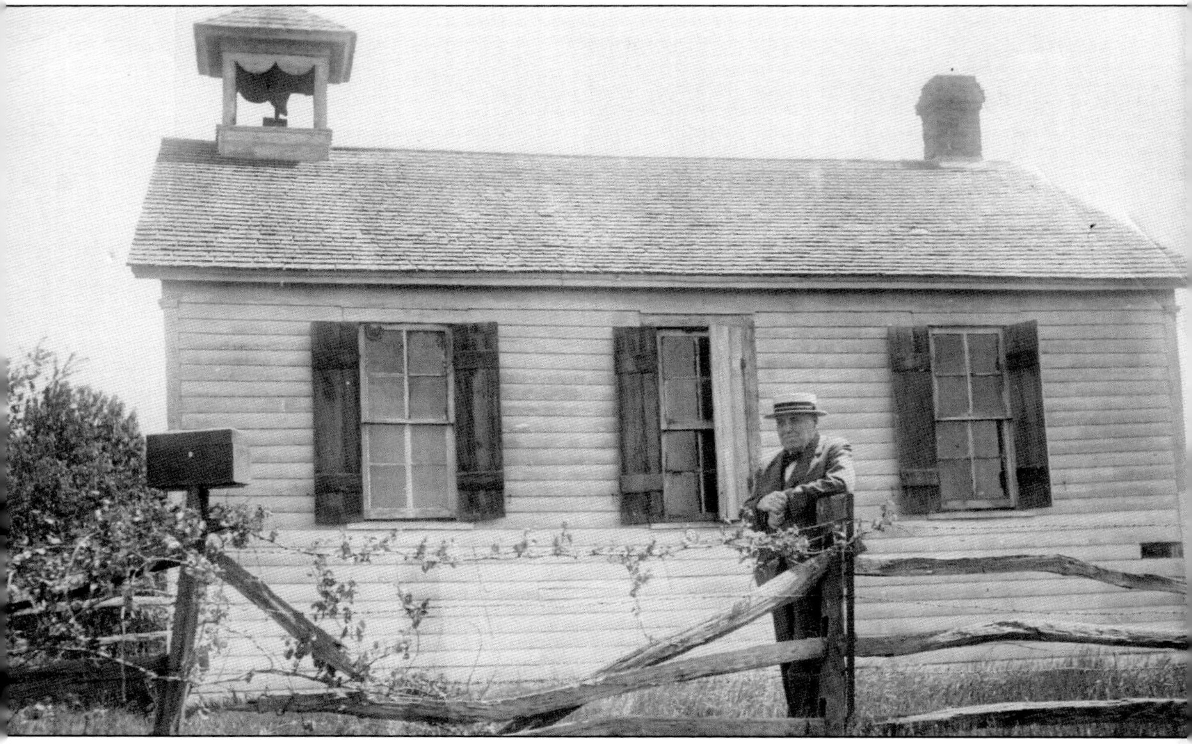

A.M. Henderson leans on a fencepost in front of the Sheldall Schoolhouse. Atop one of the fence posts is a walnut ballot box used in the election of Abraham Lincoln in 1860. In the early 1900s, the Sheldall School became a repository of pioneer period artifacts from the Story City area. Today, that tradition continues as the surviving school building is owned by the Story City Historical Society and is operated as a museum.

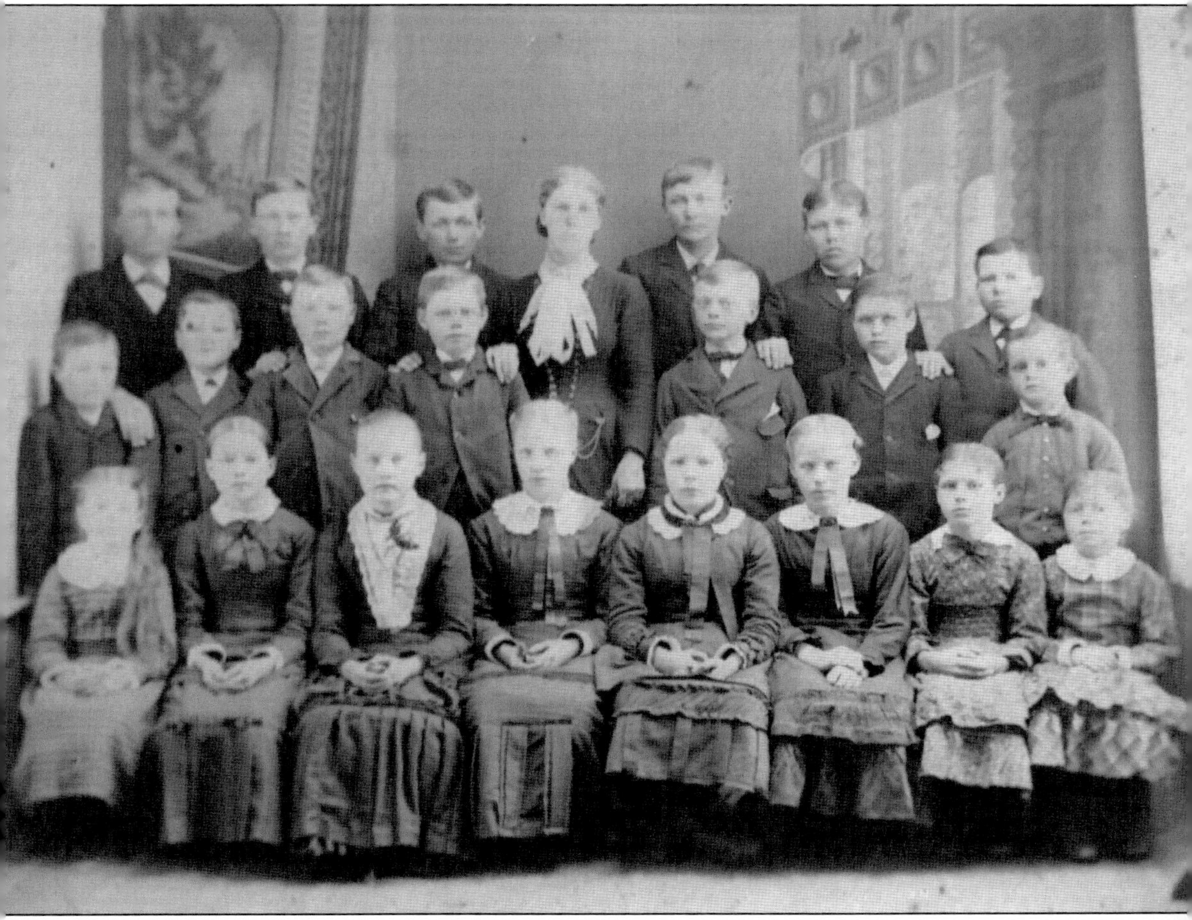

This class photograph taken in a local photography studio shows Sheldall School students in March 1884. The names of the students are listed in the archives of the Story City Historical Society.

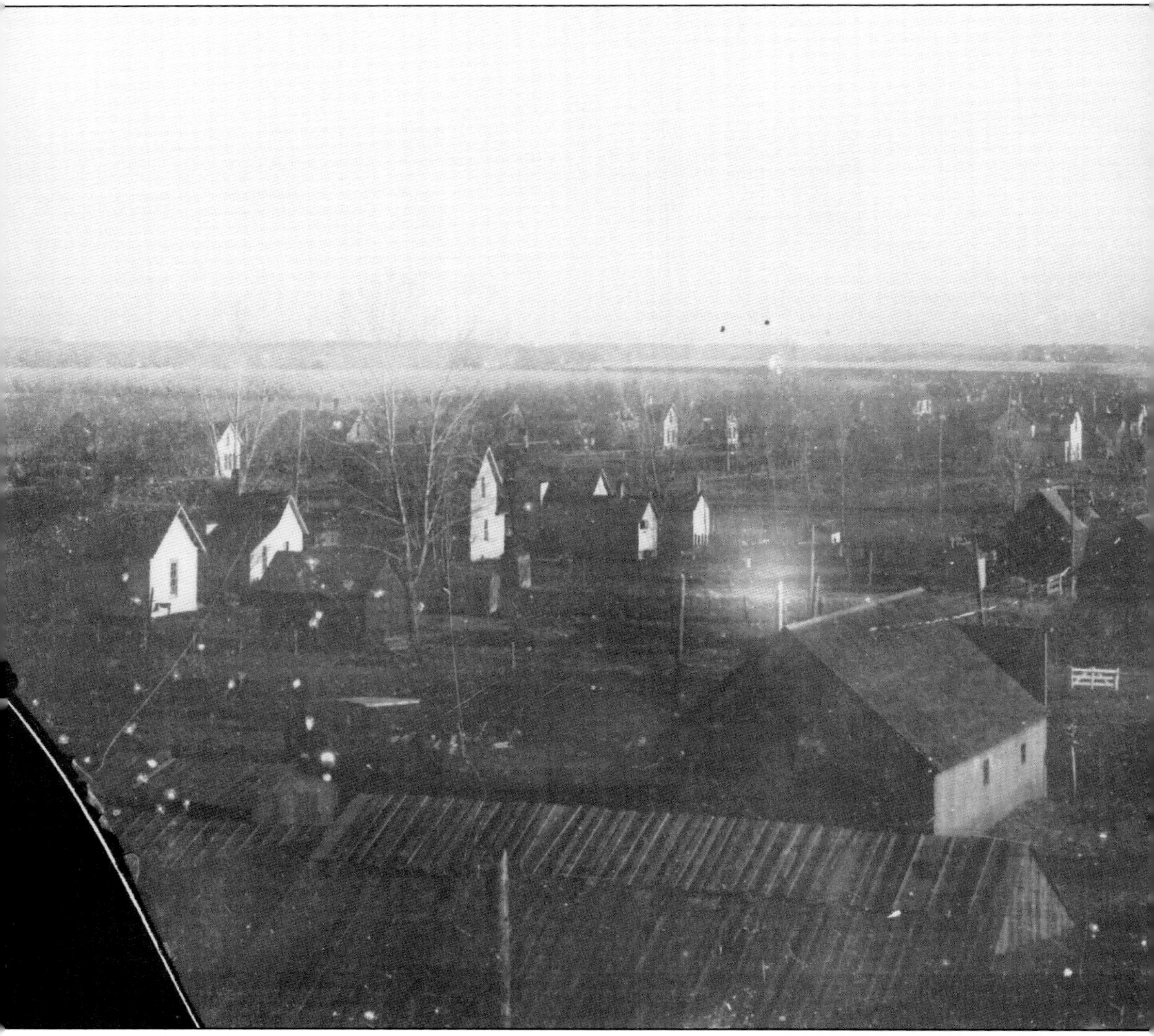

This early bird's-eye view of the Story City community shows the types of architecture in the area and how city lots were laid out. Many city lots were larger and incorporated small-scale agriculture to supplement the family's diet.

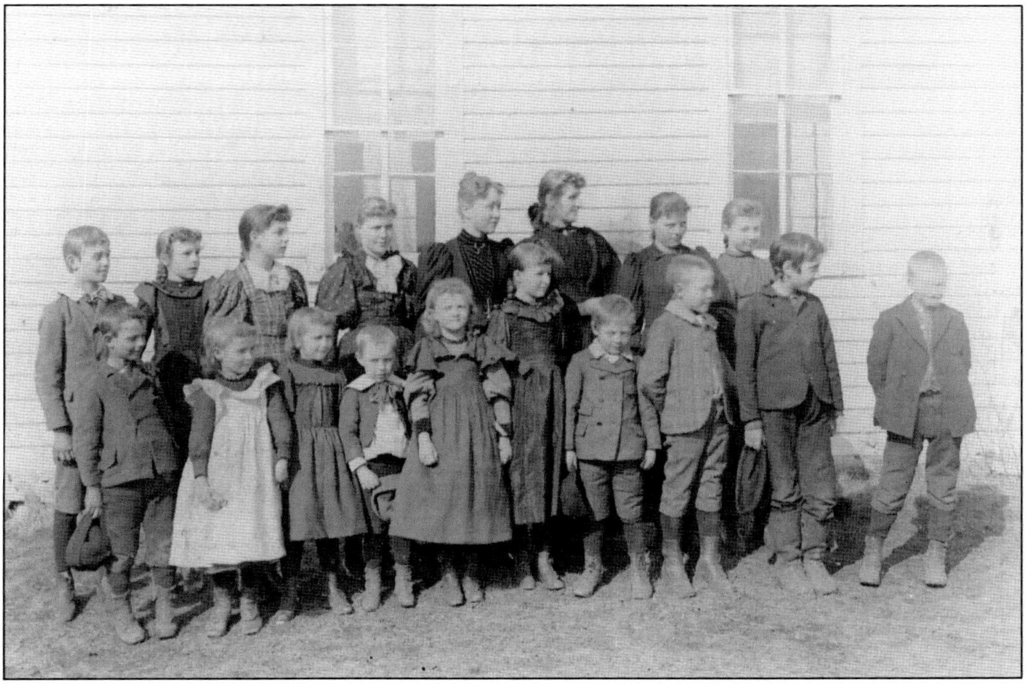

This early, unidentified class stands next to a one-room schoolhouse in the Story City area. Students were expected to not only learn but also to engage in chores around the building, such as maintaining the cast-iron stove for heat during the brutal Iowa winters.

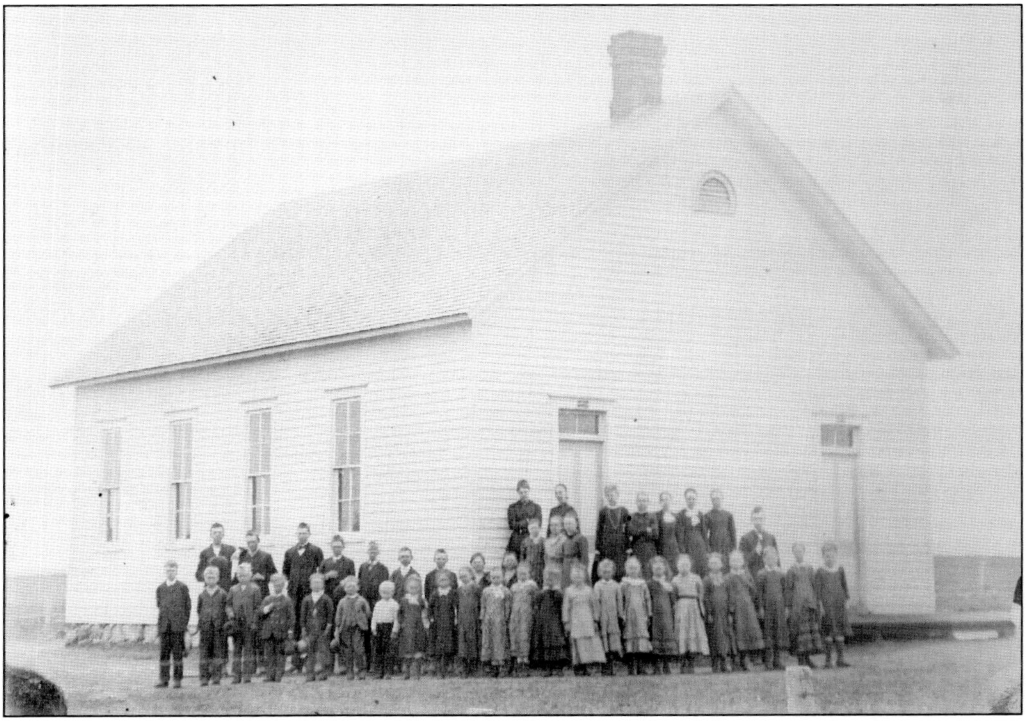

Students line up in front of the Branjord School for a photograph in 1881. The Branjord Schoolhouse was north of Story City.

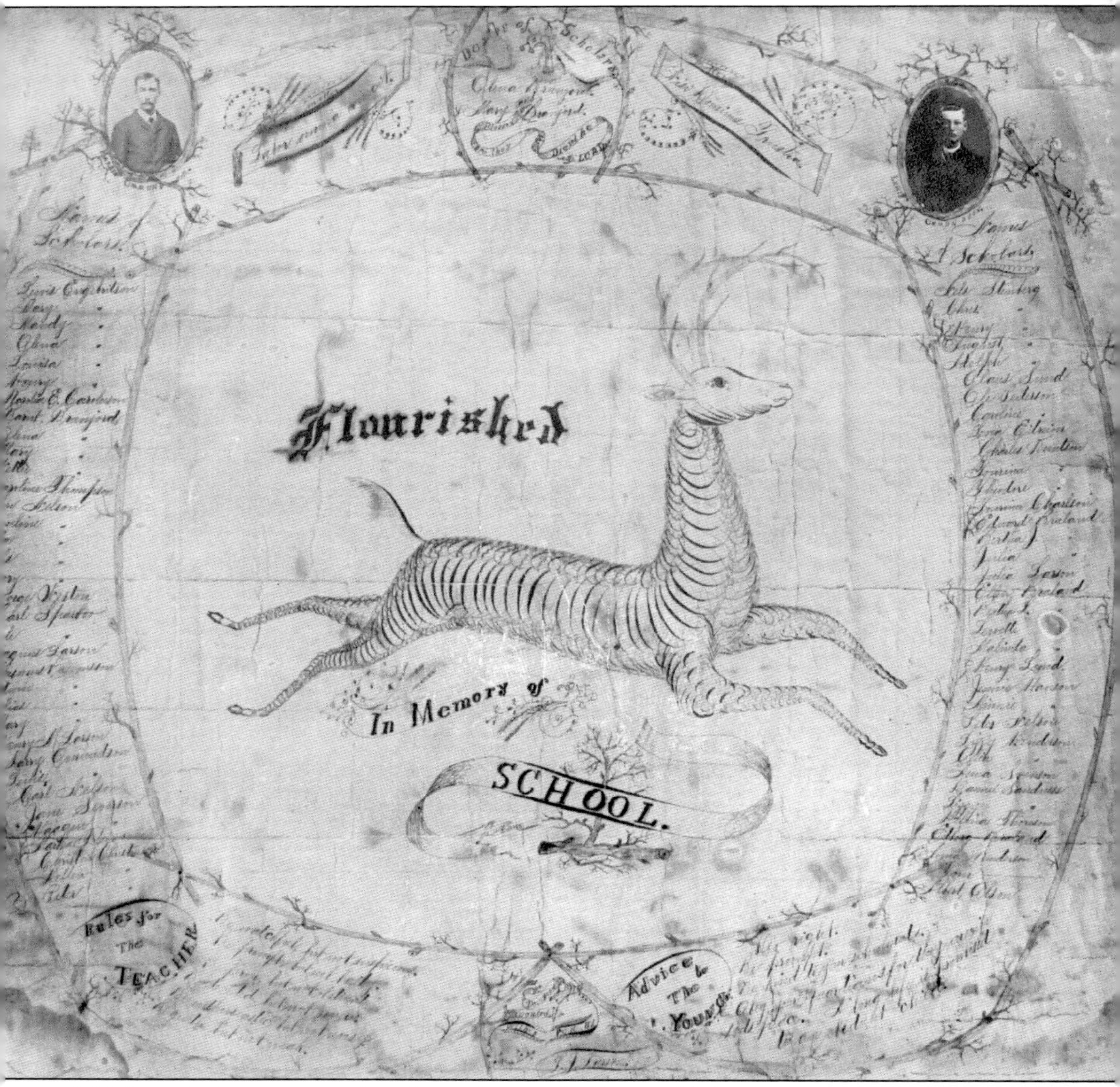

This historical paper poster lists the students at the Branjord Schoolhouse in the early 1880s. In the center is a deer illustration, which was used by students to master penmanship.

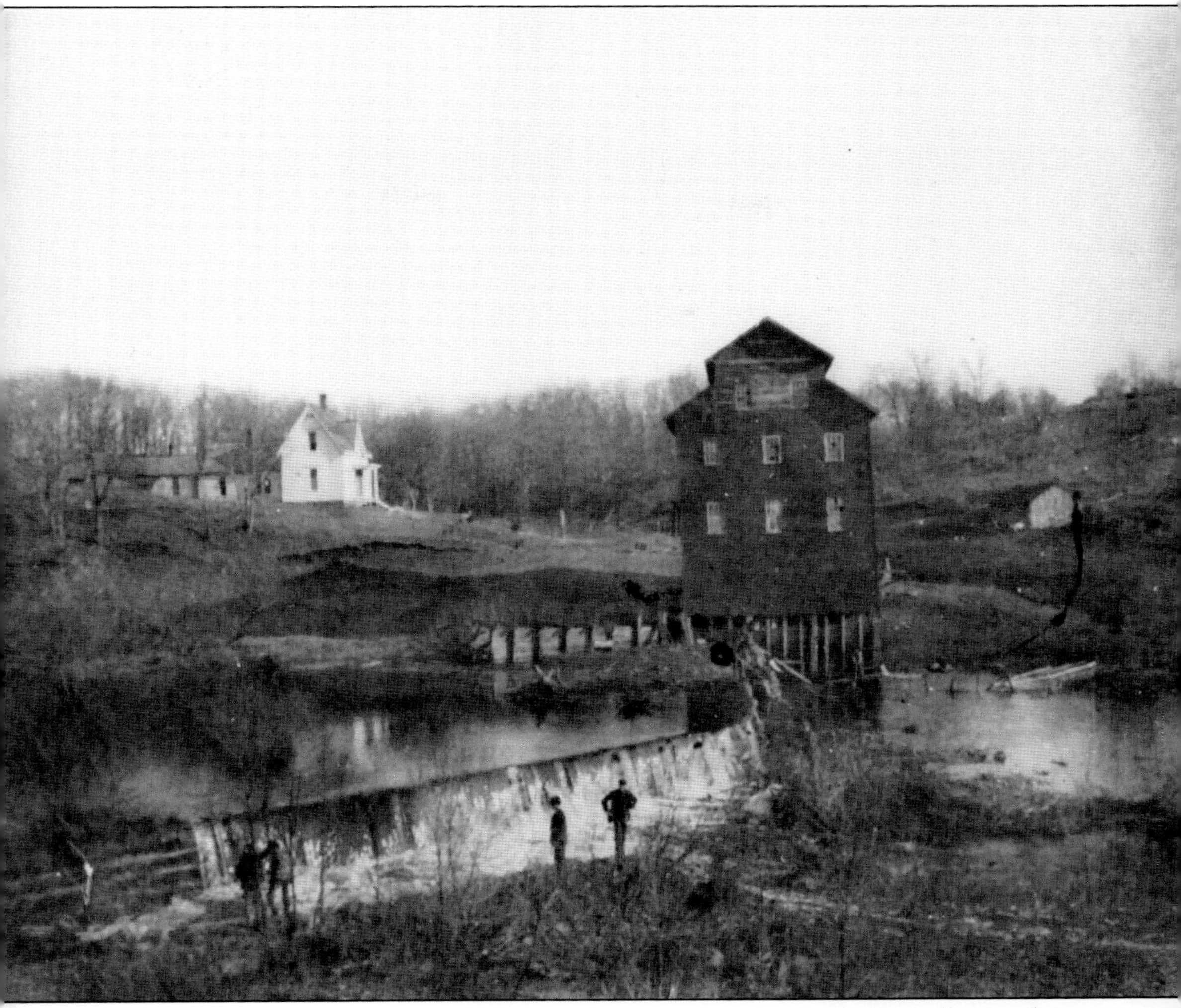

Soper's Mill, seen here in the 1870s, was an important resource for area farmers, allowing them to mill grain. Originally, a log dam stretched across the Skunk River, which required a large amount of maintenance due to floodwaters and floating ice in the spring. The site fell into disuse in the 1890s and remained abandoned for several decades until the building was razed. The site still exists today and is a county park south of Story City.

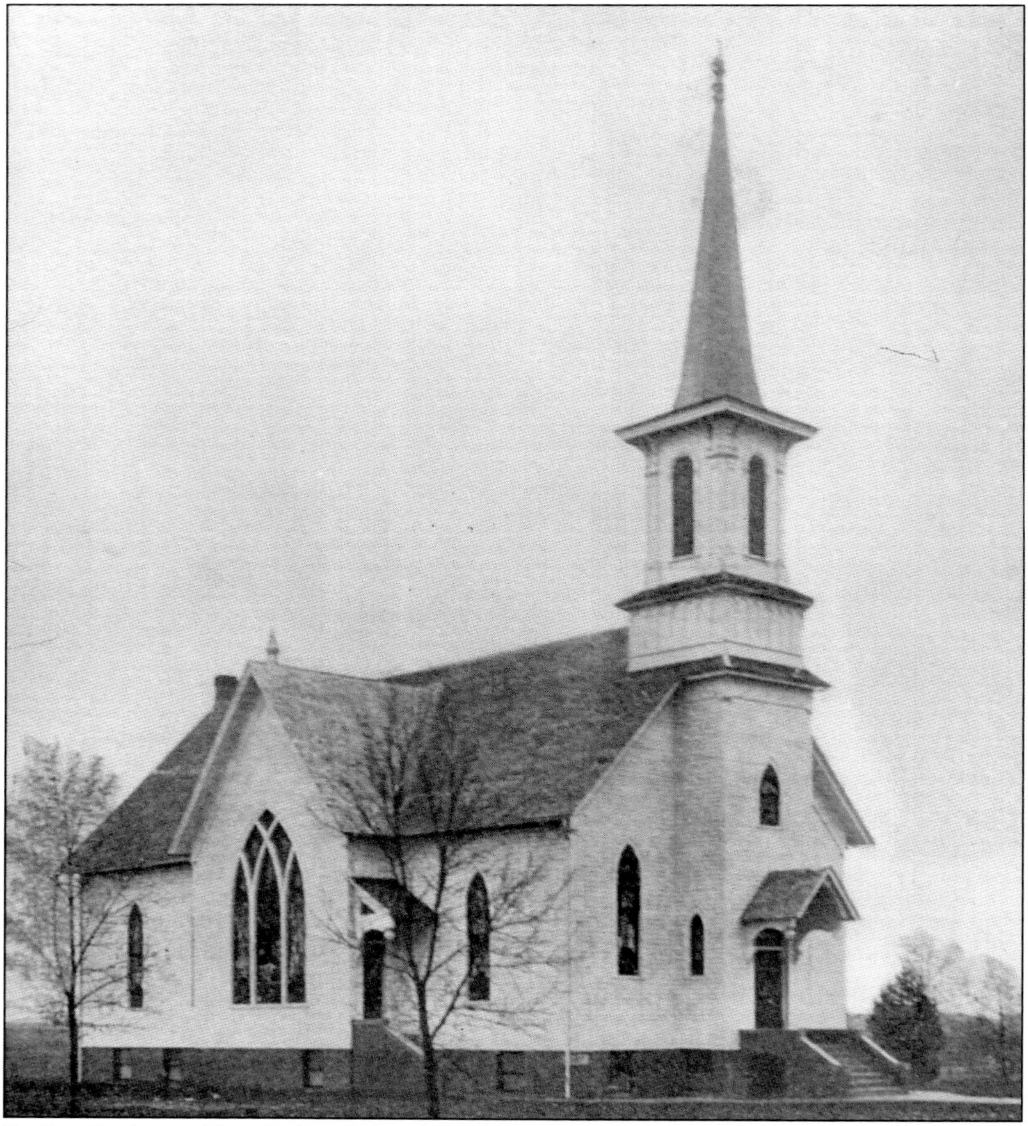

St. Petri Lutheran Church, founded in the 1850s, was the first Christian church in the Story City area. Until the construction of this larger building in the 1870s, the church met in the Sheldall Schoolhouse, where many early pioneers were baptized.

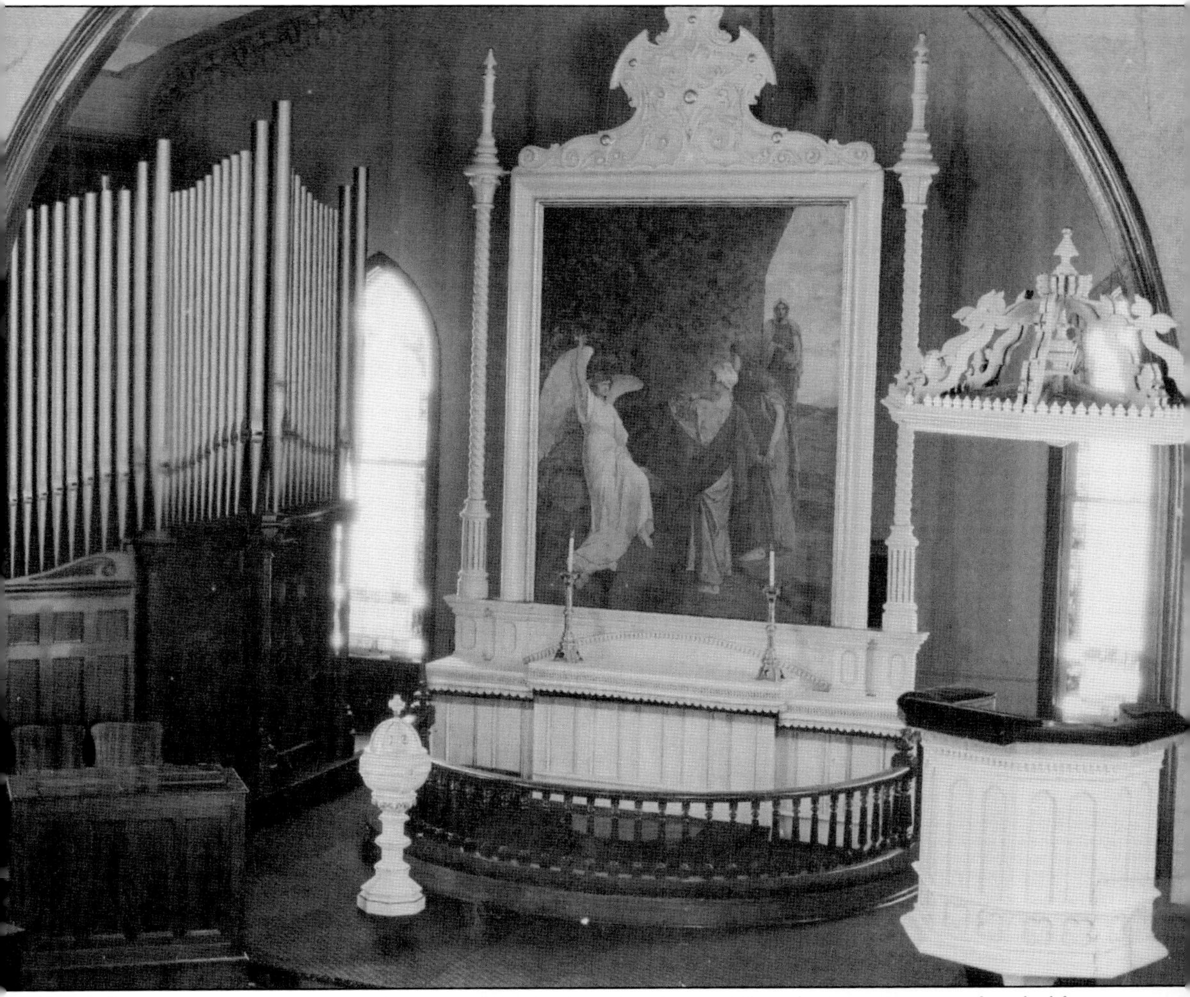

This is an interior view of the new 1870s St. Petri Lutheran Church. Services were first held in a local citizen's home until the Sheldall School House was constructed. In the 1870s, economical lumber from eastern markets allowed for the building of this large church. St. Petri had two church locations for part of the 19th century, one in Story City and one south of the community. The southern location was later moved to the town of Gilbert, a short drive south of Story City.

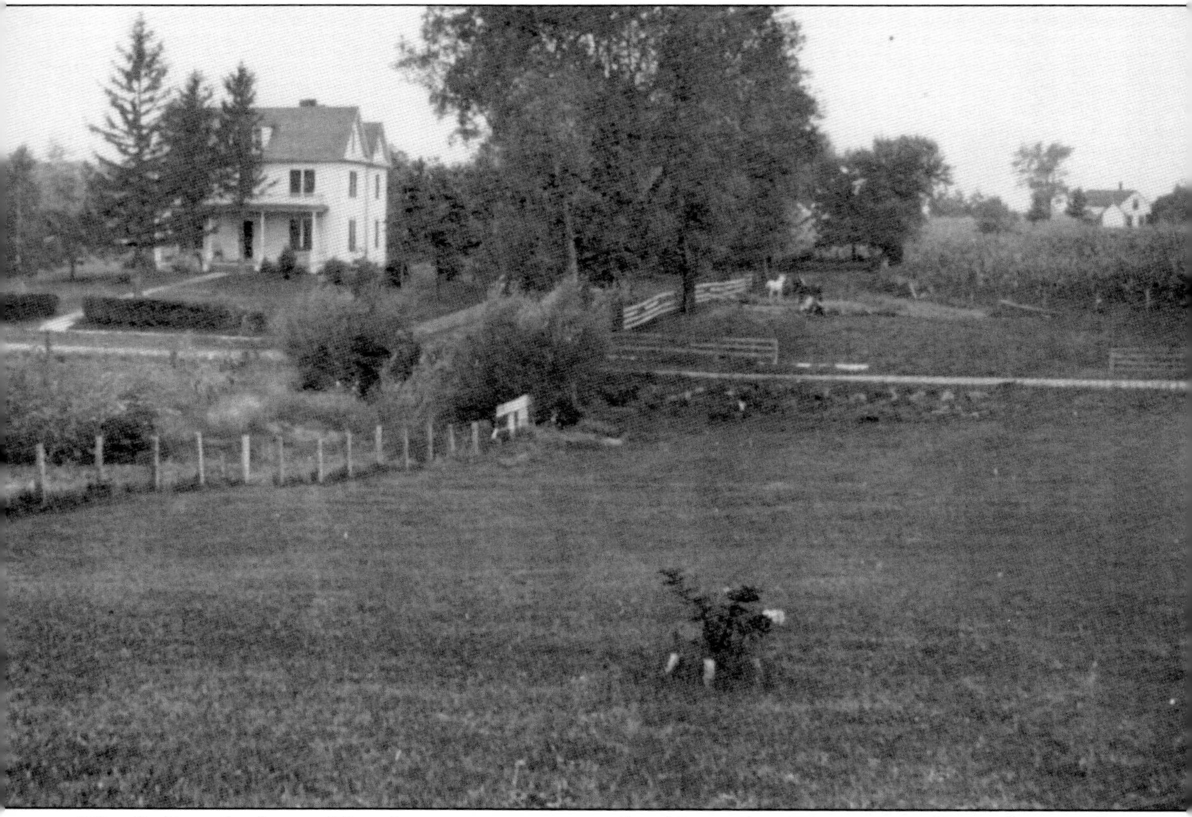

The St. Petri Lutheran Church parsonage was outside of Story City. This image offers a glimpse of what rural life was like in the area countryside. Early fencing included planks and split fence rails, and even hedgerows were experimented with as a way to protect farm fields and contain livestock.

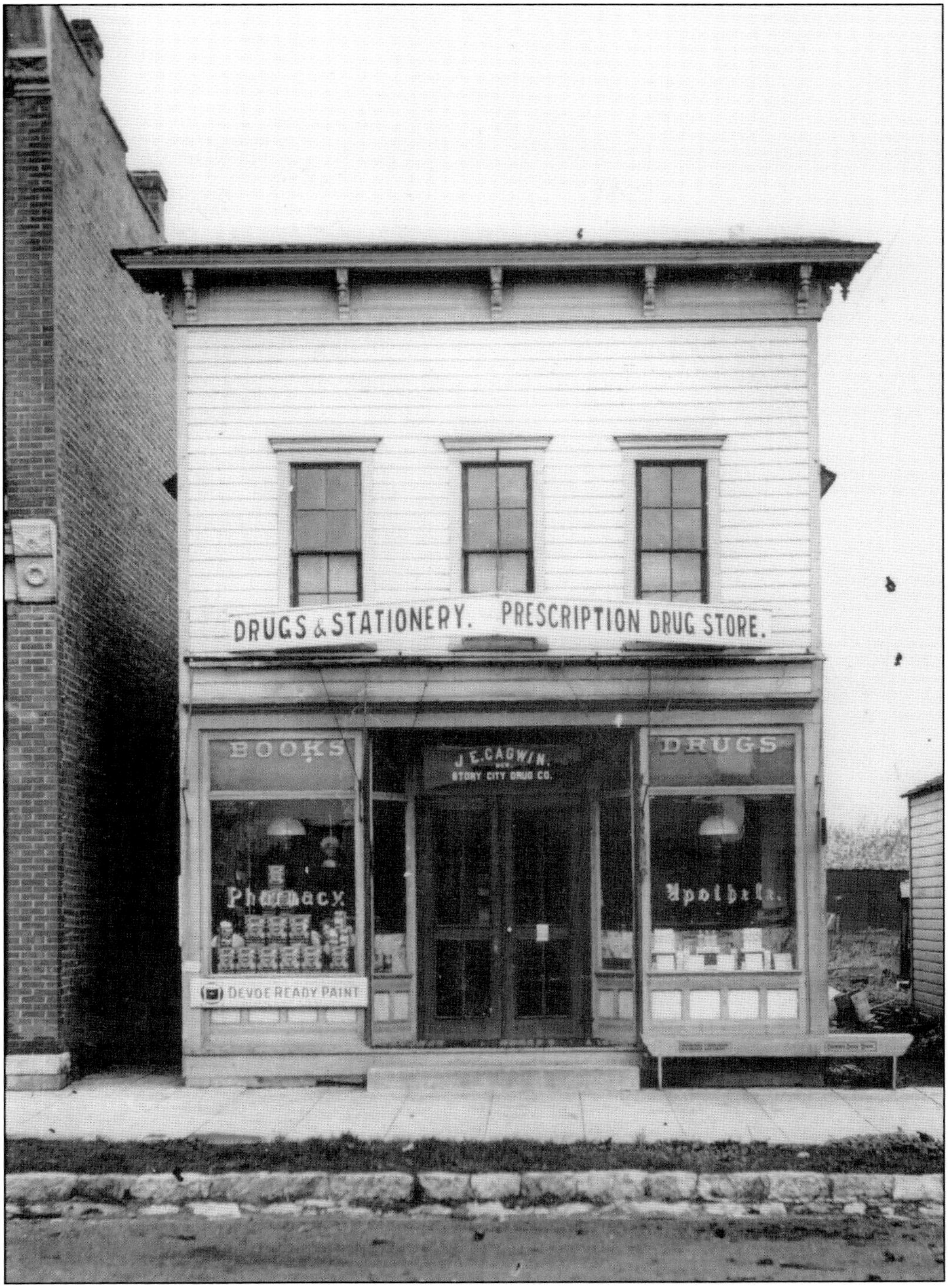

Located along Broad Street, the Story City Drug Company was managed by E. Cagwin and housed in a typical wood-frame commercial building from the mid-1800s. The local drugstore was where Story City residents could purchase medicine, seek health advice, purchase books and stationery, and acquire newly marketed ready-mixed paint, poison for nuisance control, and various forms of tobacco.

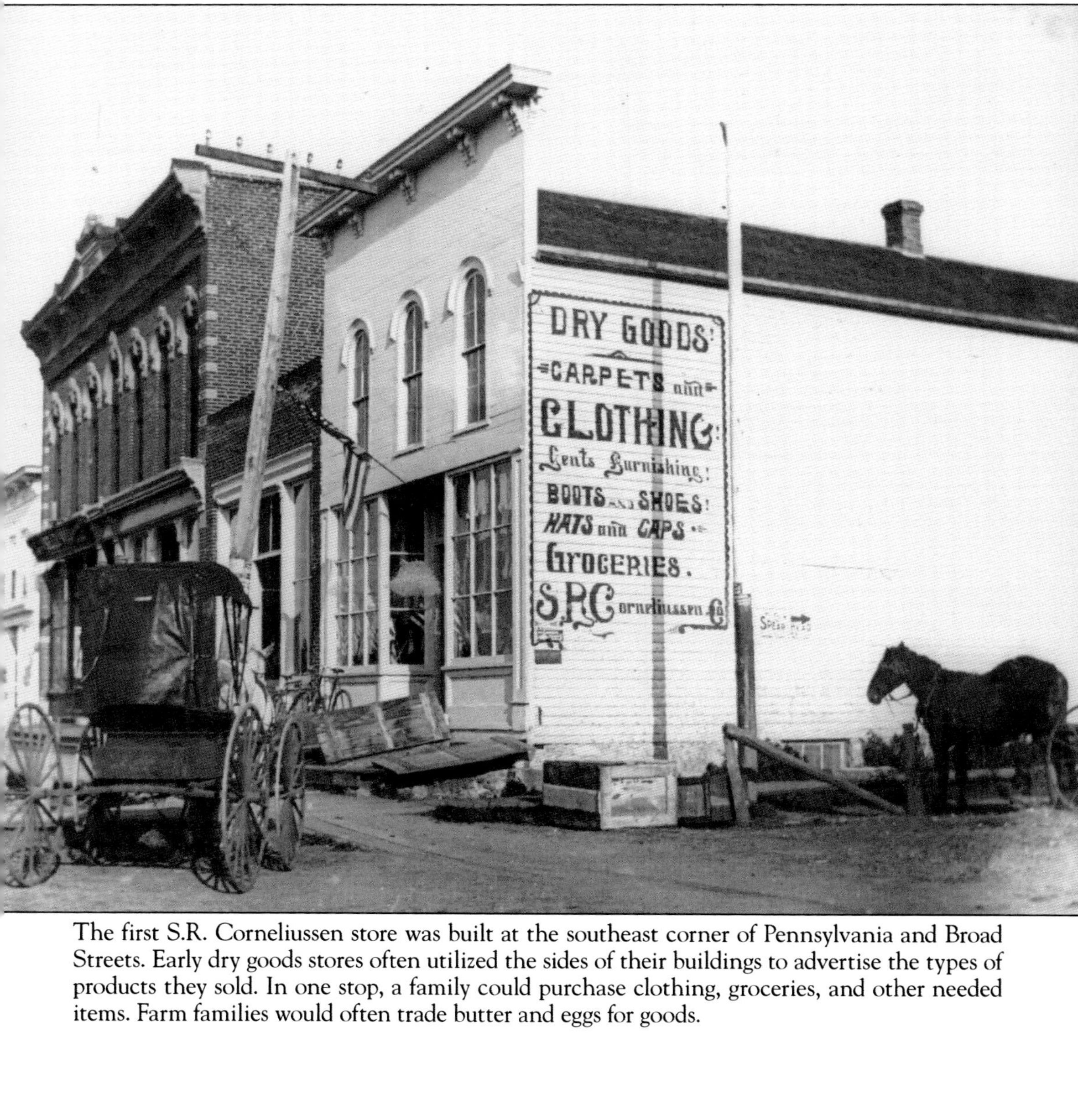

The first S.R. Corneliussen store was built at the southeast corner of Pennsylvania and Broad Streets. Early dry goods stores often utilized the sides of their buildings to advertise the types of products they sold. In one stop, a family could purchase clothing, groceries, and other needed items. Farm families would often trade butter and eggs for goods.

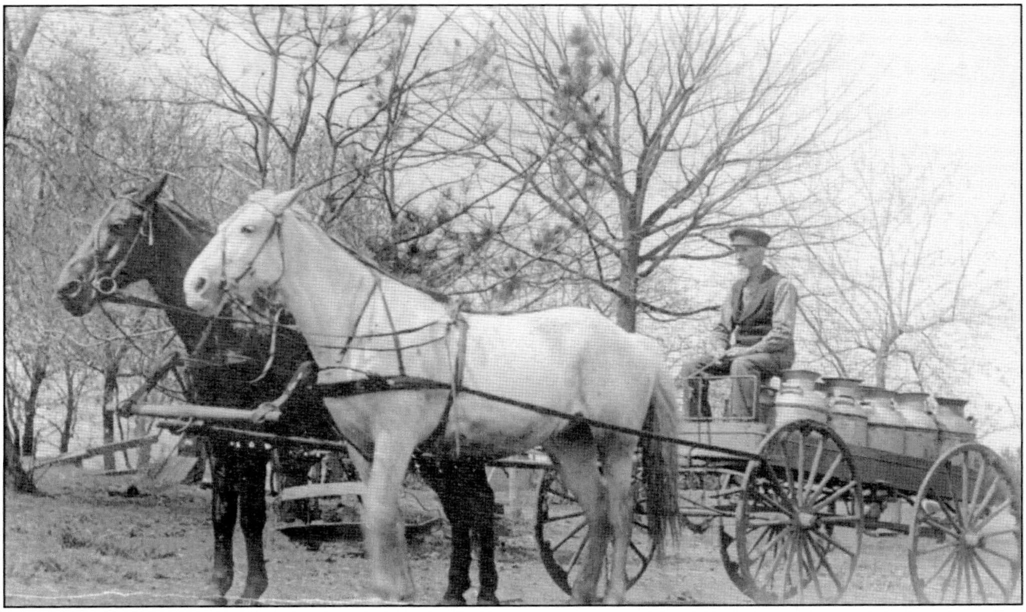

Dairy products were an important commodity for farm families in the Story City area. In the early days, cream and butter were valuable trade items to be exchanged at a local general store or used to pay down ledger-book credit. Cream and milk were transported in large metal cans across the countryside to creameries in Story City.

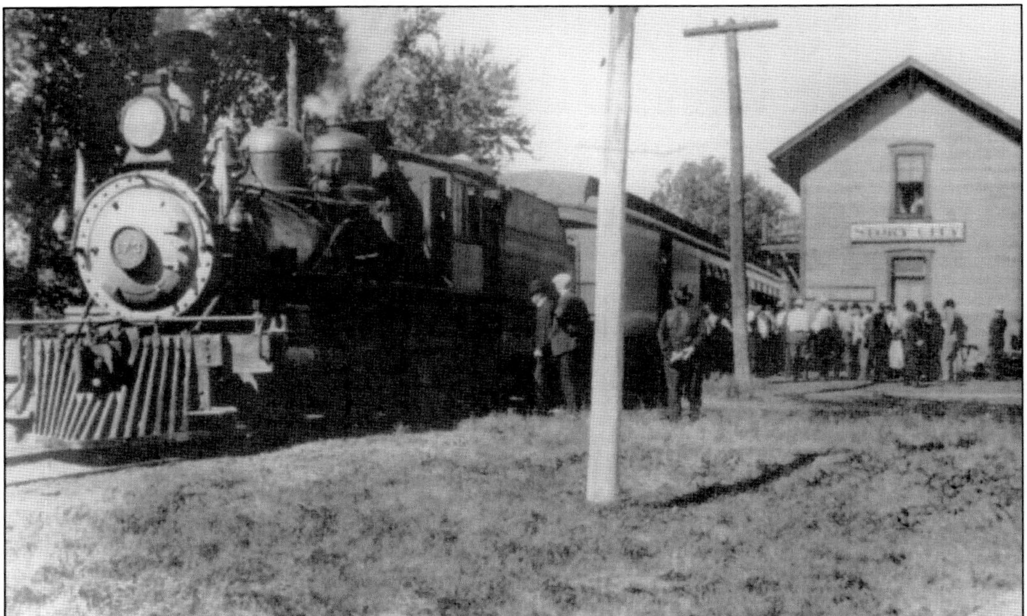

This narrow gauge rail line was replaced in the early 1880s with a standard rail service, through a great deal of effort by Story City businessmen and the mayor, Capt. William Wier. The first depot was called the Hook and Eye and was in the middle of Broad Street, where the railroad line still runs through the community. Later, in 1886, the Iowa Central Railroad came to Story City from Marshalltown, better connecting it to eastern markets. Near the corner of Fourth and Market Streets was a roundtable for turning engines around for the return trip out of Story City.

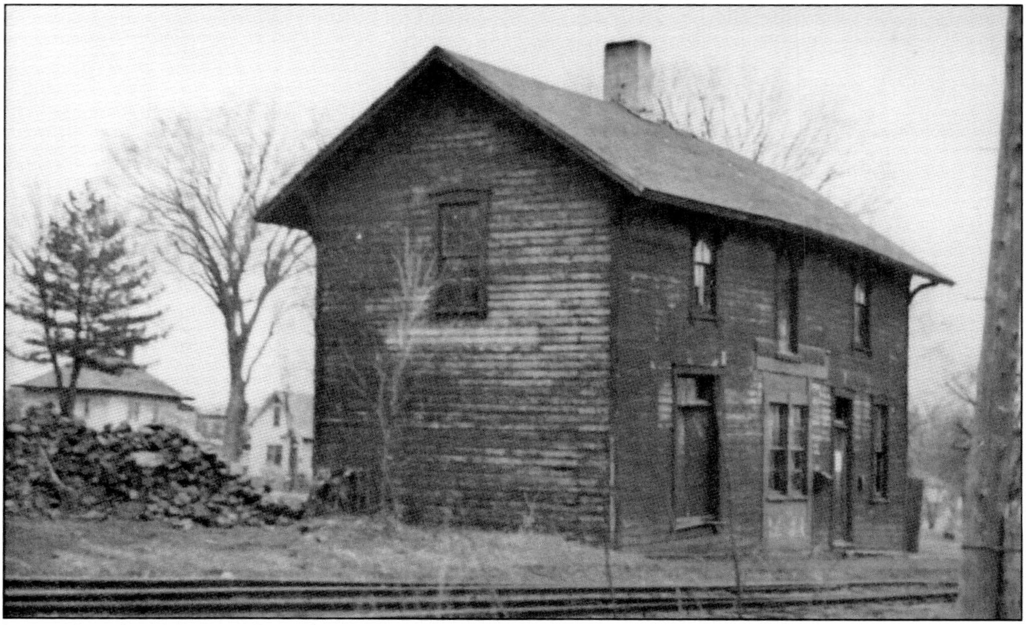

More details of the Hook and Eye railroad depot are seen here. Typically, depots would have one side of the interior devoted to passengers and the other side for freight. The depot was on the north side of Fourth Street near Garfield.

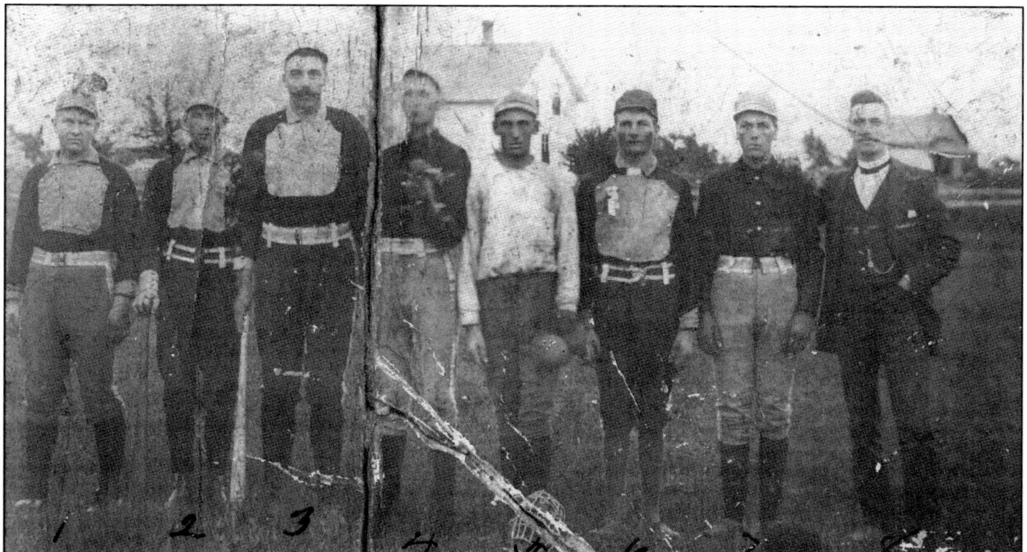

Baseball has been a popular pastime in Story City since the Civil War. In this photograph of the first baseball team in the community, possibly from the 1870s or 1880s, a young Freeman Fuller (third from left) towers above the other players.

Two

Prairie to Corn Belt

Following the addition of a railroad line to Story City and the community's incorporation into a town, a great deal of economic growth continued. Newly arrived residents in Lafayette Township developed the prairie and timbered bottoms into productive farms utilizing new mechanized agricultural equipment, much of which was sold by the community's first mayor, Civil War veteran Capt. William Wier, in his implement store.

The community of Story City played a vital role in agriculture, providing a venue for commodities to be sold to expanding markets. Newly built stores along Broad Street attracted businesses that supported the farm economy of the area, providing products and services to farmers. This new growth was noticed by railroad companies, and additional lines were established.

A hub of activity in northwest Story County, the community continued to grow, attracting more and more immigrants and others from around the country. This unique cultural melting pot allowed newspapers to flourish both in English and Scandinavian languages, and a variety of churches were constructed. A community school building was built and country schools were standardized, providing quality education to those living in the fast-developing area. In 1883, a fire department was established and local law enforcement maintained the town's temperance laws.

All across the former prairie landscape of the Story City area, farms were built with lumber brought in by the railroad from river towns along the Mississippi River. Large barns were constructed to provide shelter for abundant crops of hay and grain, and colorful windmills pumped water to increasing animal herds. Barbed wire was introduced, replacing the old hand-split wood rail fences of the pioneer period and providing an affordable option to protect fields from the ever-shrinking number of free-ranging livestock in the area. In the second half of the 19th century, the tall grass prairie would be replaced by tall corn fields.

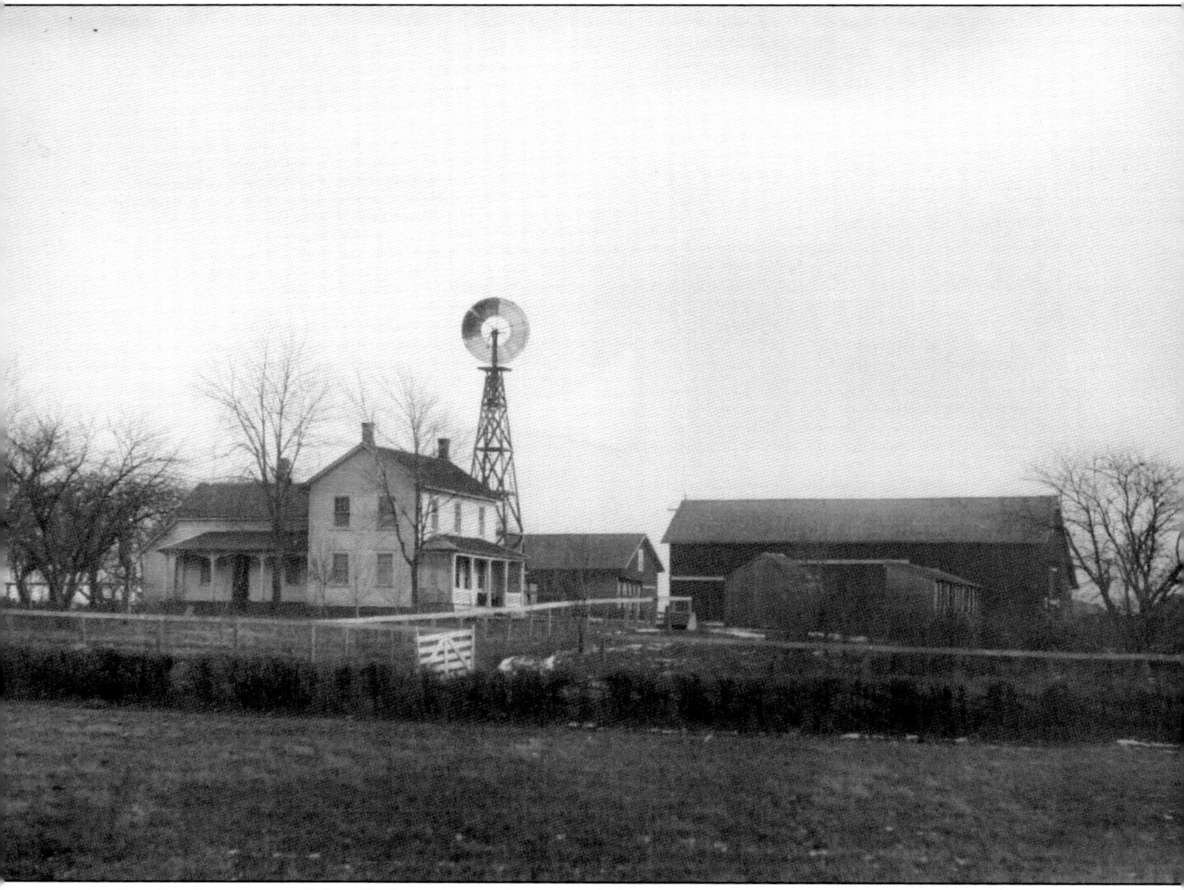

In the third quarter of the 19th century, farmsteads began increasing in size as economical lumber was brought in via rail to construct large barns and homes.

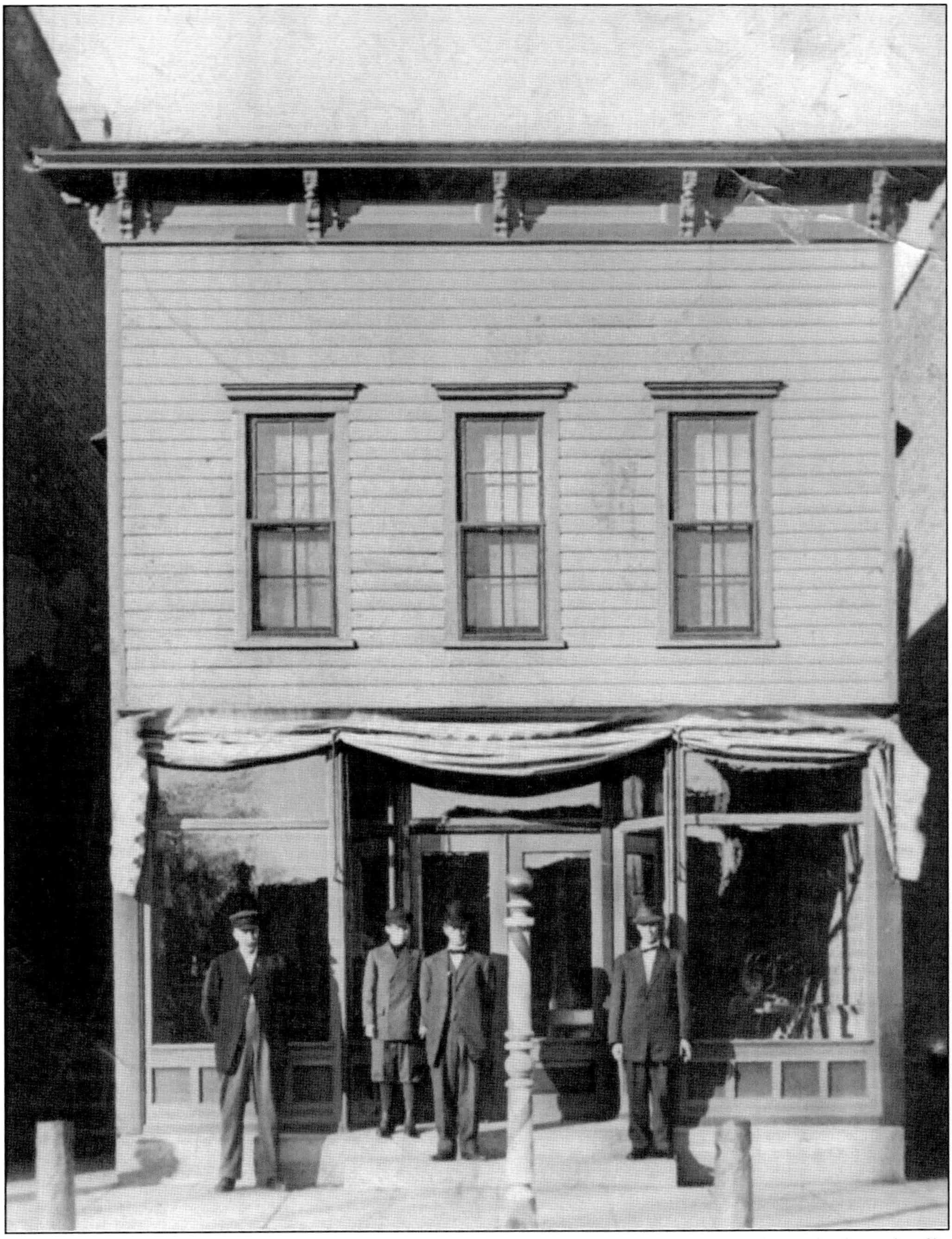

Fuller's barbershop on Broad Street featured a barber's pole that was easy to see along the boardwalk, which predated sidewalks.

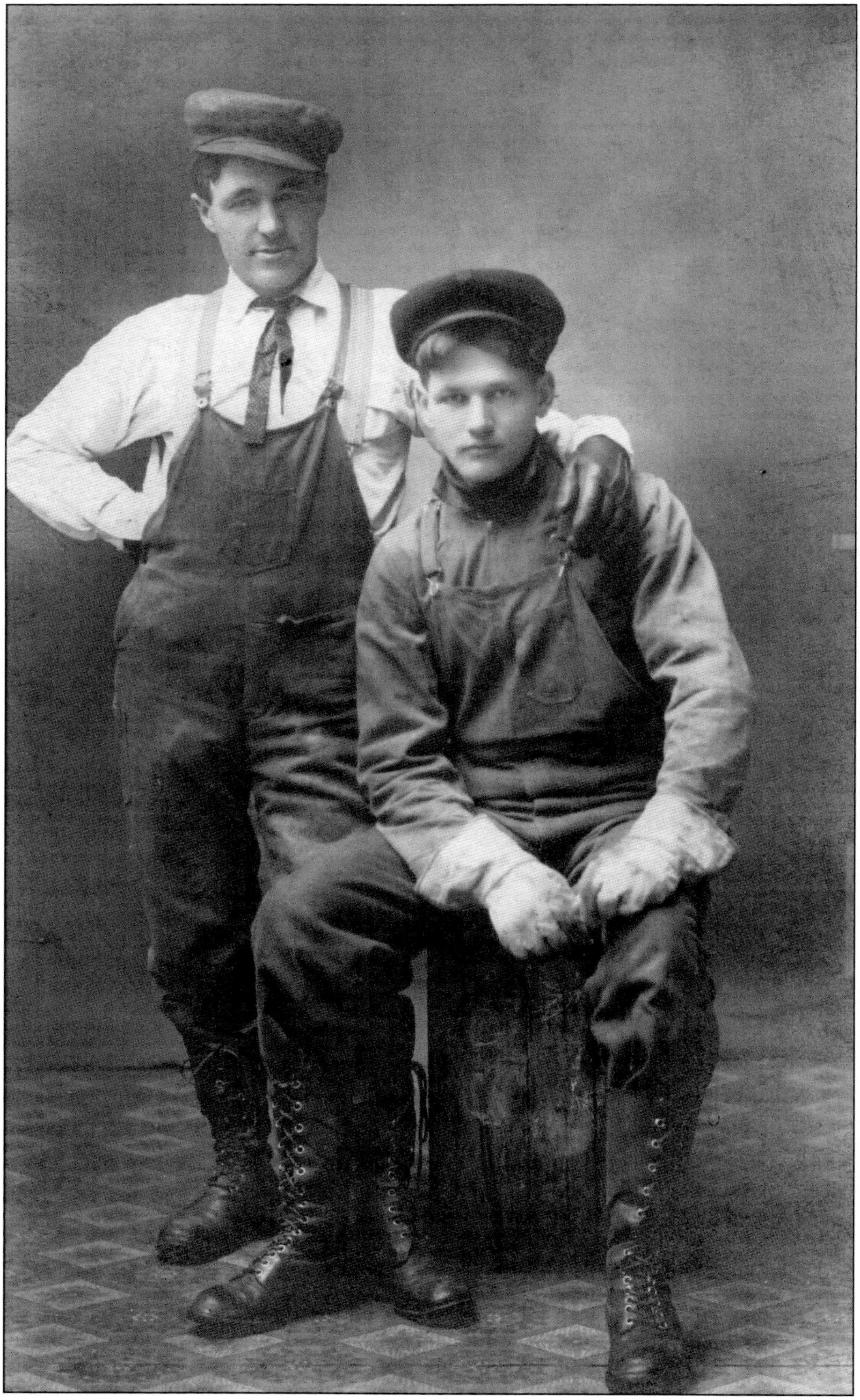

This portrait shows the dressing style of working-class men in the late 19th century. Denim overalls were often worn as an outer layer over trousers, and neckties were commonly worn by laborers.

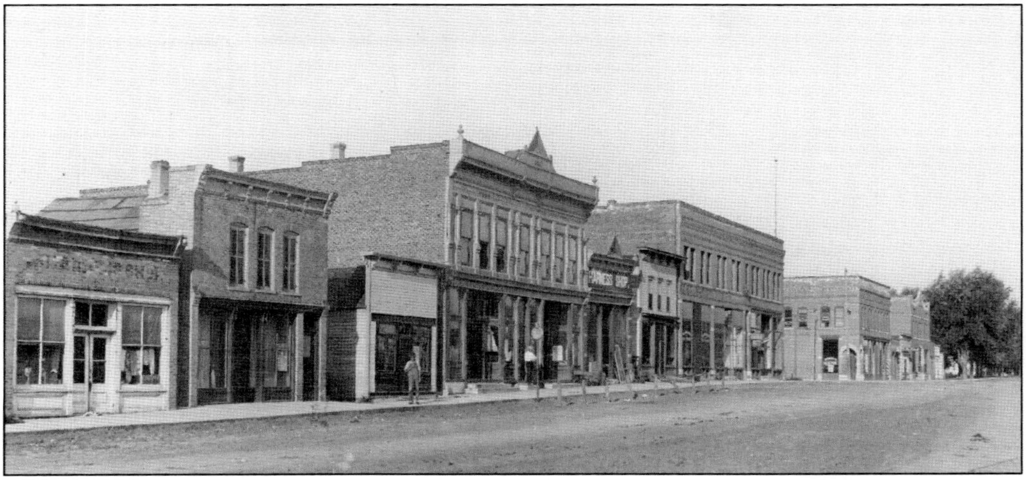

This view down the south side of Broad Street shows dirt streets, boardwalks, hitching posts, and a mix of wood and masonry architecture. In this photograph, the Pioneer Building and Swan Opera House (currently the Charlson Building) are prominently featured.

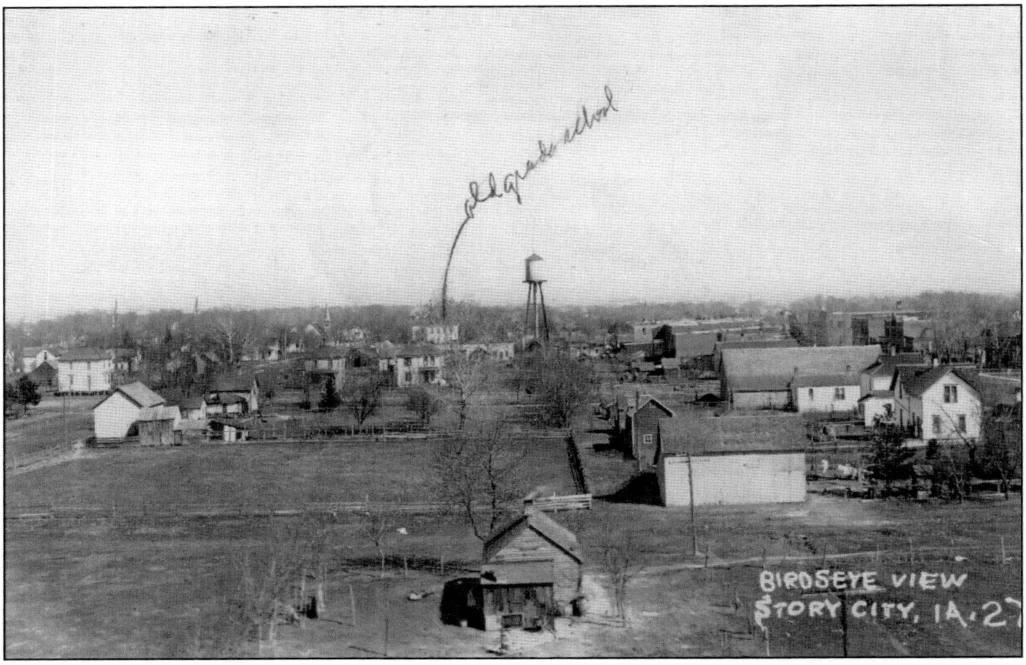

This bird's-eye view of Story City looking east shows residences and a few businesses, showcasing the mix of architecture, fencing styles, commercial buildings, and the renovation of smaller, framed homes from the pioneer period into outbuildings such as stables and workshops.

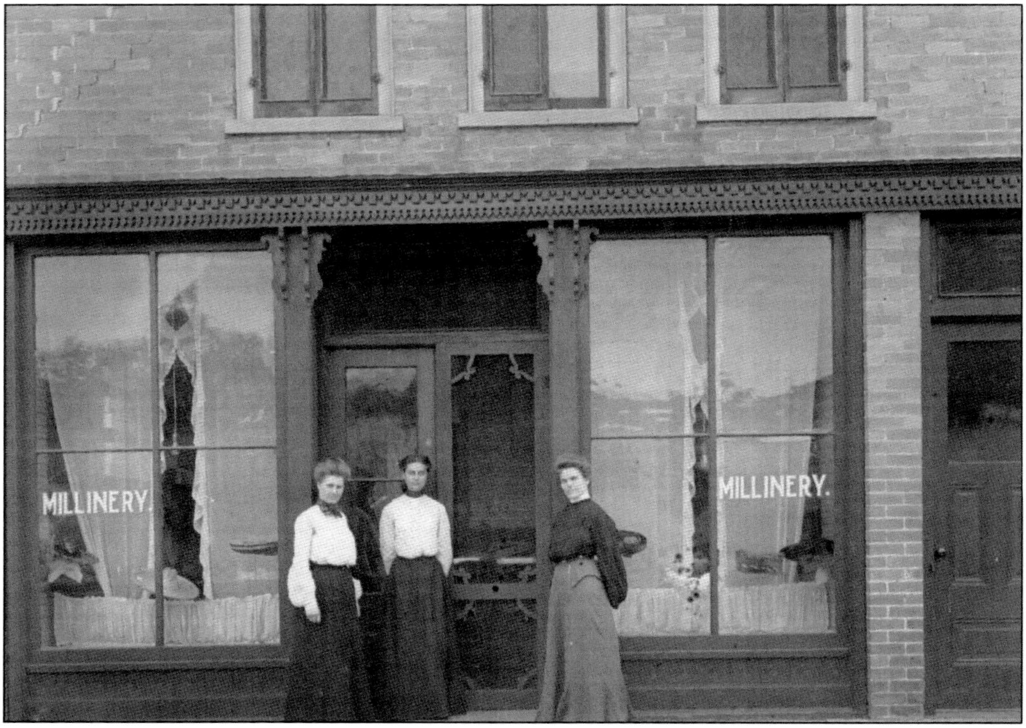

In an age when women wore unique hats with a variety of feathers and ribbons, this millinery shop was a popular venue for Story City women. Posing out front are, from left to right, Anna Mathre, Yvette Nordskog, and Julia Mathre in the front doorway.

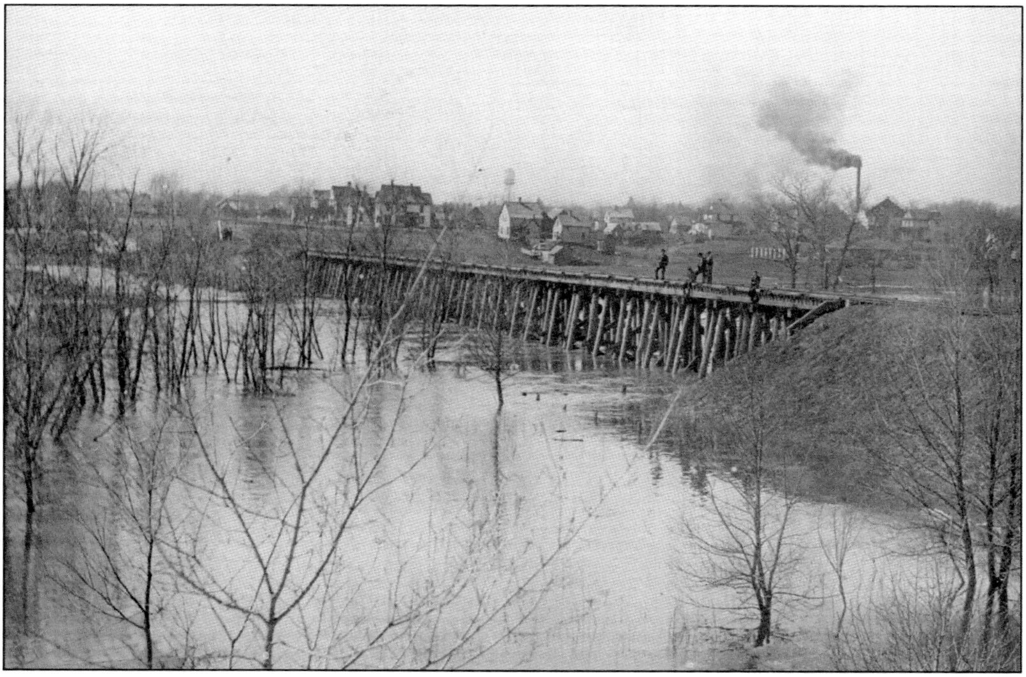

The Skunk River has overflowed its banks into Story City a number of times. This image shows the railroad trestle over the river leading into town during one such flood.

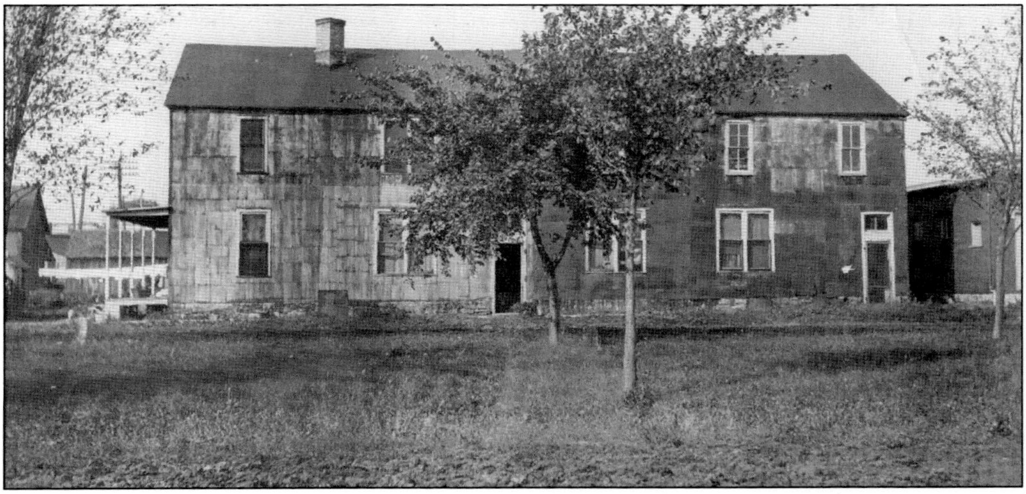

The Story City cracker company was founded by a former Lutheran pastor at the intersection of Elm and Broad Streets on the south side of town. The company was successful for a number of years until the baker left to join a larger cracker production company.

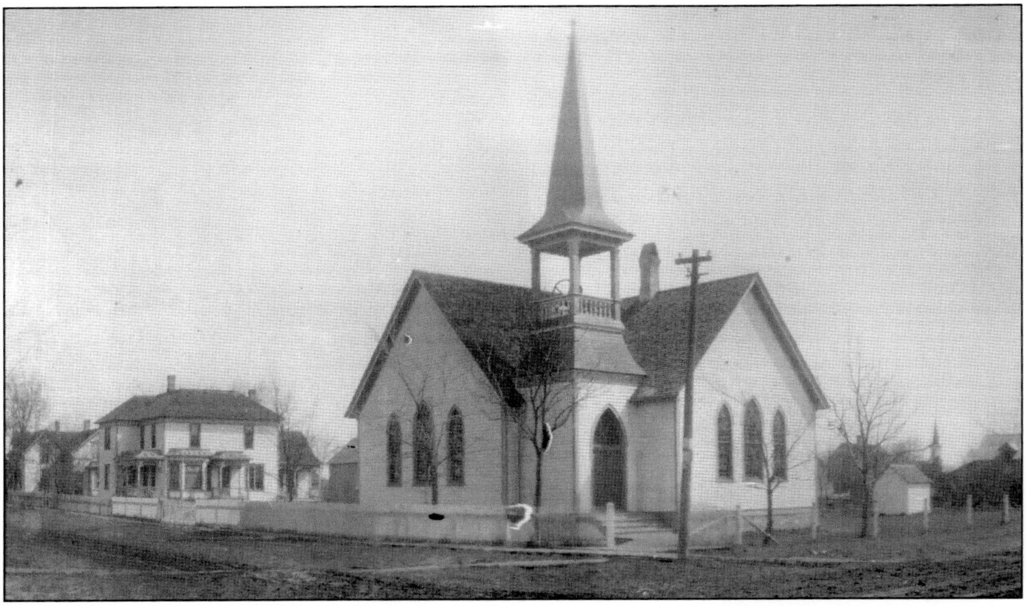

Bethel Lutheran Church was one of three Lutheran churches established in Story City with 19th-century roots. Lutheran churches were very popular with the large number of Scandinavian immigrants who settled in the region.

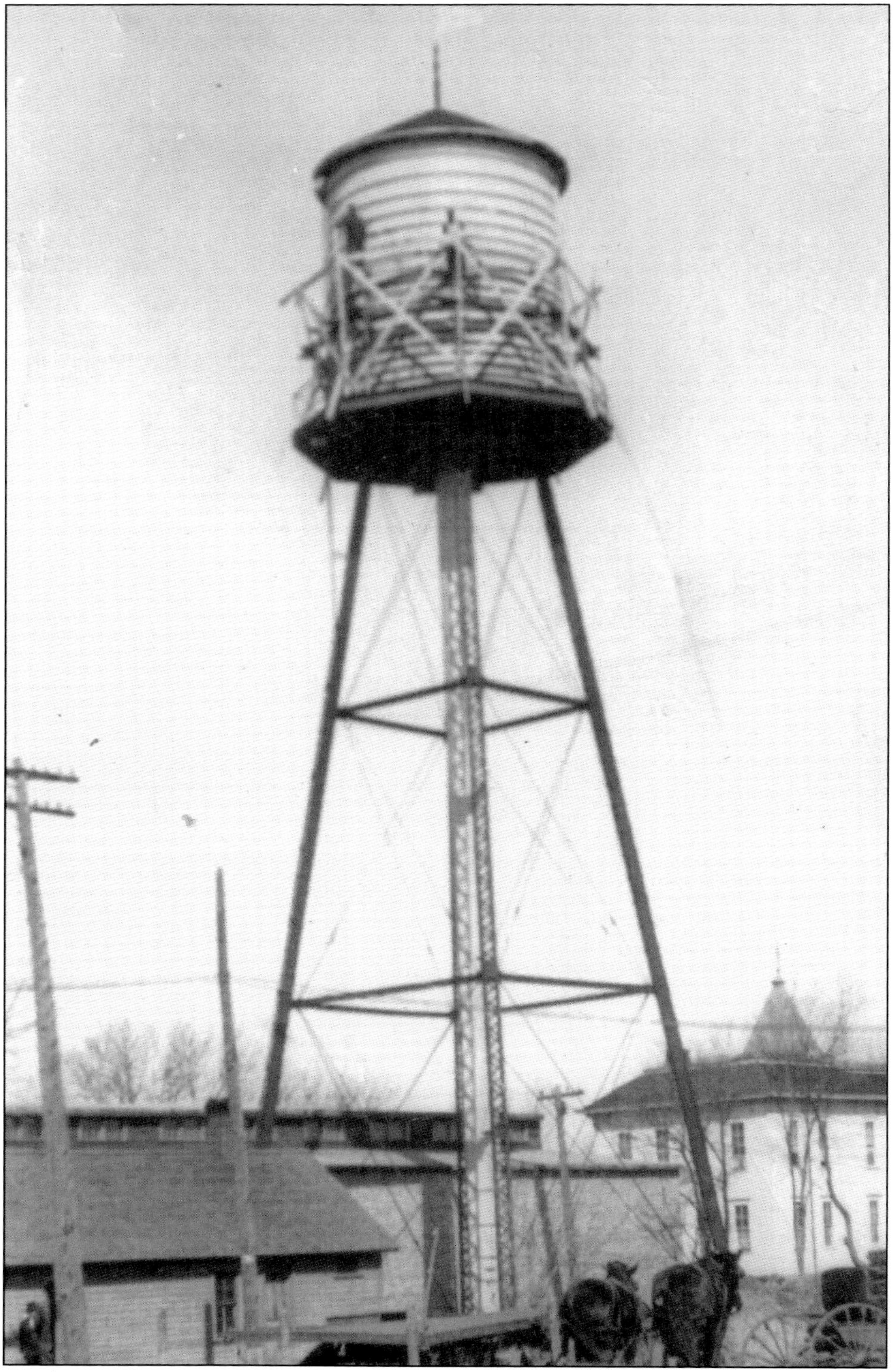

This early water tower in Story City has a tank made of wooden staves secured with metal bands. Located in close proximity to the 1881 Story City School, this wooden water tower was eventually replaced because of maintenance concerns.

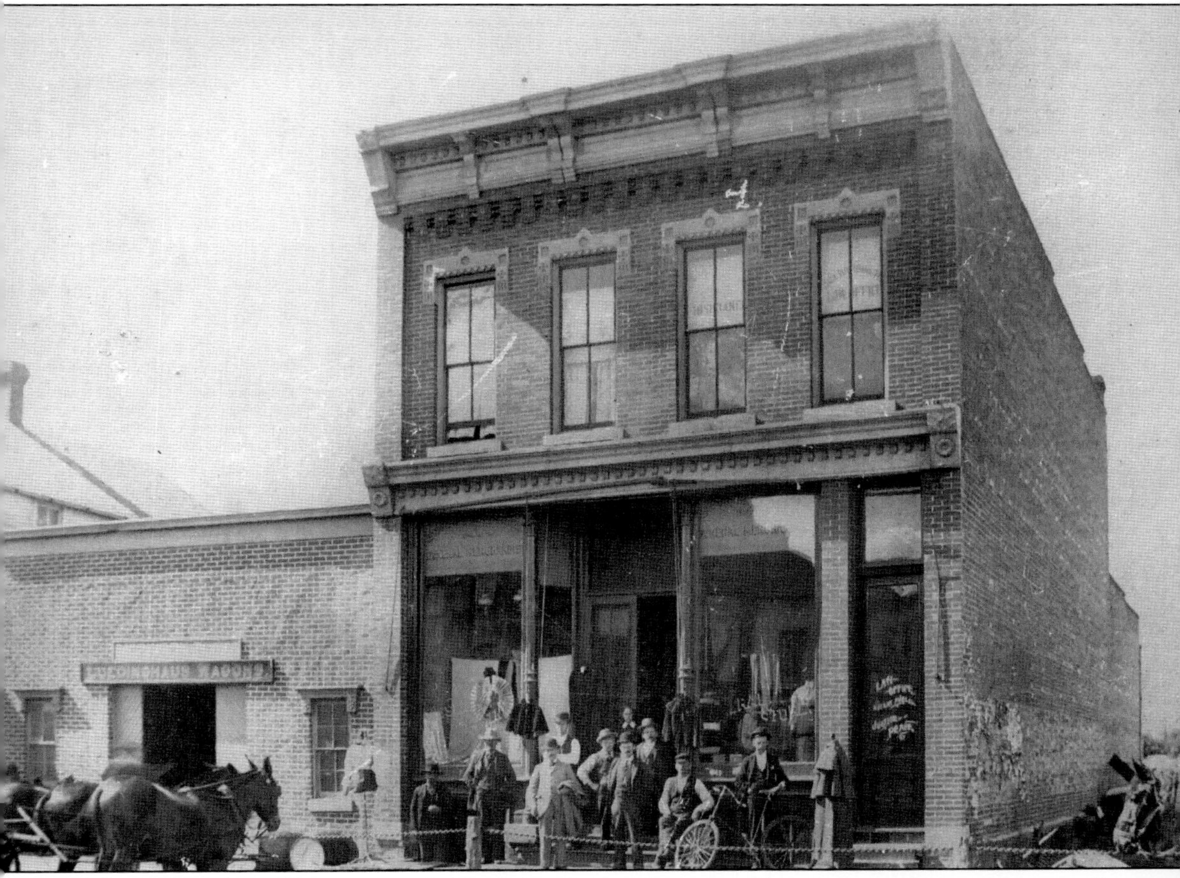

The Leudinghaus Wagon Shop (left) was beside the Cassem and Jensen general store. Many small towns had a wagon or carriage factory where readymade wheels acquired from eastern factories were incorporated into locally produced horse-drawn vehicles. A livery barn stood here before the brick buildings were constructed.

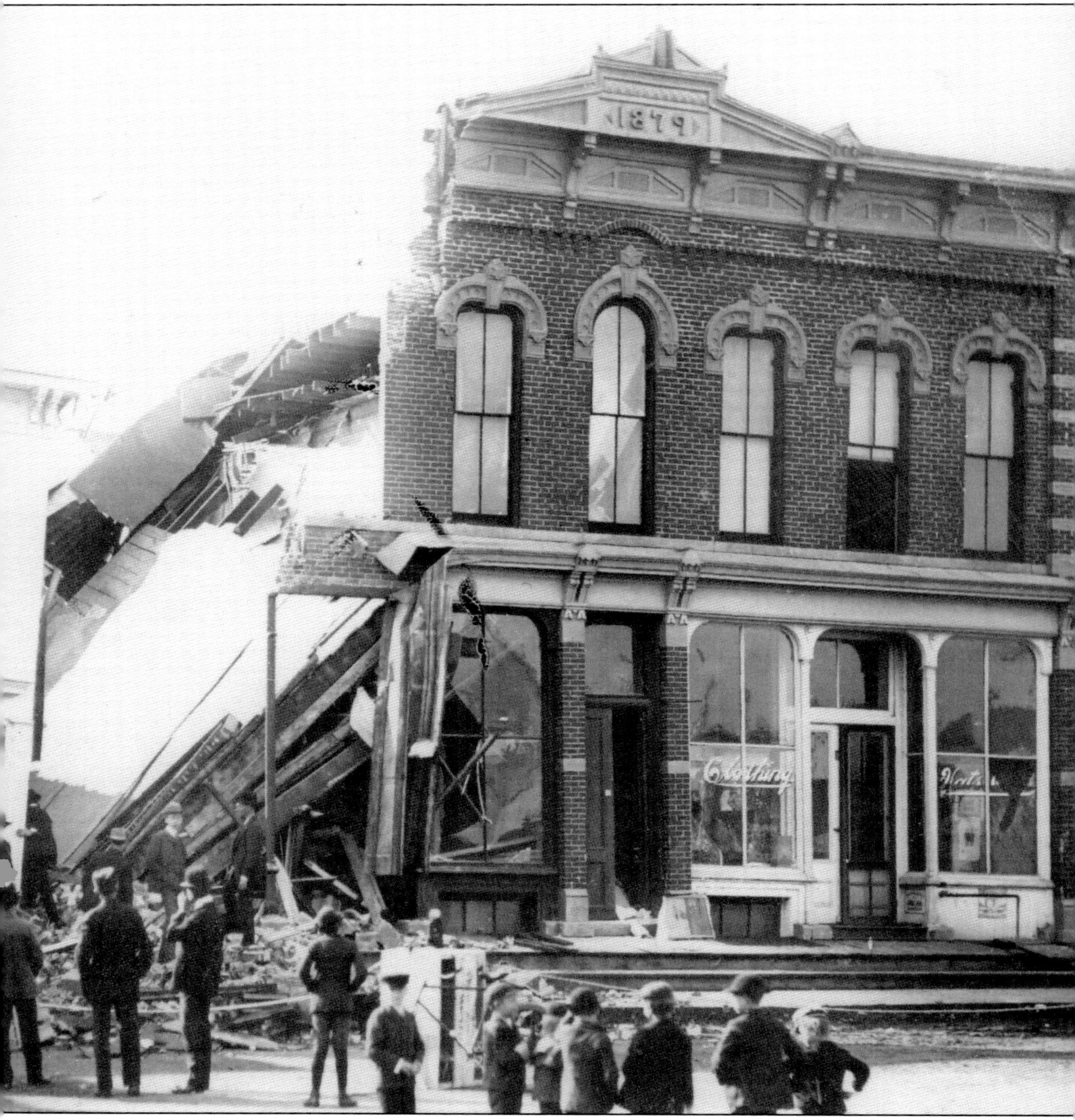

Following repair work on a basement wall, the first brick building in Story City, built in 1879 at 606 Broad Street, collapsed, fortunately while it was unoccupied. The collapse drew a large crowd. The Pioneer Building was constructed on the site and still stands today.

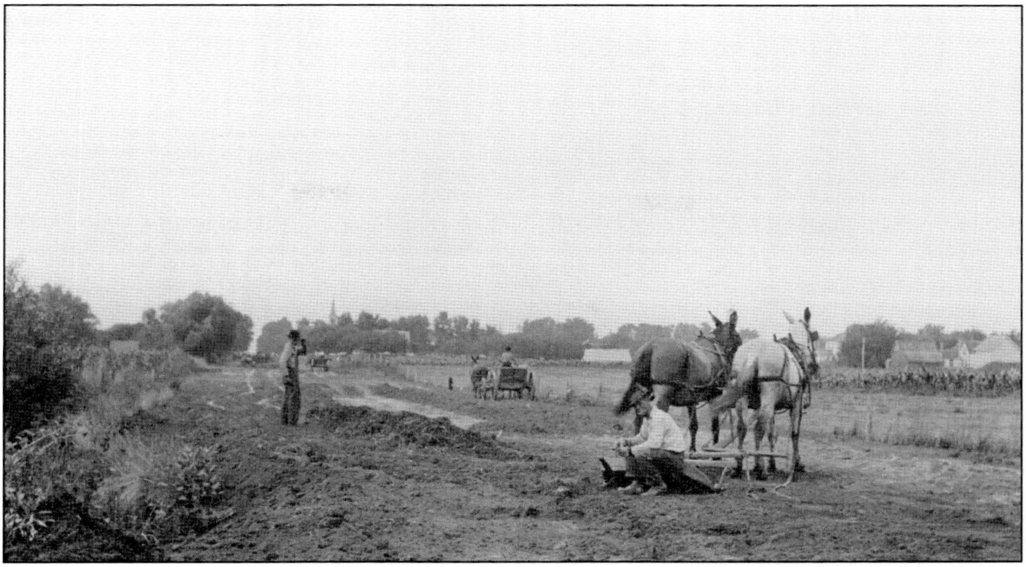

This image shows a road crew grading North Lafayette Street just outside of Story City. Early roads quickly turned into mud, which was nicknamed "gumbo" by locals. There are accounts of wagons and horses getting stuck after the spring thaw or after periods of heavy rain.

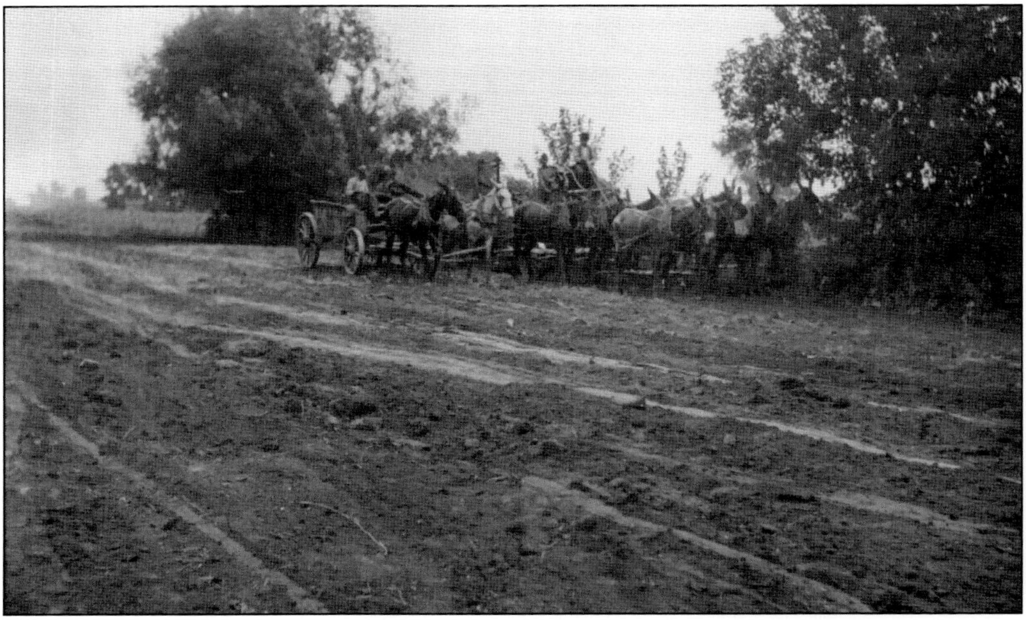

A horse-drawn machine conveys soil into the bed of a heavy dray wagon to add dirt to a pothole in another location. In the late 1800s and early 1900s, a number of patents for road-repairing equipment were issued.

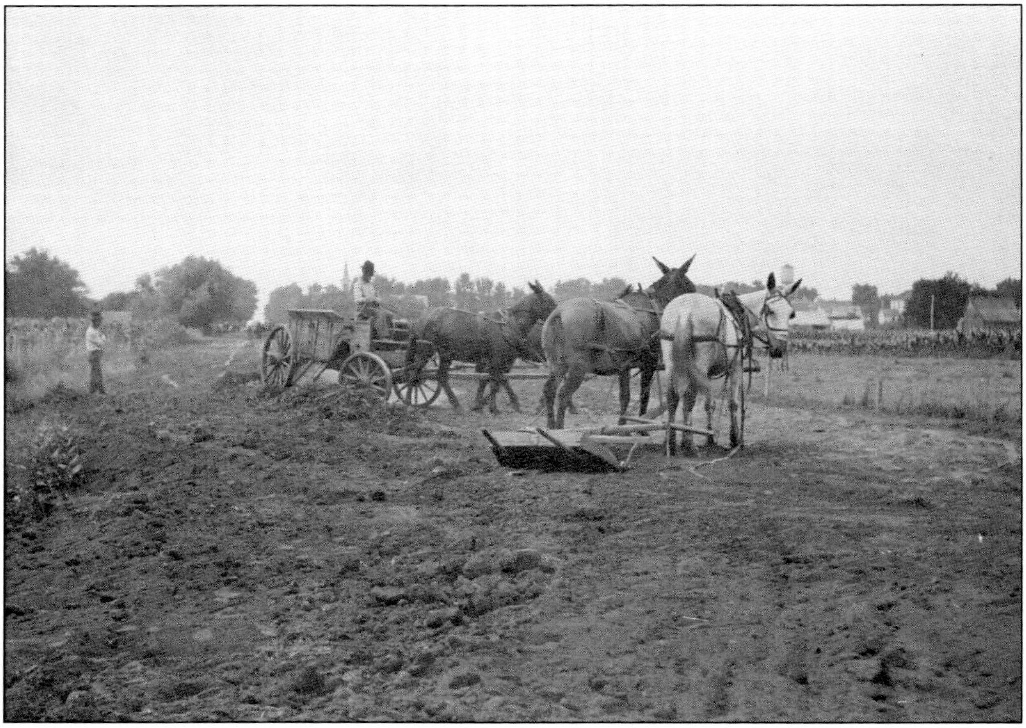

Before modern earthmoving equipment, slip skids were used to move soil. Resembling a wheelbarrow with two handles, this simple machine allowed the operator to scoop a load of earth and then drag it by draft animals to wherever it required dumping.

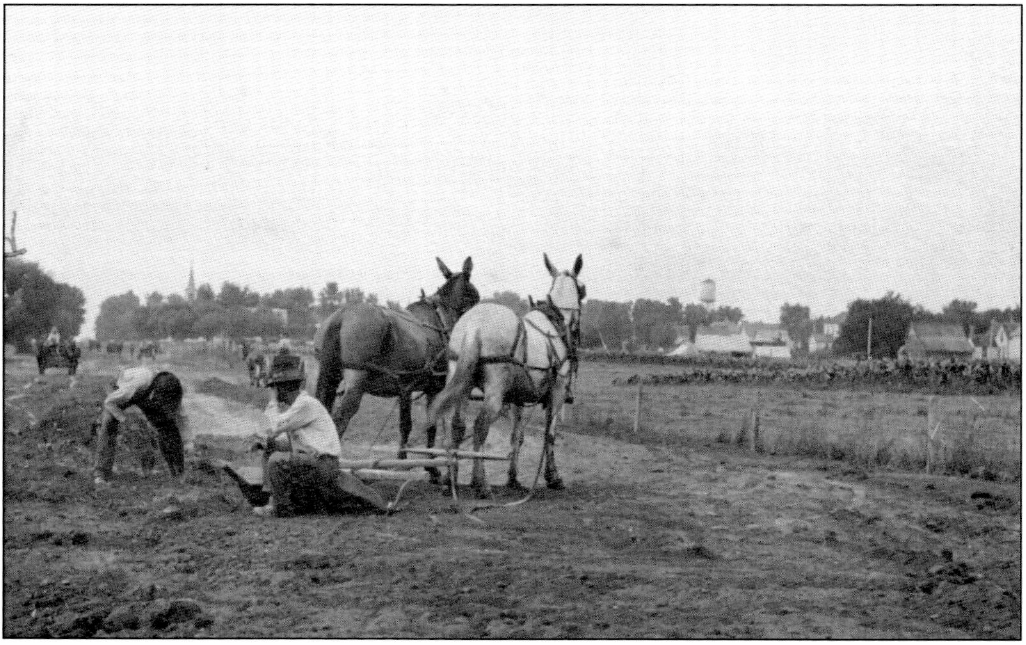

The outskirts of Story City are seen in this image of a road crew taking a break. The skyline shows the steeple of a Lutheran church, the wooden water tower, a few outbuildings, some crops, and a few homes.

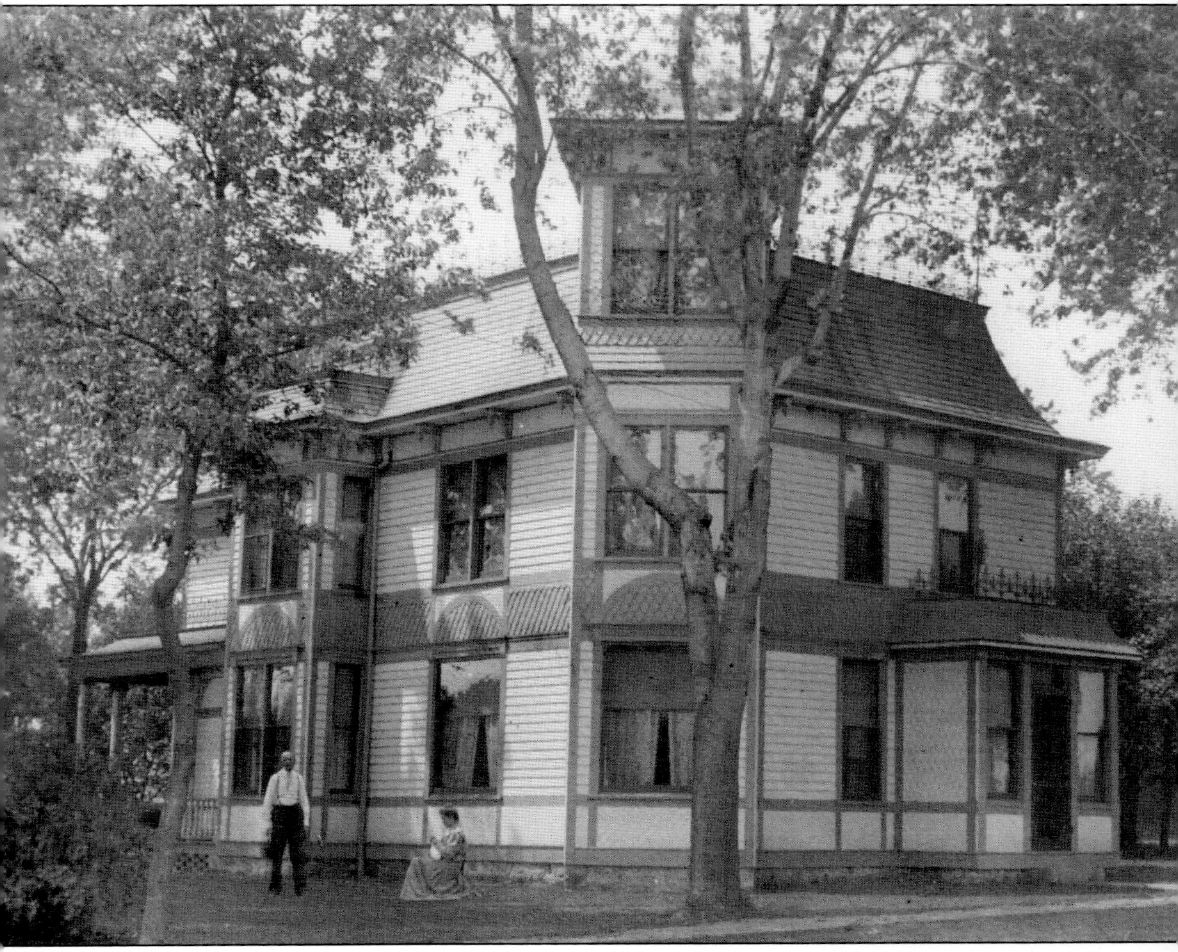

This Victorian home was built by the Wierson family and still stands today, about a block south of city hall.

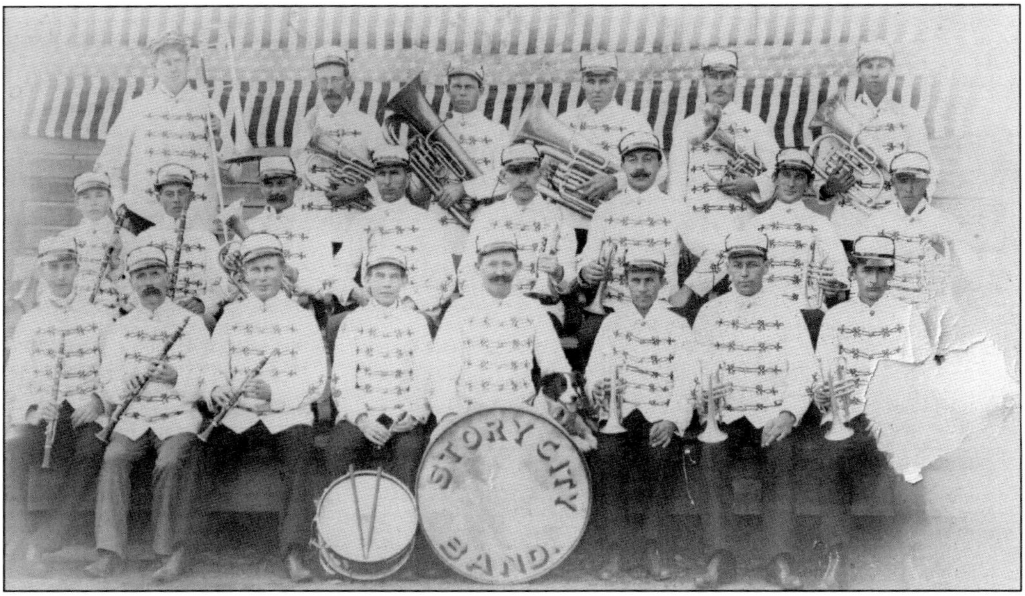

Story City has strong musical heritage. This image, taken on the east side of the Minneapolis and St. Louis Railroad depot, shows the community band in 1893. Community bands were popular entertainment at a number of events.

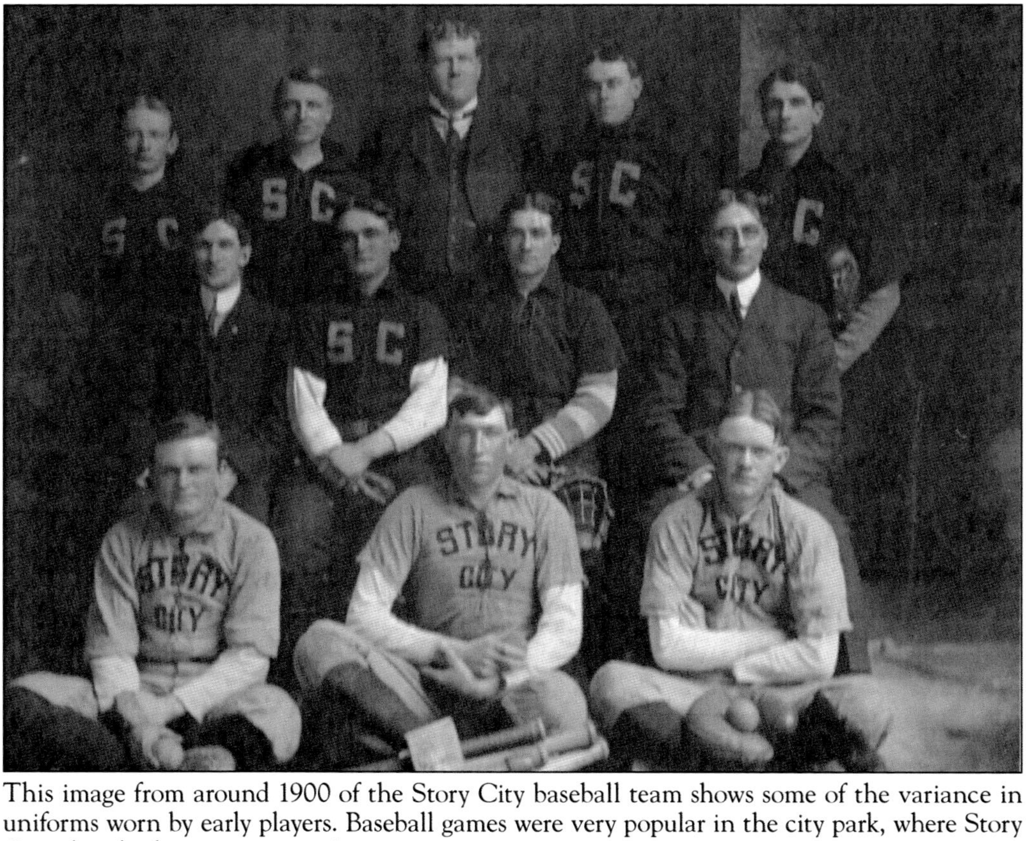

This image from around 1900 of the Story City baseball team shows some of the variance in uniforms worn by early players. Baseball games were very popular in the city park, where Story City played other communities' teams.

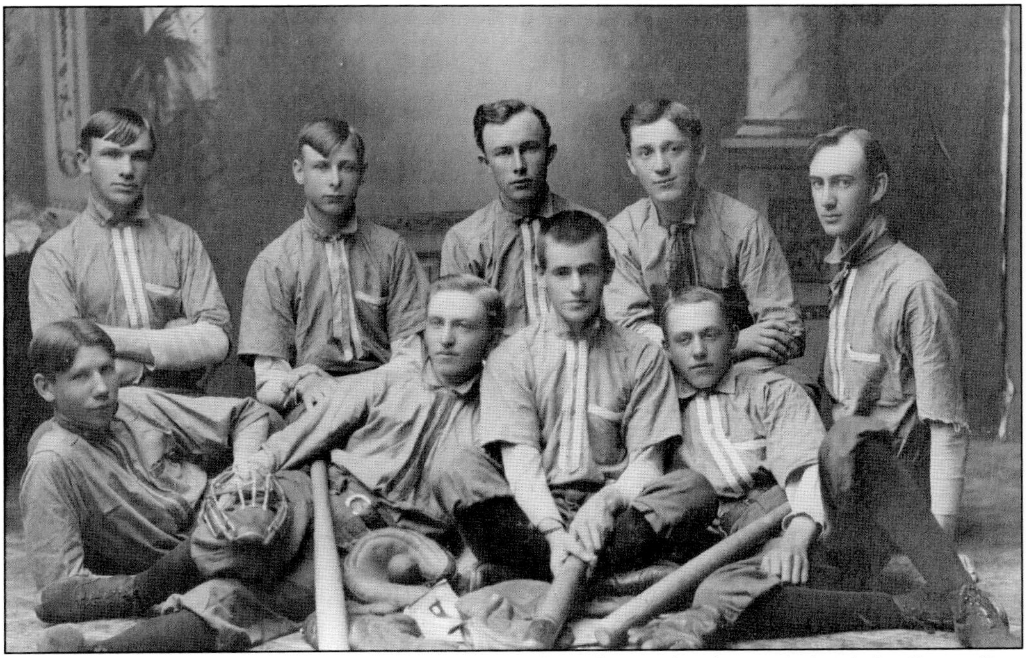

One player has shortened his sleeves to stay cool in this early photograph of the Story City baseball team. The combination of over-shirts and long-sleeved undershirts was typical of men's fashions in the 1800s.

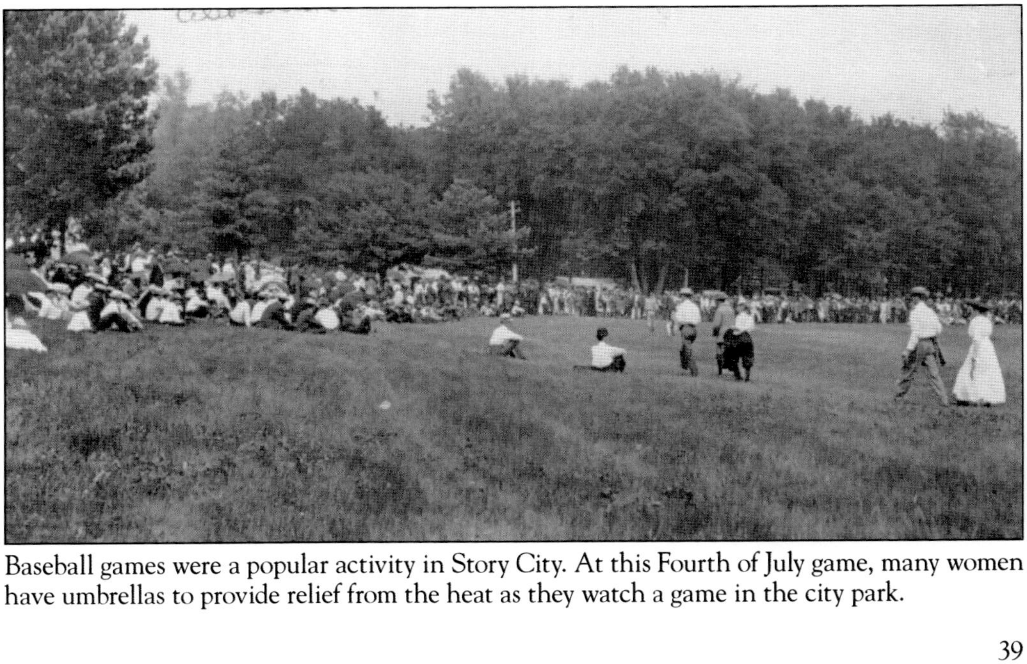

Baseball games were a popular activity in Story City. At this Fourth of July game, many women have umbrellas to provide relief from the heat as they watch a game in the city park.

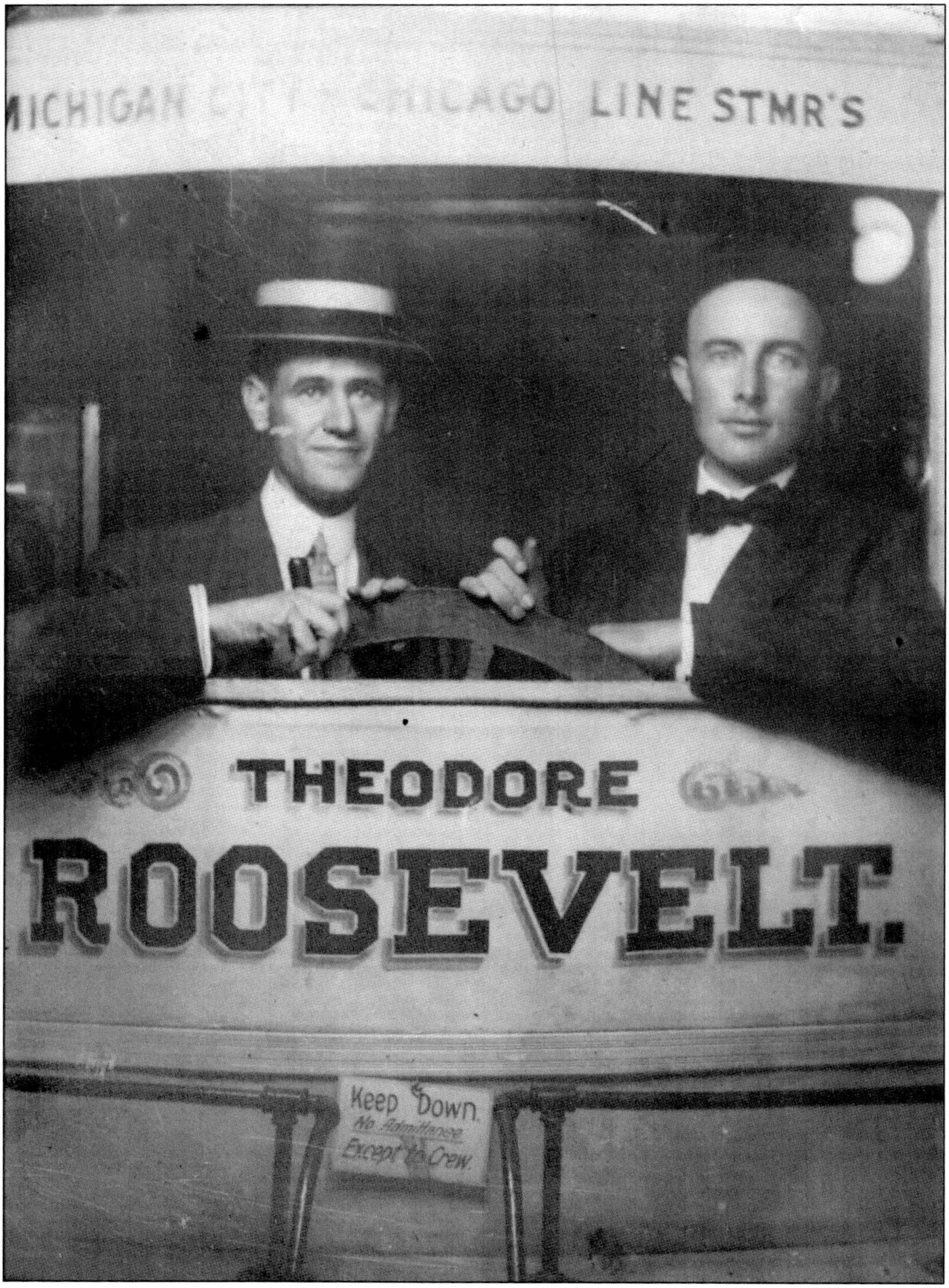

Novelty photographs generally taken at fairs and carnivals were common in the late 1800s and early 1900s. These economical images often incorporated painted cutouts in which the subjects could place their heads for a comical photograph.

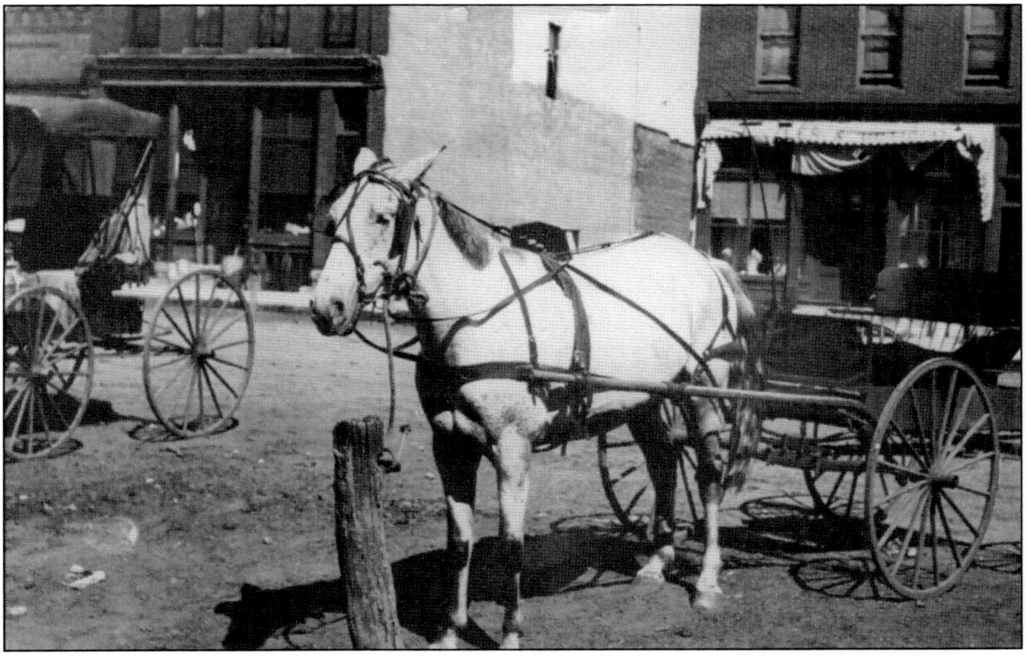

These wooden hitching posts with iron rings along Broad Street secured horses while the owners conducted business in Story City.

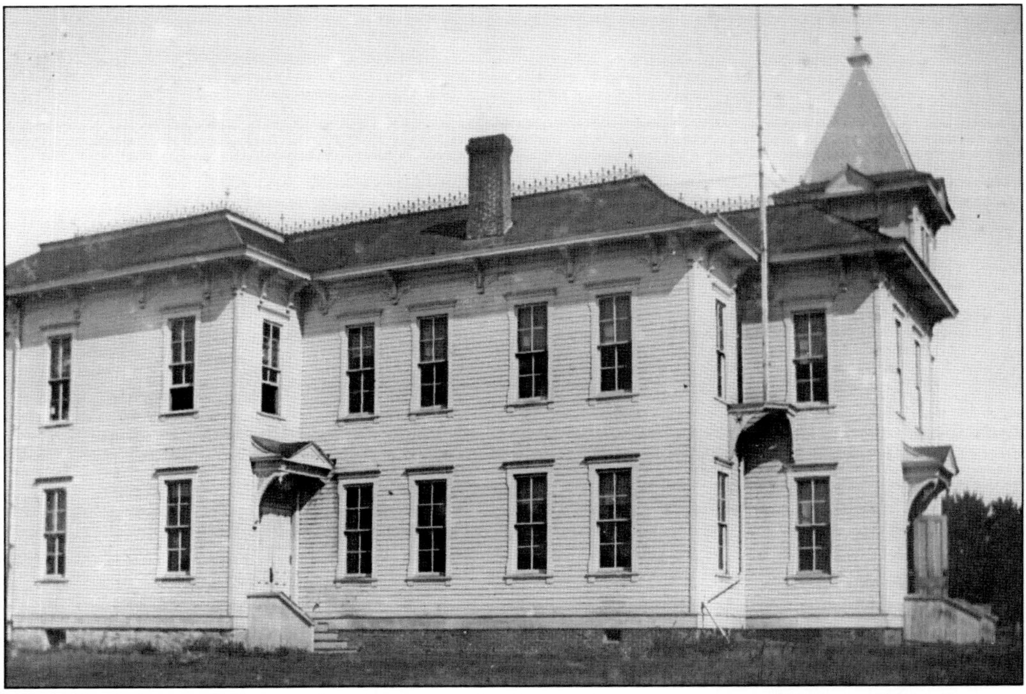

In 1881, a large wood-frame schoolhouse was built near the intersection of Story and Elm Streets. It was first an all-community school, but as the town's population grew, an upper level school was built in another part of town, and this building was used as an elementary school before finally being razed. The metal ornamentation along the roof was typical of the period for residential houses, but much of it was melted during scrap drives for both world wars.

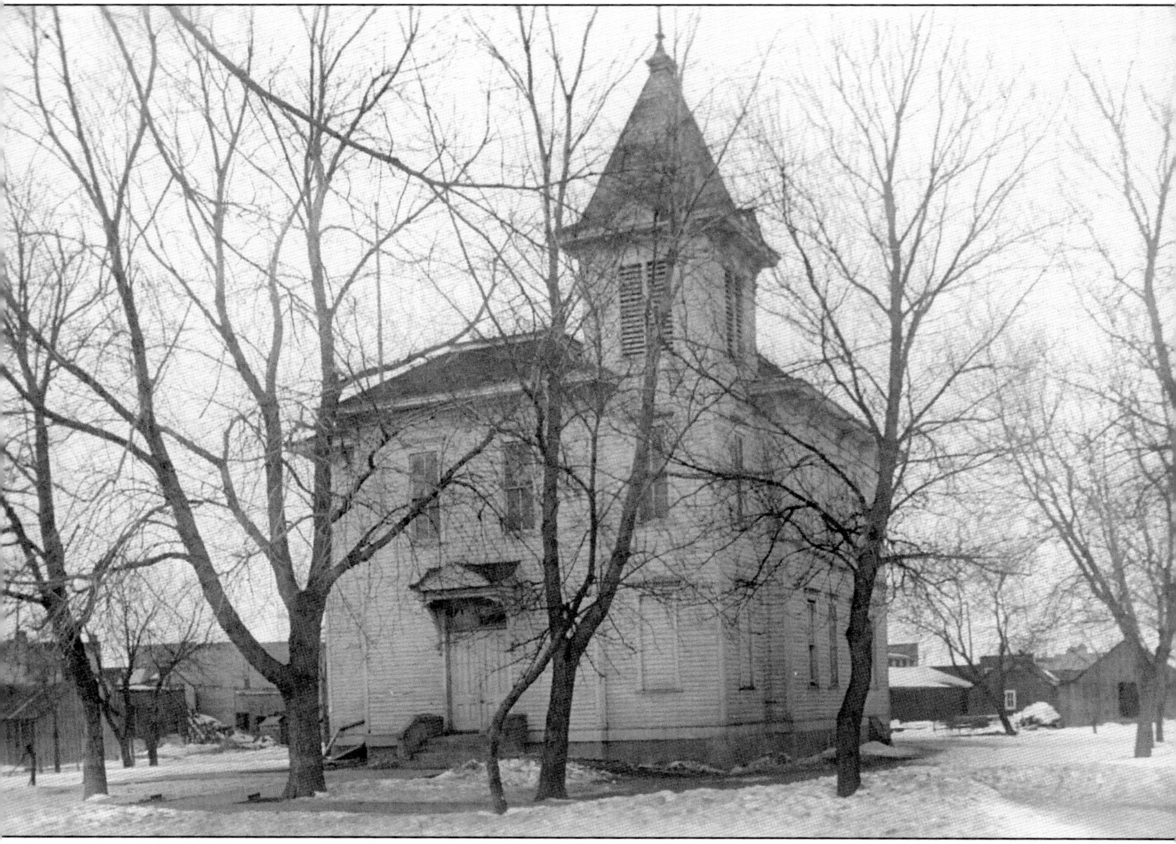

The 1881 Story City schoolhouse is seen here along with a view of the neighborhood around the building, consisting of the rear access of the Broad Street commercial district. The school's bells were located in the tower.

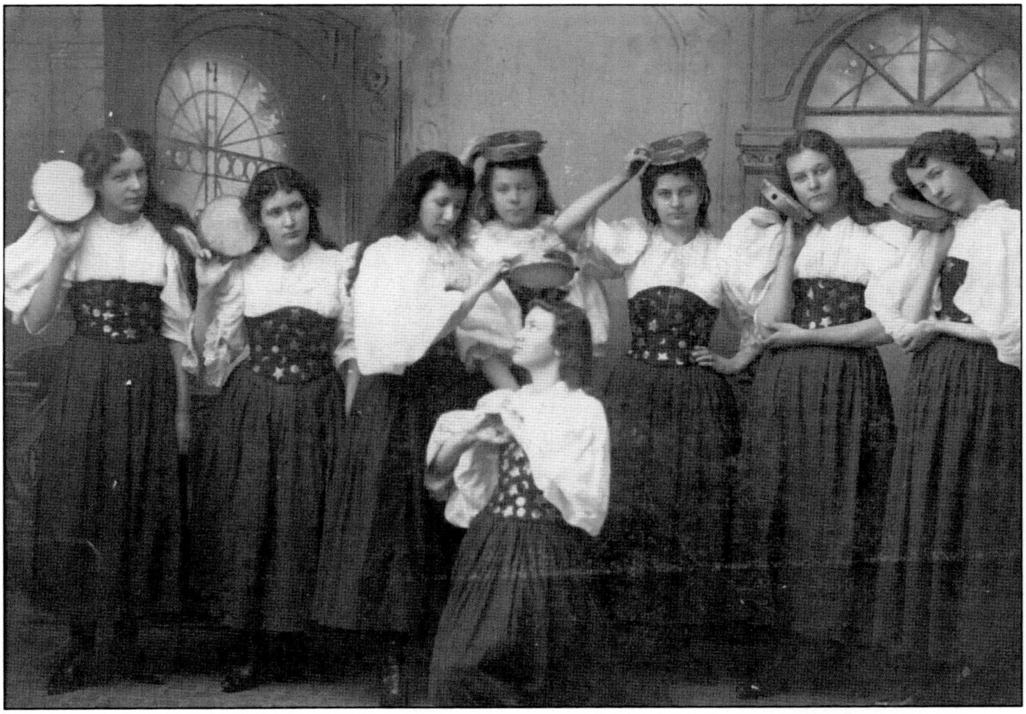

The cast of the 1896 Story City High School play pose with tambourines. While the title of the play is unknown, exotic plays were popular during this period.

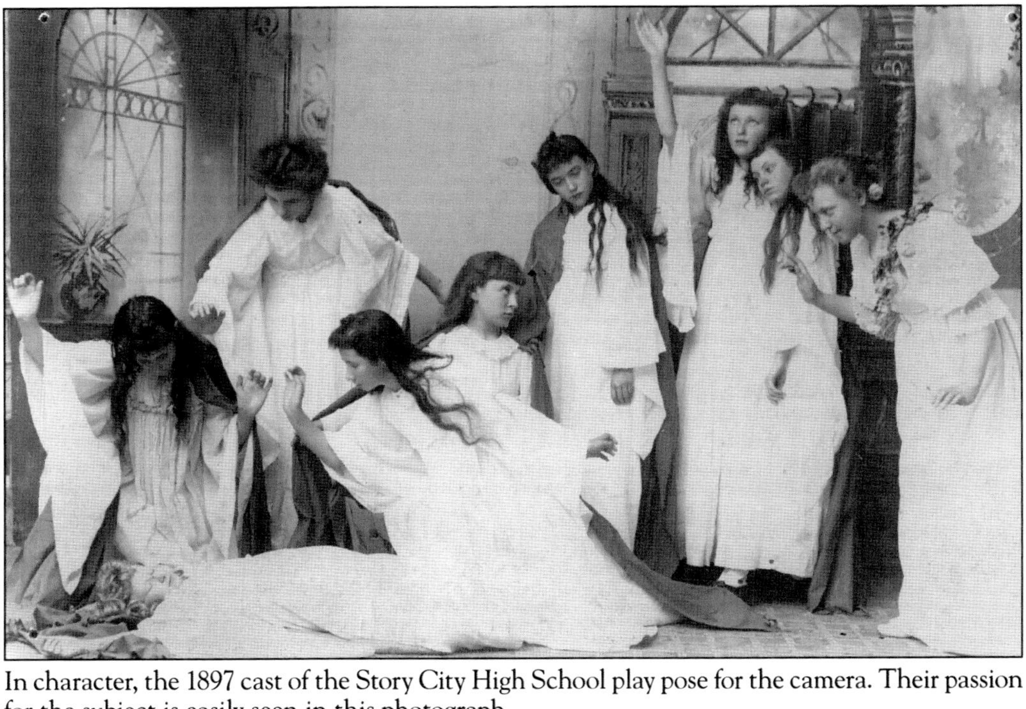

In character, the 1897 cast of the Story City High School play pose for the camera. Their passion for the subject is easily seen in this photograph.

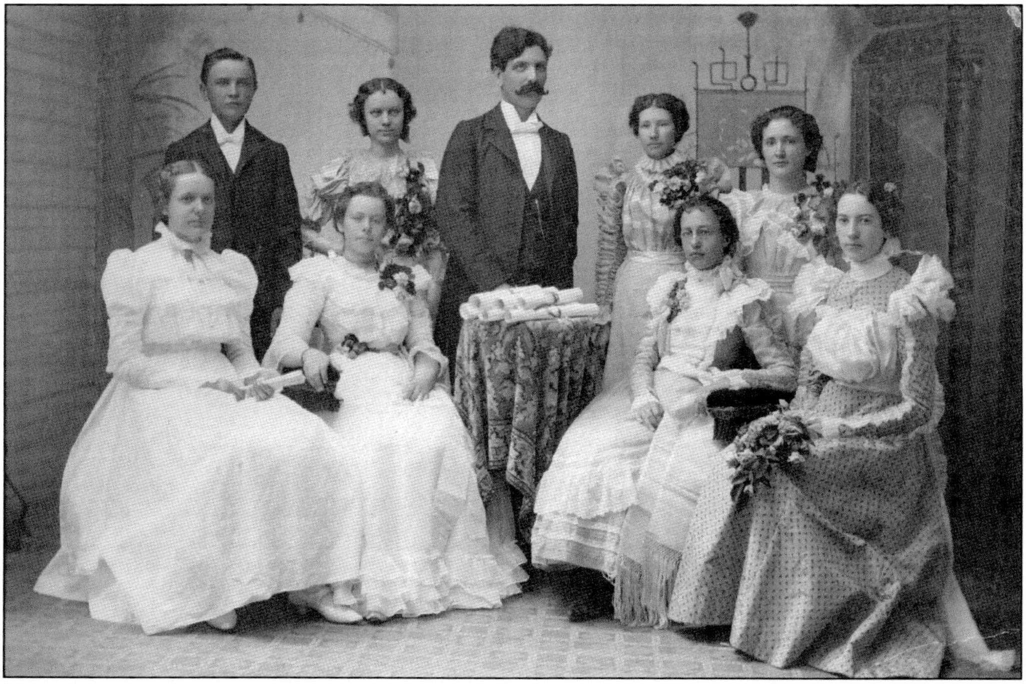

An 1890s graduating class of Story City High School students pose in this formal photograph. The backgrounds of these photographs were generally comprised of painted canvas panels decorated in a variety of ways.

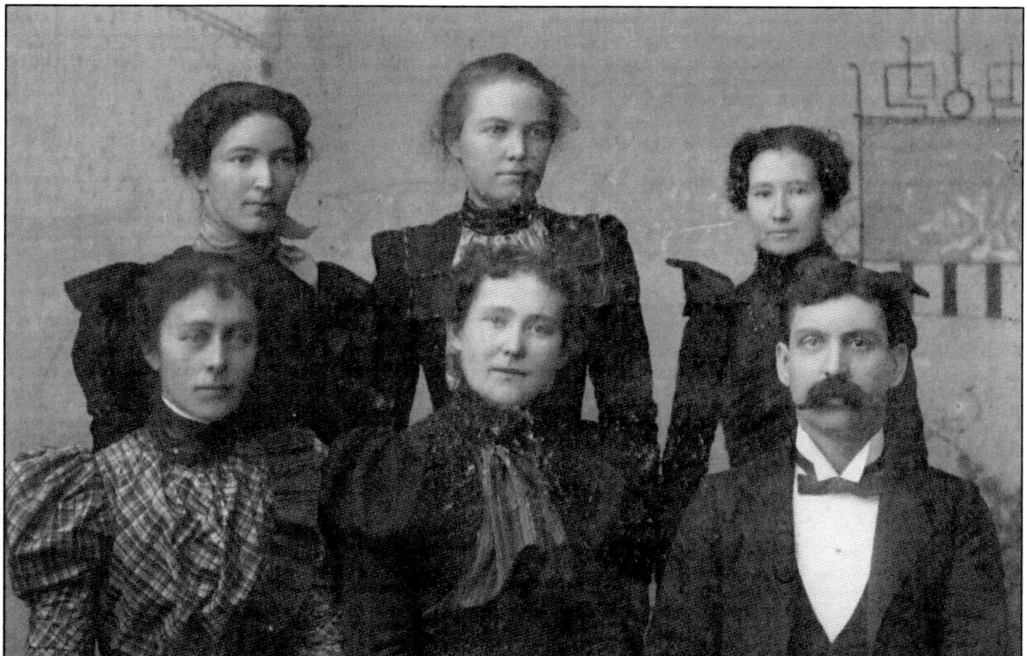

Story City teachers pose in a portrait gallery in the fall of 1898 with the principal, Mr. Gardner (first row, far right). Severie Hanson Parker, a recent graduate of the high school at the time, is behind the principal.

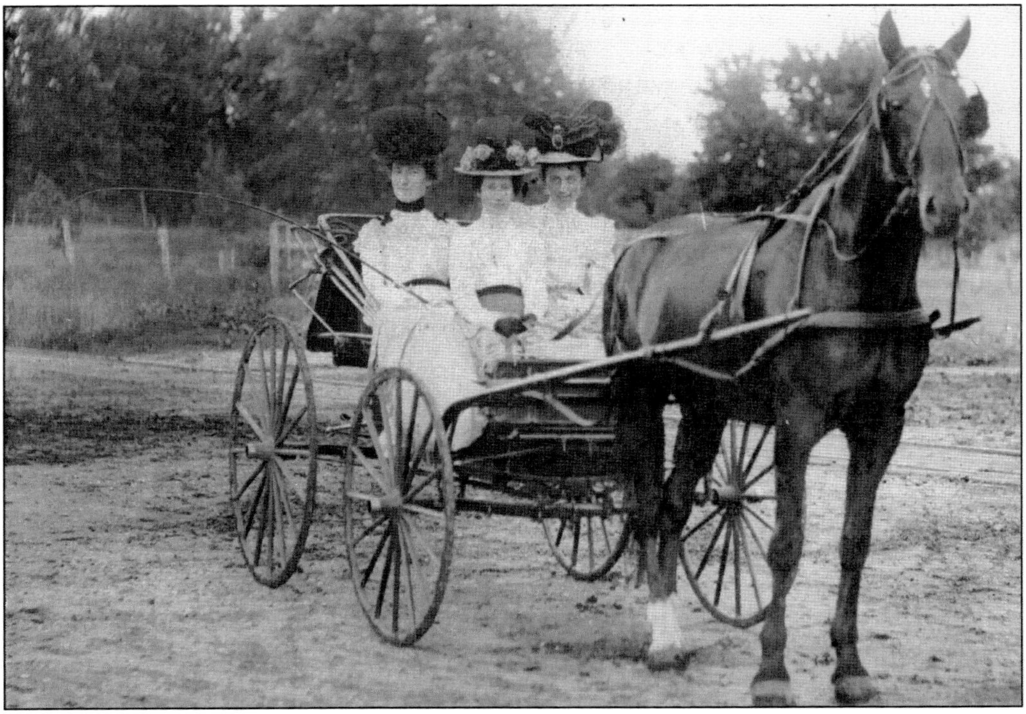

Three Story City teachers pose for the camera in a buggy pulled by a very alert horse. In the 1890s, buggies were popular and could be rented from a livery stable for a trip or if you were a visitor who had arrived on the railroad.

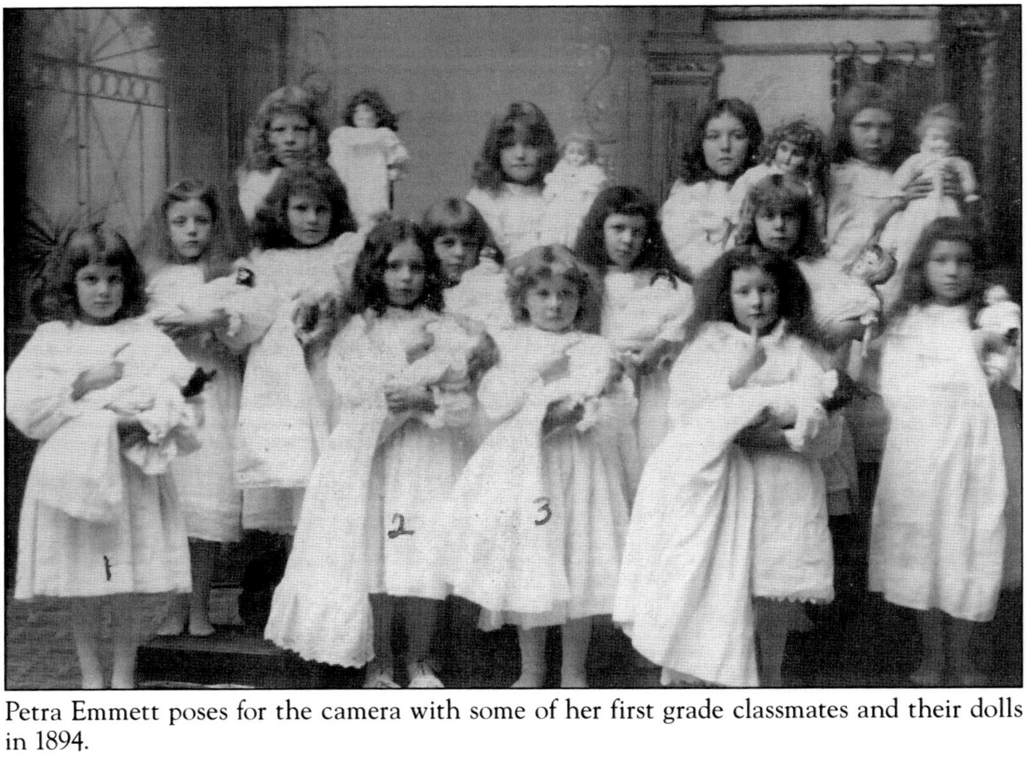

Petra Emmett poses for the camera with some of her first grade classmates and their dolls in 1894.

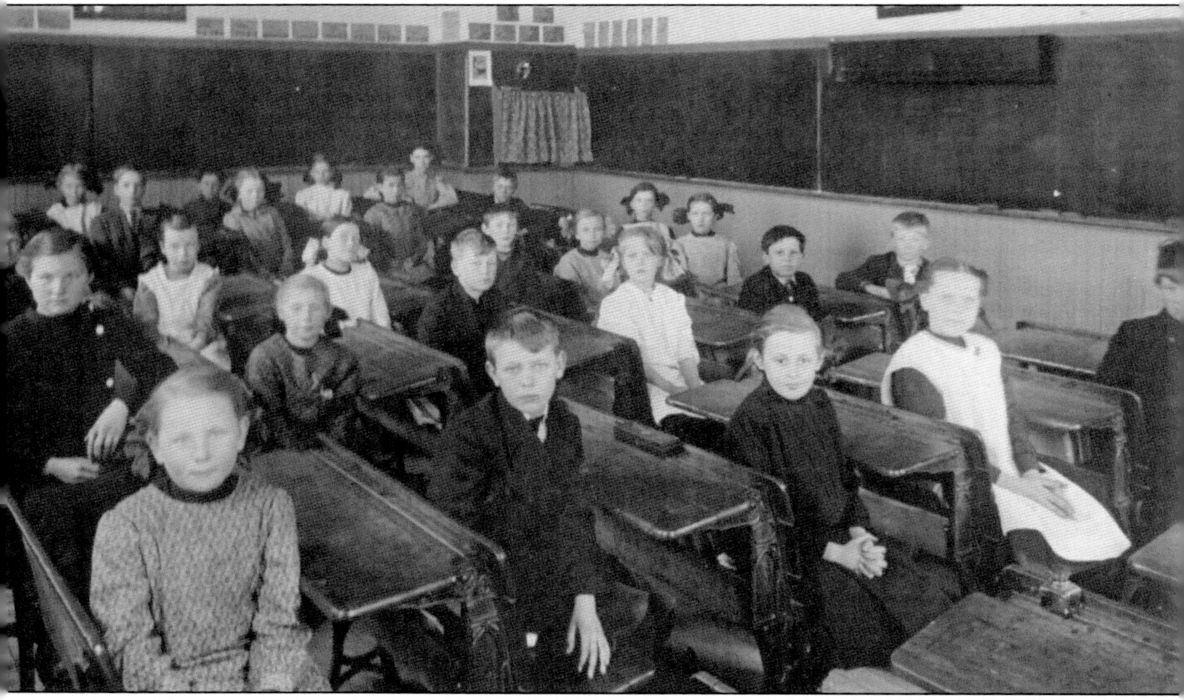

A tired-looking fifth grade class taught by Miss Olive Holm poses in their classroom in the 1881 Story City school building.

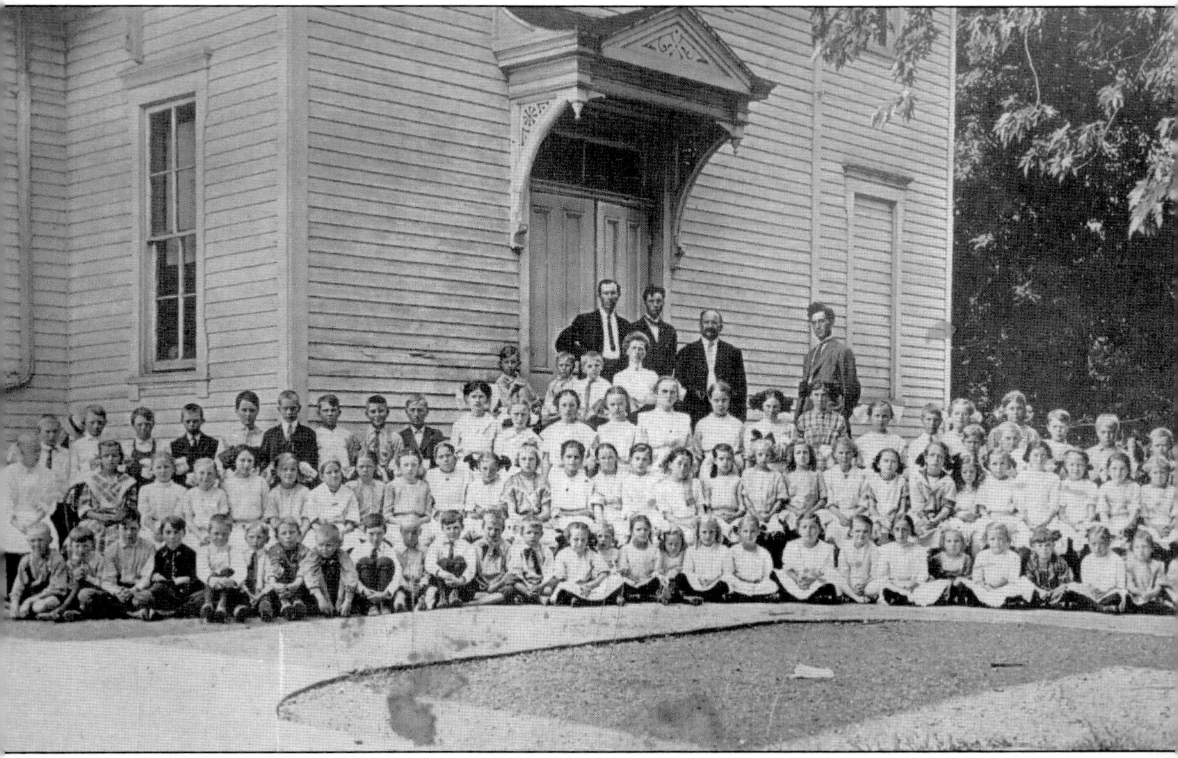

The entire student body of Story City Elementary School, along with their teachers, Prof. Fero, Cal Hanson, and Miss Johnson Larson, pose in front of their building at 627 Elm Street. A playground was south of the building and a wooden water tower stood nearby.

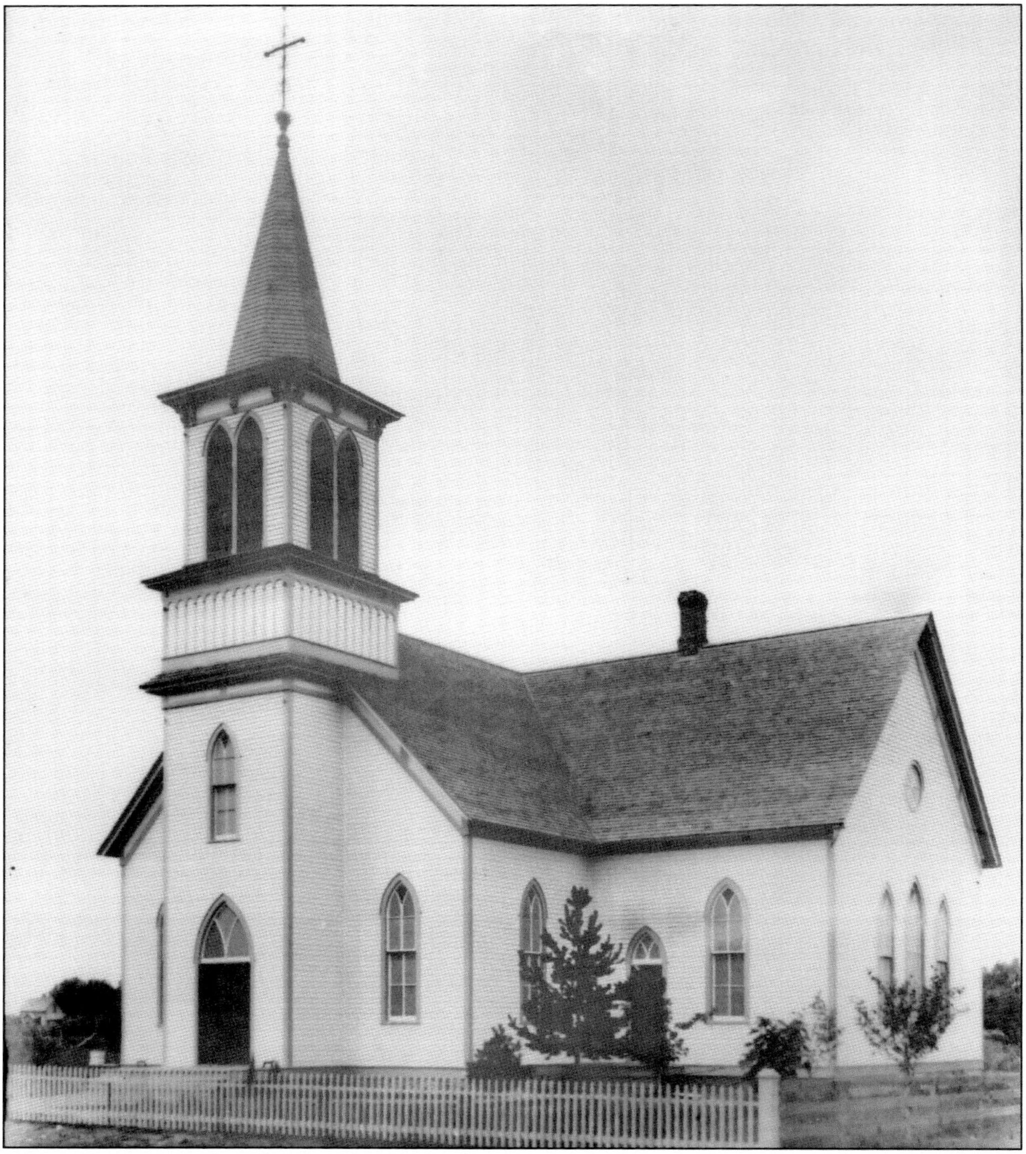

The early Immanuel Lutheran Church, at the corner of Lafayette and Broad Streets, is seen here in 1899. This building was later torn down and replaced by a brick building.

Three

Community Building

The early 1900s was a time of continued growth in Story City as the population increased, businesses expanded with new opportunities, and much of the current historic Main Street business district was constructed. A large number of brick commercial buildings were built in 1913 and some, like the Story City Theater, remain in business today. These businesses offered a great deal of support to the agricultural economy of the area, providing goods, services, and entertainment.

By this time, there was little native prairie left. Farmers were reaping the benefits of a greater variety of mechanized machinery, which significantly reduced the workload of previous generations. Steam engines were utilized more than horse-powered equipment for the threshing of grain, and tractors were making a slow emergence, although most farmers still depended on teams of draft horses.

Automobiles were beginning to gain popularity, allowing a greater range of travel around the area, often sharing the roads with horse and buggies in the transitional period. Doctors, salesmen, and others whose professions required fast transportation were quick to utilize this technology. However, the muddy roads of both the rural and urban areas of the community could slow the rate of speed significantly. In the early 1900s, Broad Street was paved and the hitching posts along the Main Street district vanished forever.

With the availability of the automobile, Lake Comar, two miles south of town, attracted tourists from across central Iowa and made Story City a popular summer resort community.

In 1917, Story City residents enlisted in the armed forces to serve in World War I, and 11 of them perished from wounds, exposure, and illness. Upon returning home, veterans went back to working in the shops, mills, and farms of the area, making a positive impact in the growth of the community. Their leadership would help guide Story City through the Great Depression.

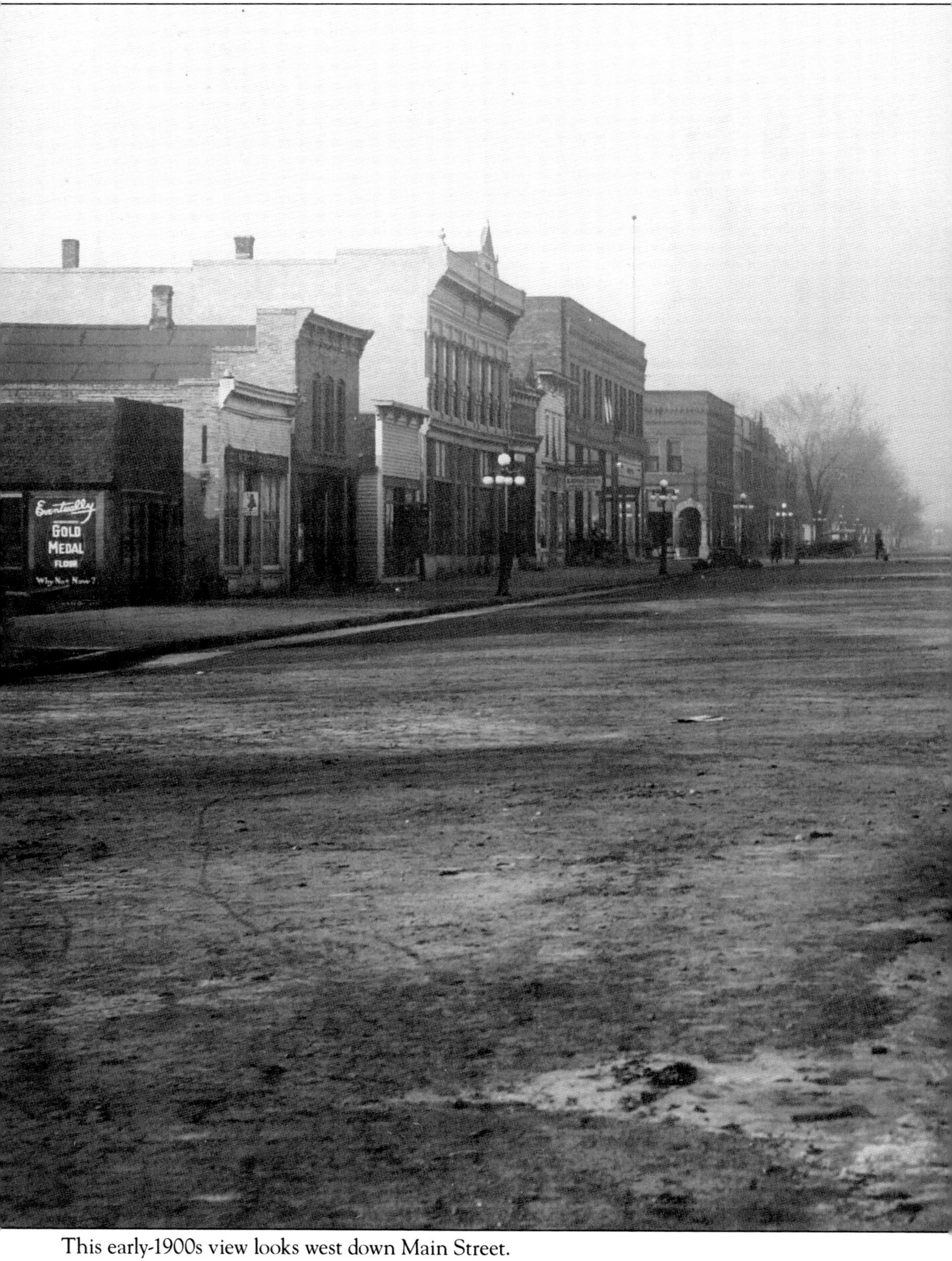

This early-1900s view looks west down Main Street.

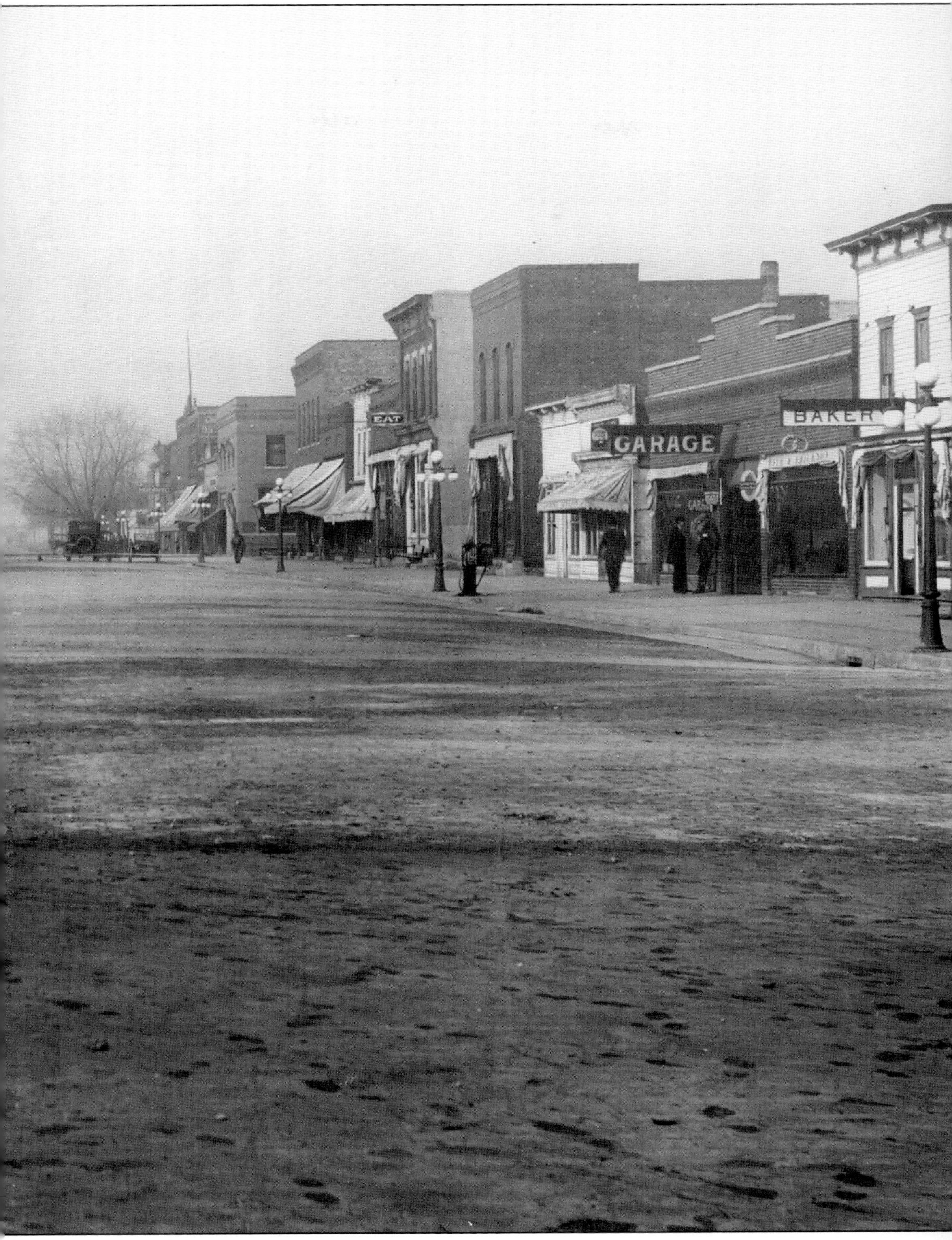
EAT
GARAGE
BAKERY

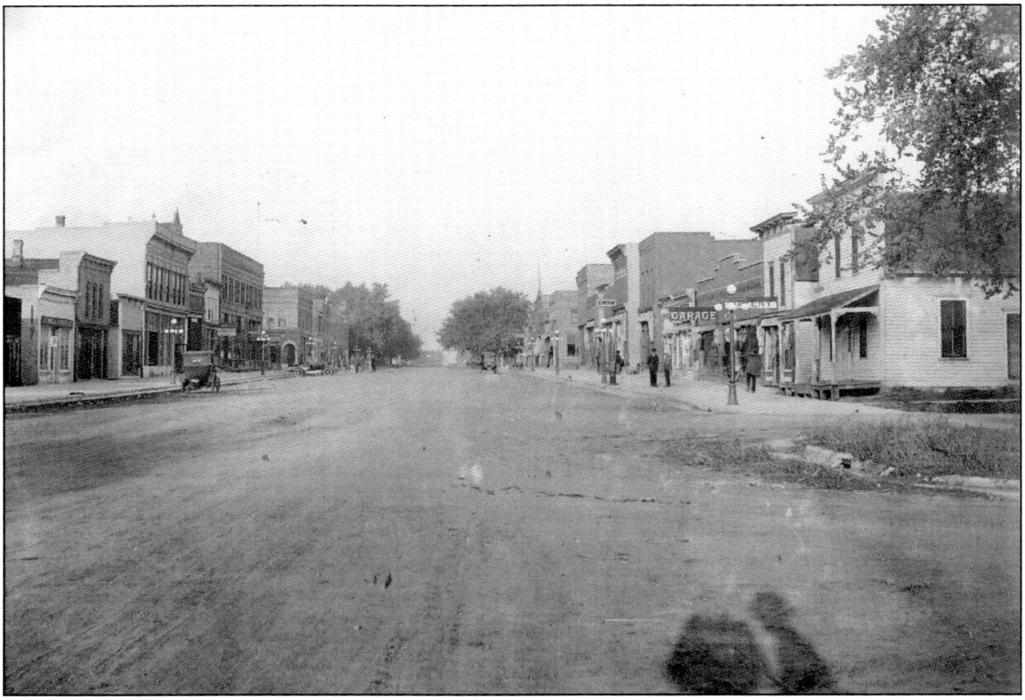

The photographer's shadow is seen in this west-facing view of the Main Street business district.

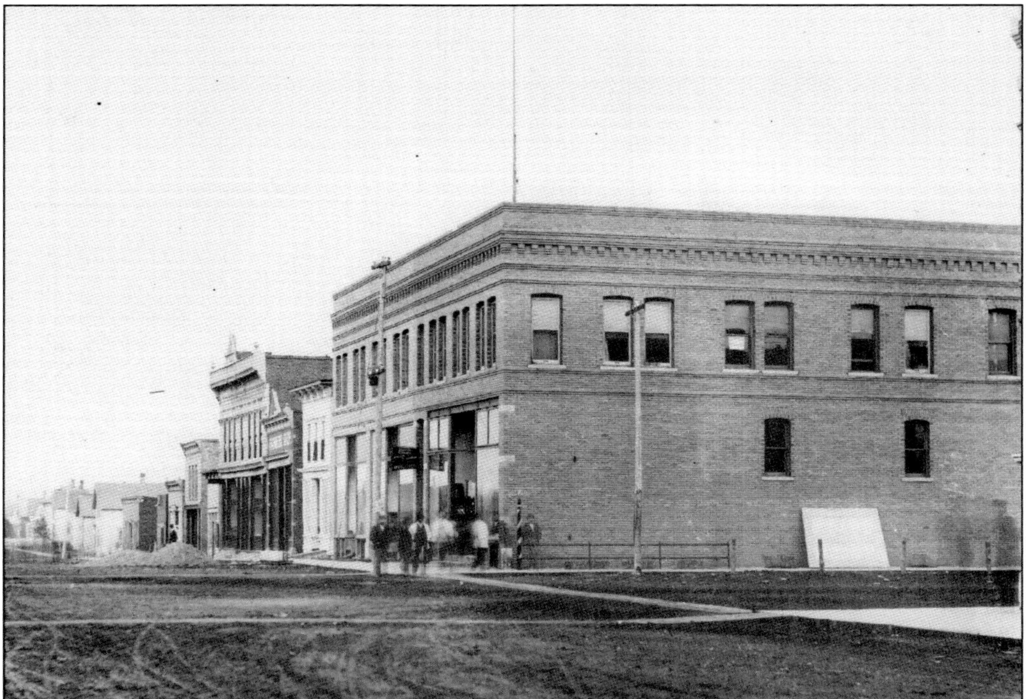

To gain access to the Pioneer Building in the early 1900s, customers walked across the muddy streets on boardwalks. This images looks southeast at the business district from Broad and Pennsylvania Streets.

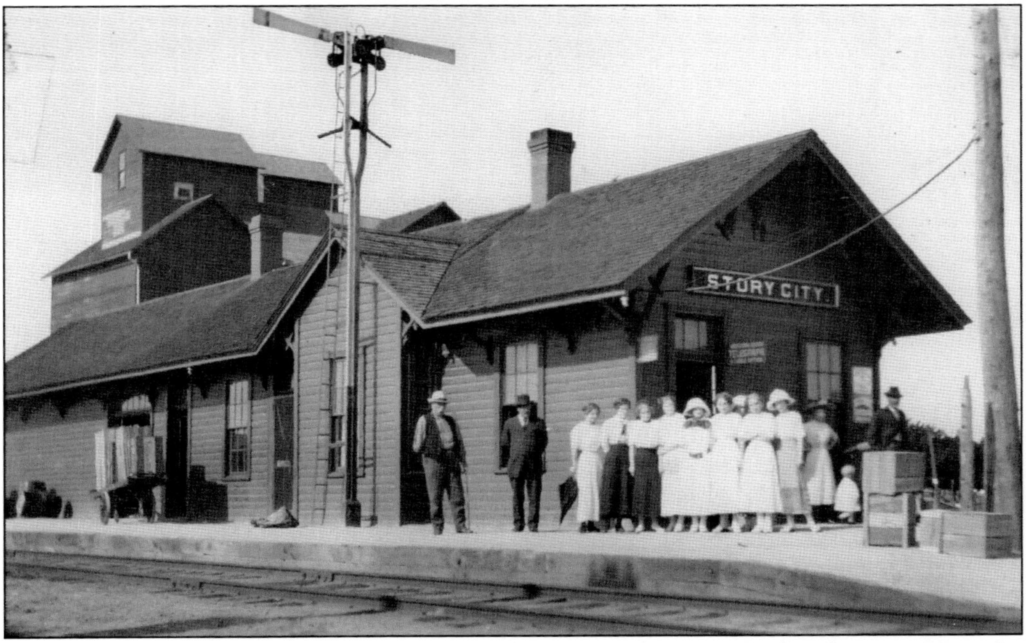

A group of young women pose in front of the Chicago Northwestern Railroad station. Note the older man with a missing arm standing next to the girls—he may be a Civil War veteran. A number of men from the area returned home from the Civil War after suffering amputations from wounds received on southern battlefields.

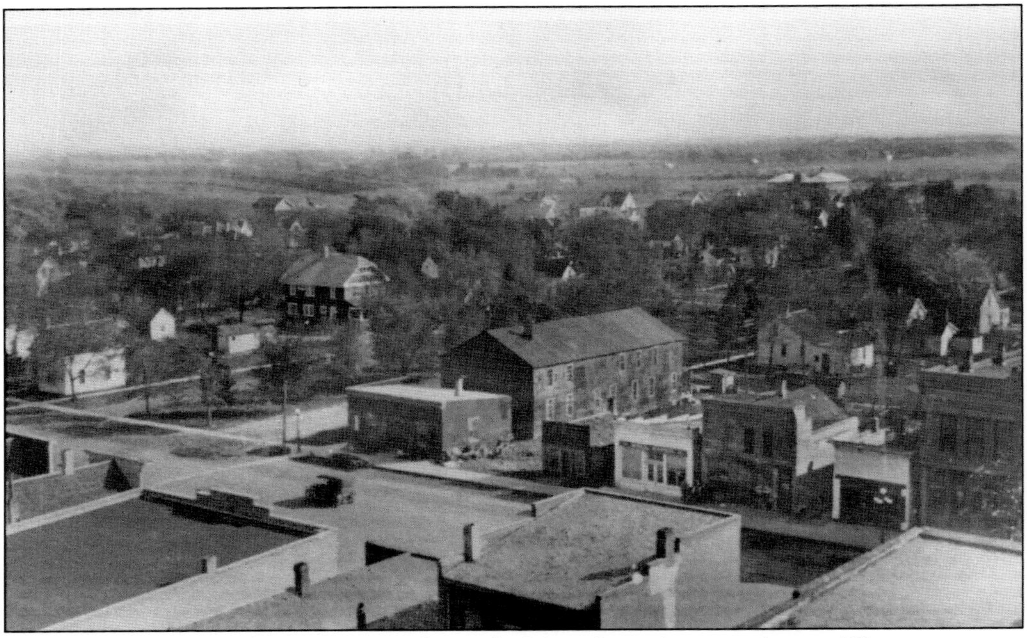

This aerial view from the water tower shows the Main Street business district. The intersection is Elm and Broad Streets and the large building to the south is the Story City Cracker Factory.

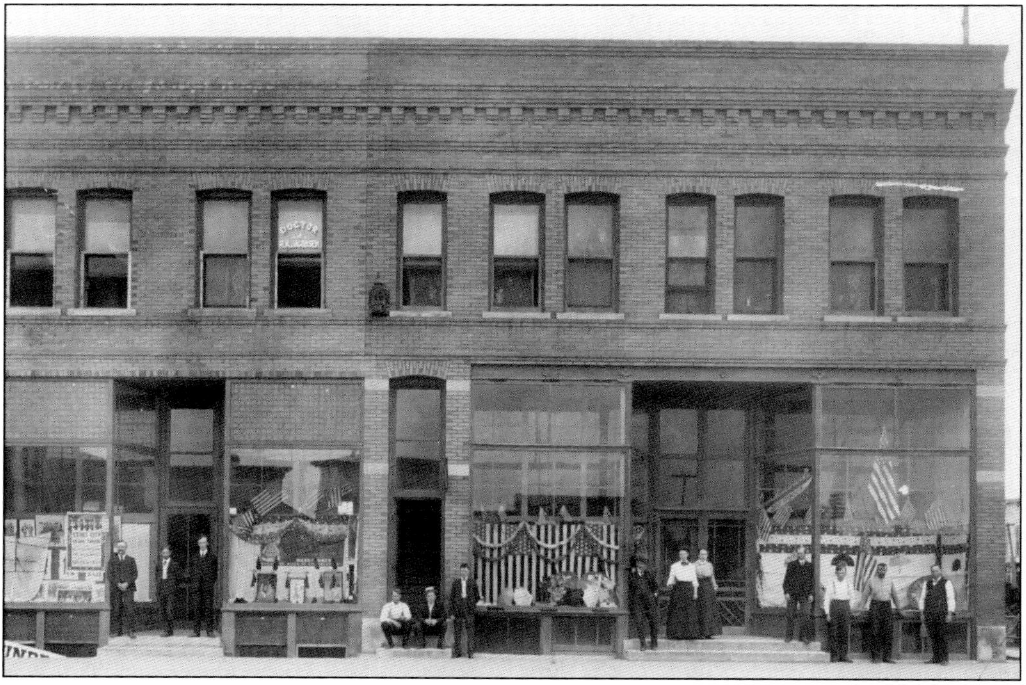

The Pioneer Building was home to a number of different establishments including Cornellisen and Co. store, a Knights of Pythius lodge, and Dr. Jacobson's office. In this image, people prepare the building for the Fourth of July parade.

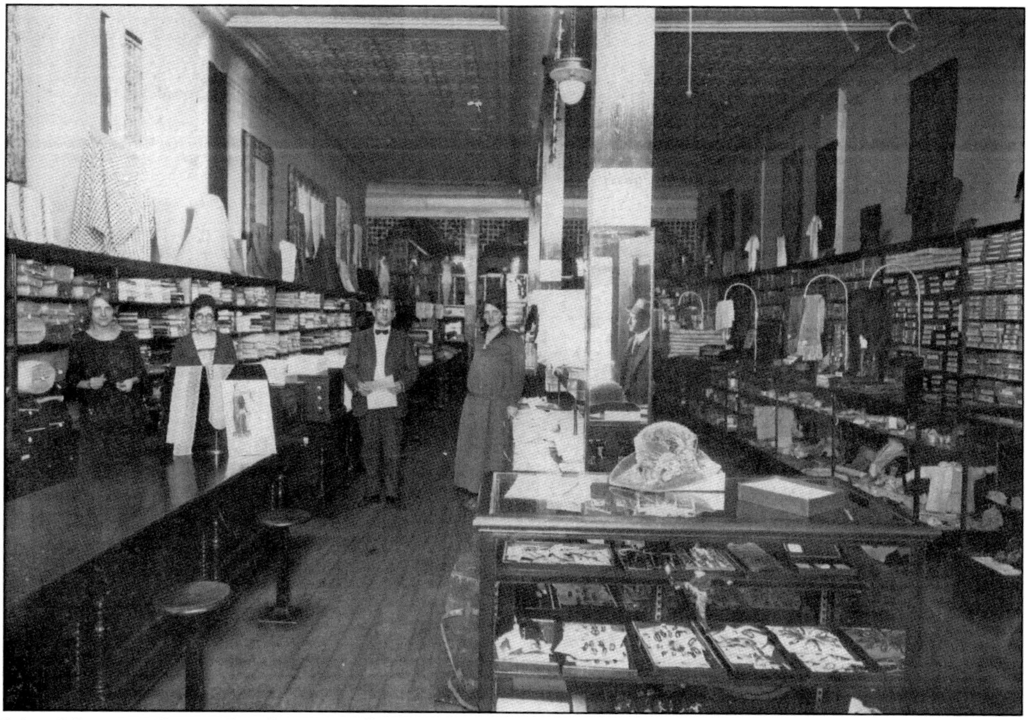

Mae Munsen, Lizzie Jacobsen, and H.J. Hauge pose for the camera in Hauge's dress shop at 521 Broad Street. The shelves display fabric, readymade clothing, and jewelry.

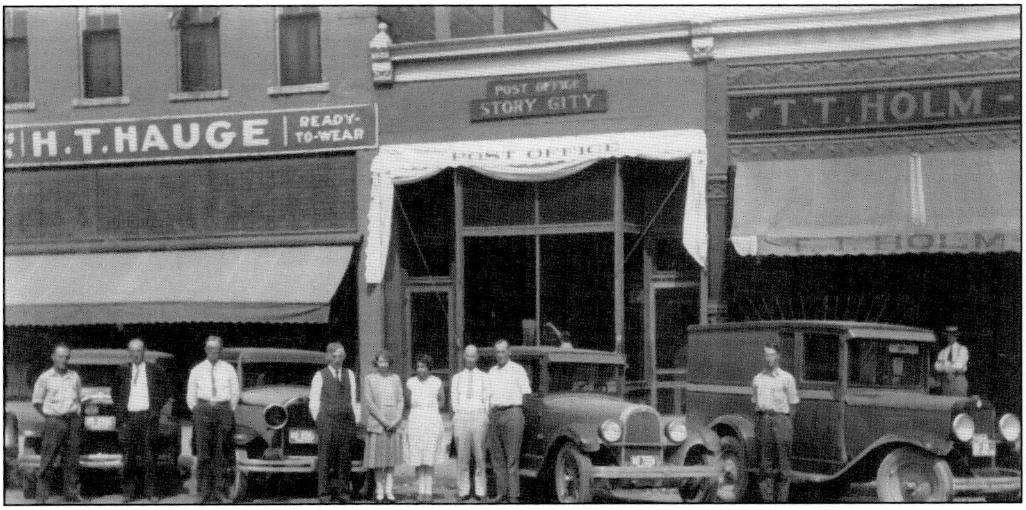

Visitors to Main Street pose in front of Hauge's dress shop, the post office, and Holm's harness shop.

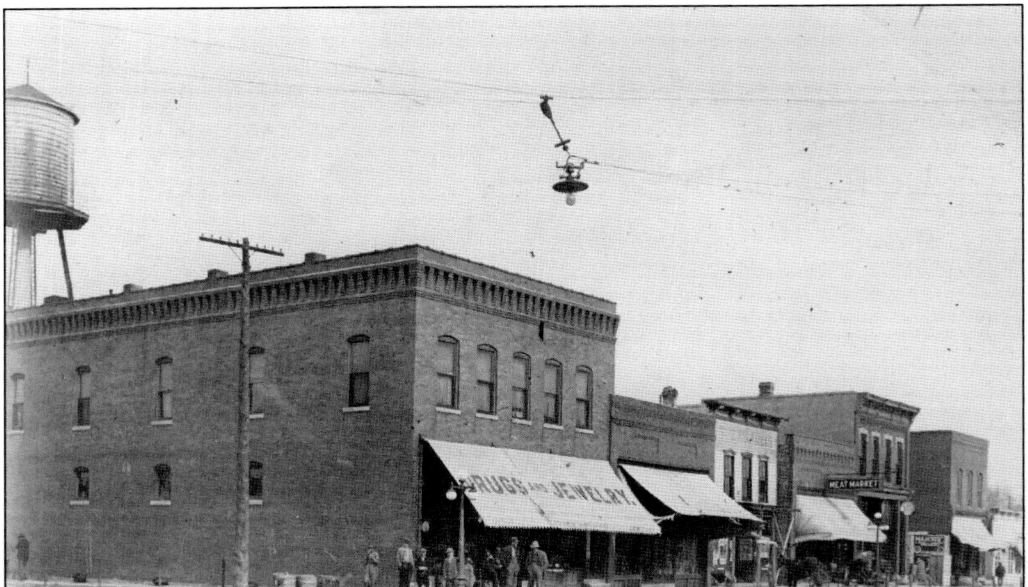

At the corner of Park and Broad Streets, a business awning reads "Drugs and Jewelry" just down the street from a meat market. Wooden boardwalks cross Broad Street and an electric light dangles above the intersection.

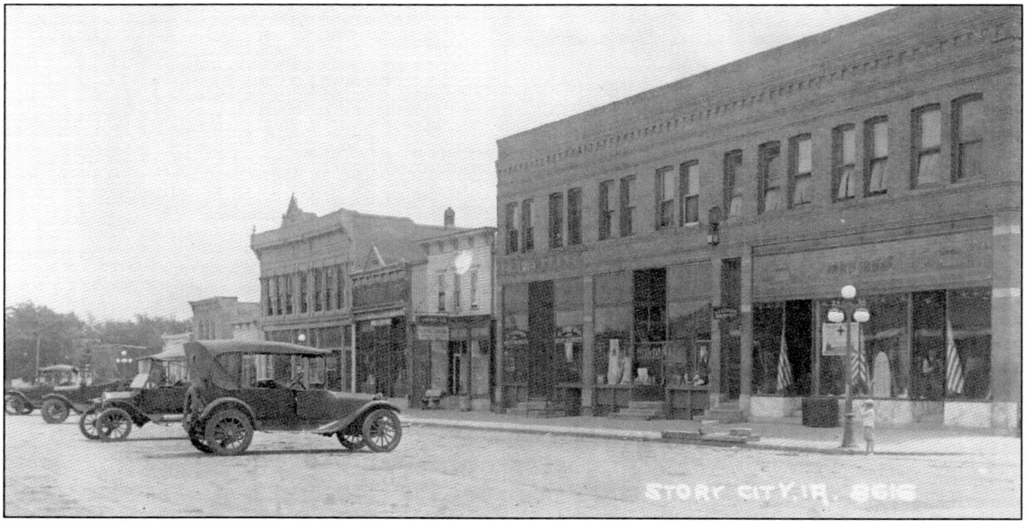

The Pioneer Store Company along Broad Street has American flags in the window and a Red Cross promotional sign. Small American flags were an economical and common decoration in Story City for patriotic celebrations, parades, and to show support for soldiers. A similar flag was found during the rehabilitation of the Charlson Building and is on display in the community's chamber office.

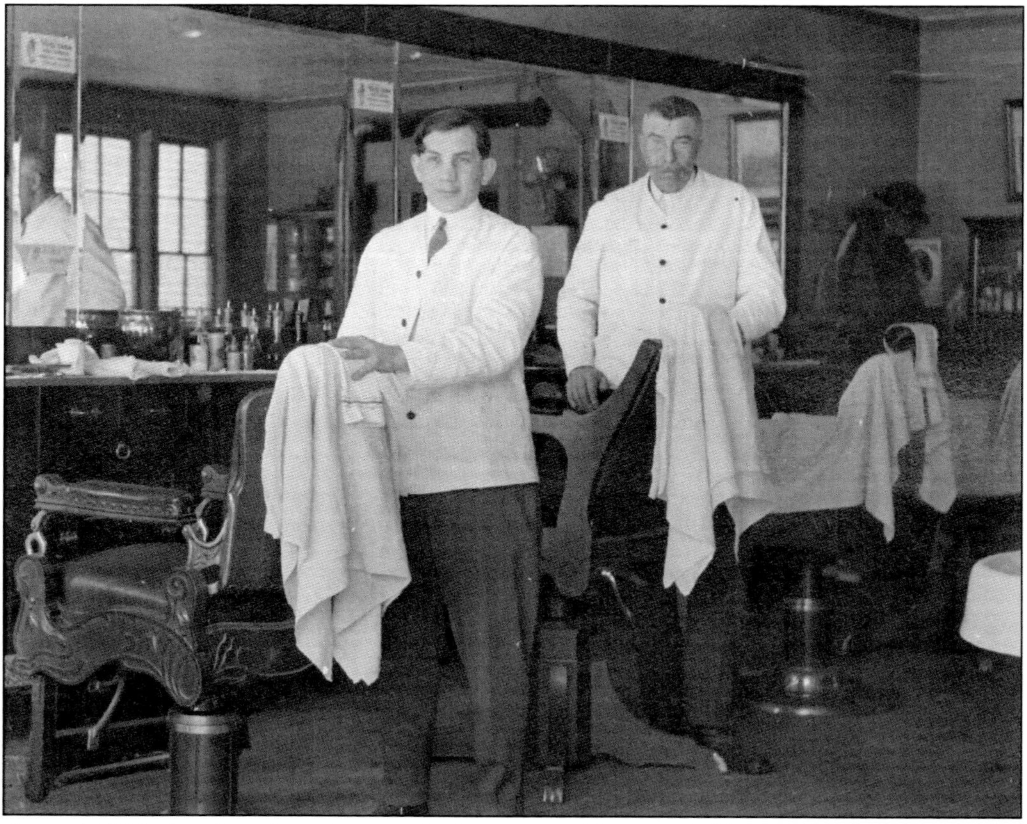
Around 1900, the place for a shave and a haircut was Freeman Fuller's barbershop. In the days before safety razors, barbershops offered a place for men to receive a straight razor shave.

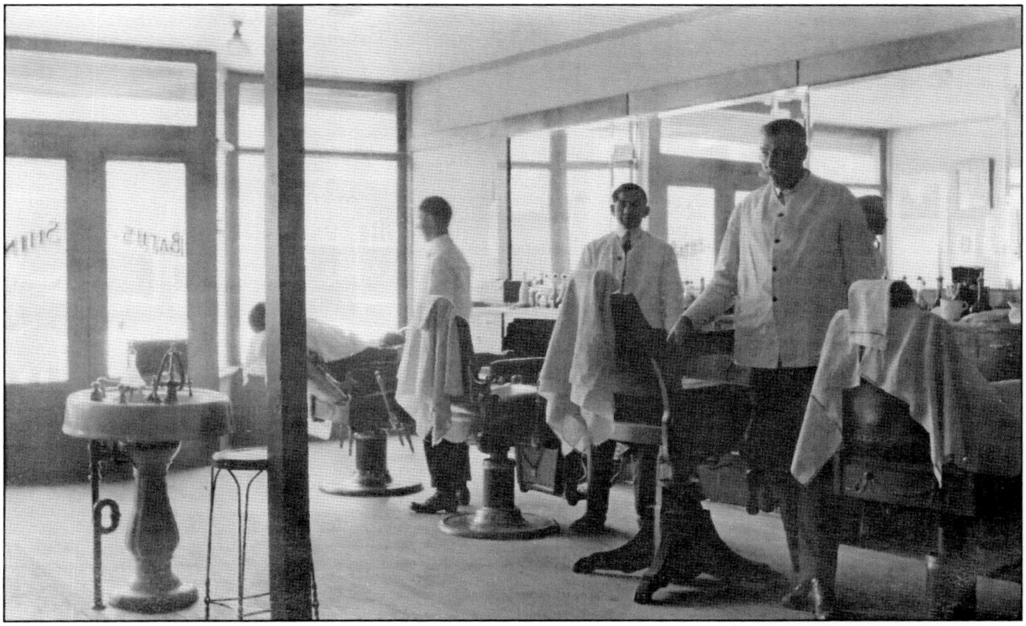

Freeman Fuller was a towering presence in his barbershop at 515 Broad Street. Barbershops were a great place for men to catch up on news in the community while receiving a trim and a clean shave.

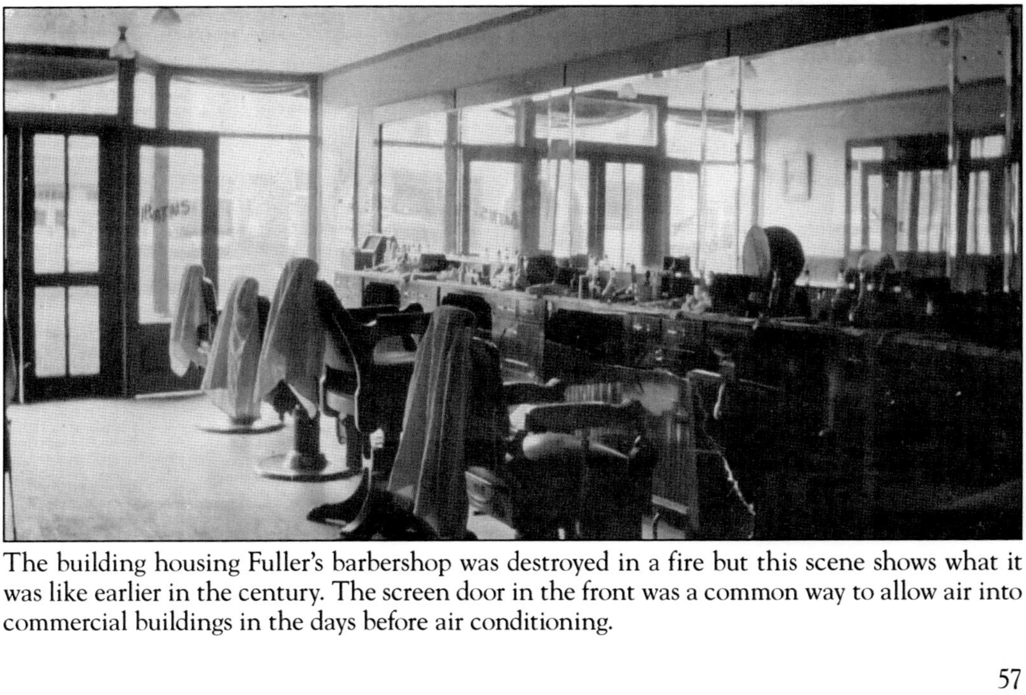

The building housing Fuller's barbershop was destroyed in a fire but this scene shows what it was like earlier in the century. The screen door in the front was a common way to allow air into commercial buildings in the days before air conditioning.

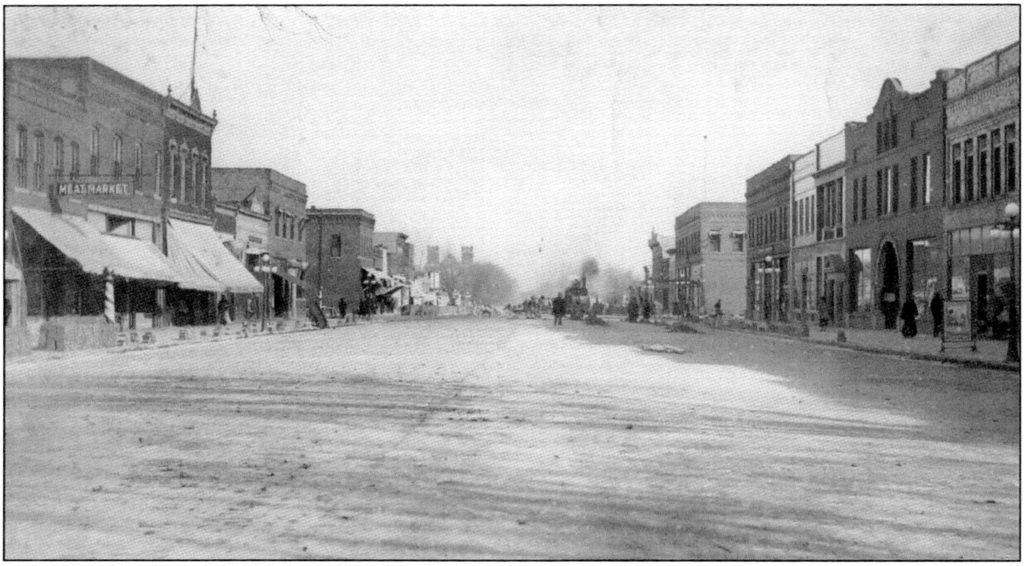

This westward view looks down Broad Street while brick streets were being installed. The striped barber pole marks Fuller's barbershop and the silhouette of Immanuel Lutheran Church is in the distance.

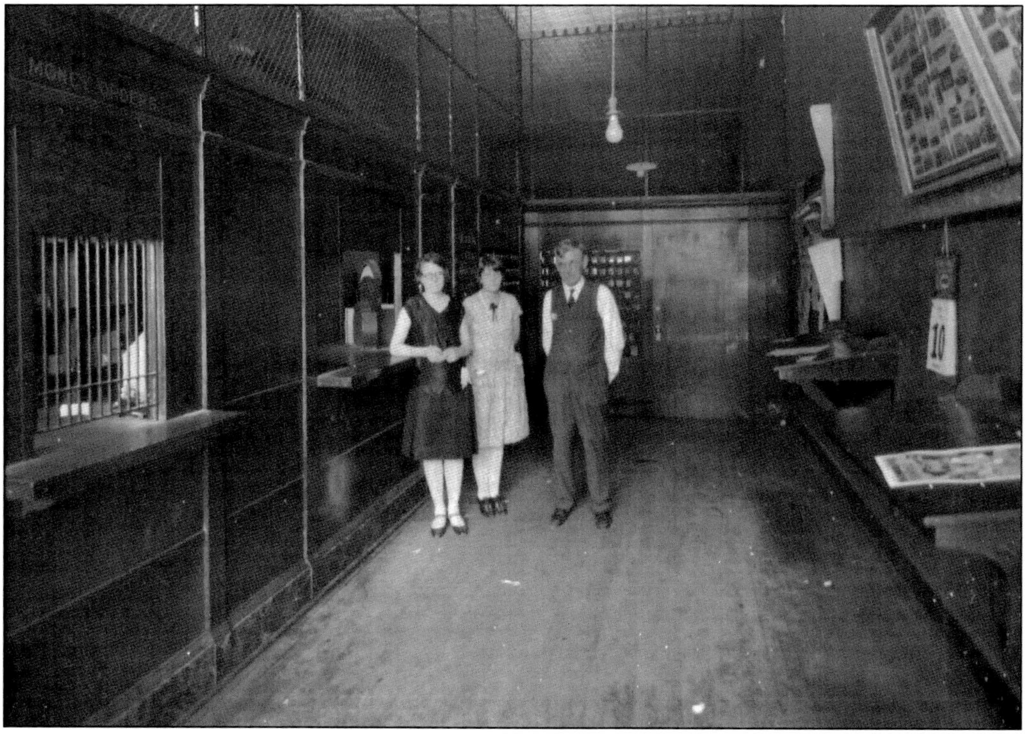

Employees stand in the lobby of the post office. The two large, framed pictures hanging on the wall show past postmasters and are still on display in the lobby of the current post office, now in a different building.

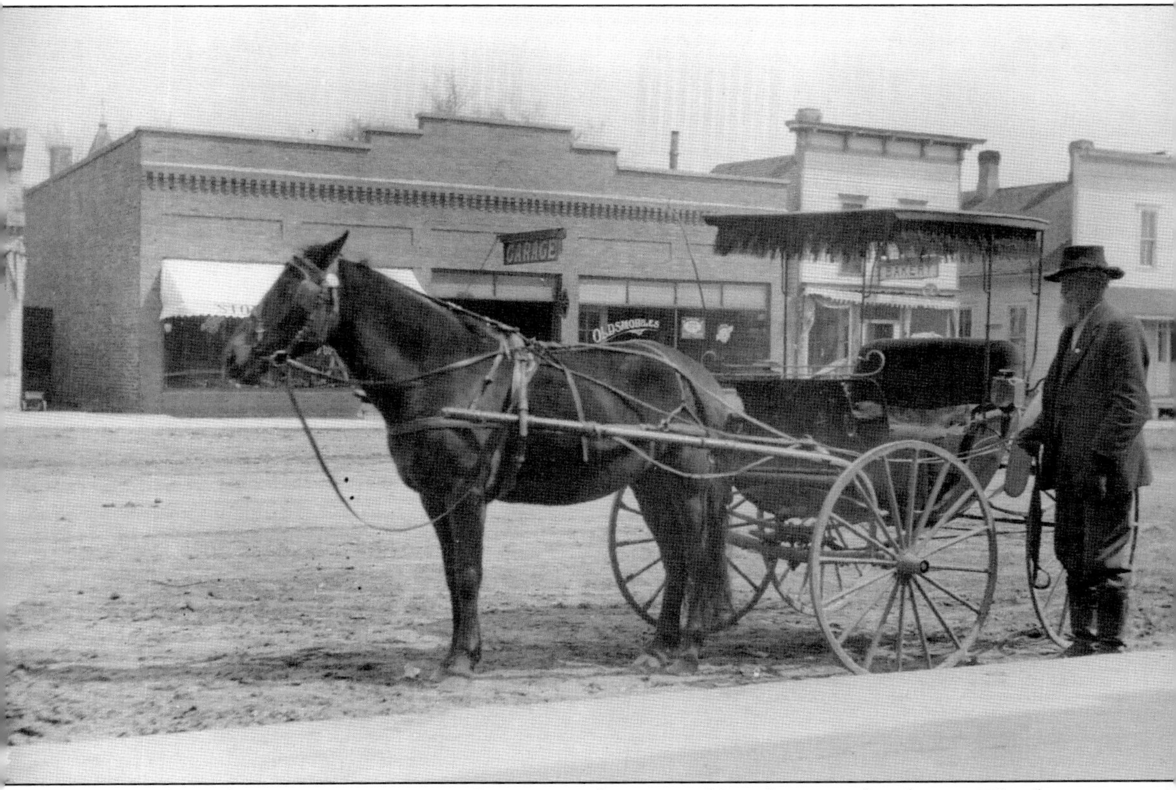

The early 20th century was a time of transition between old and new technologies. This horse-drawn buggy faces north in front of a garage on Broad Street.

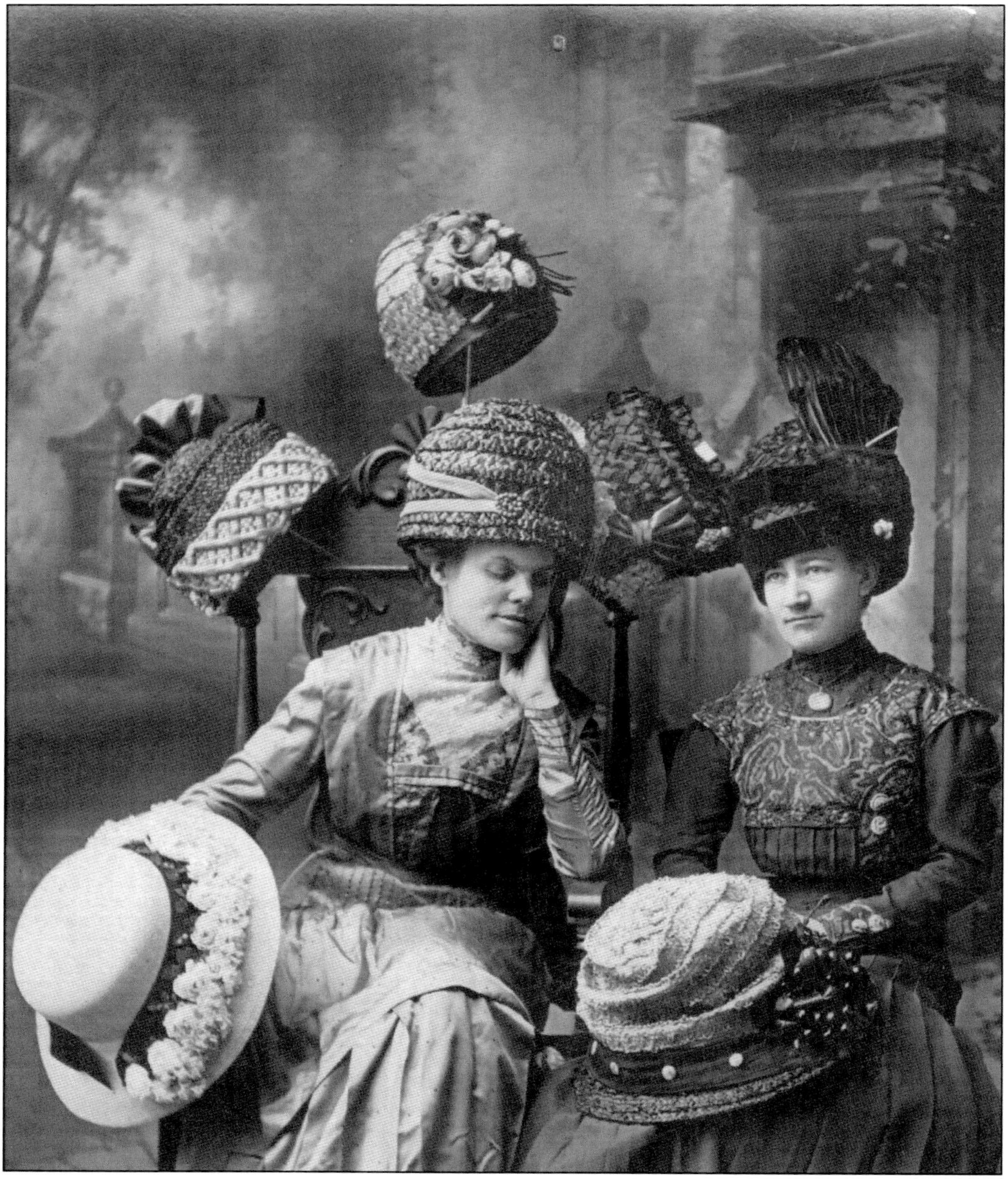

Julia and Anna Mathre pose with some of their millinery products. These unique masterpieces constructed with materials like ribbon, woven straw, silk flowers, and feathers were worn by area women in the early 1900s.

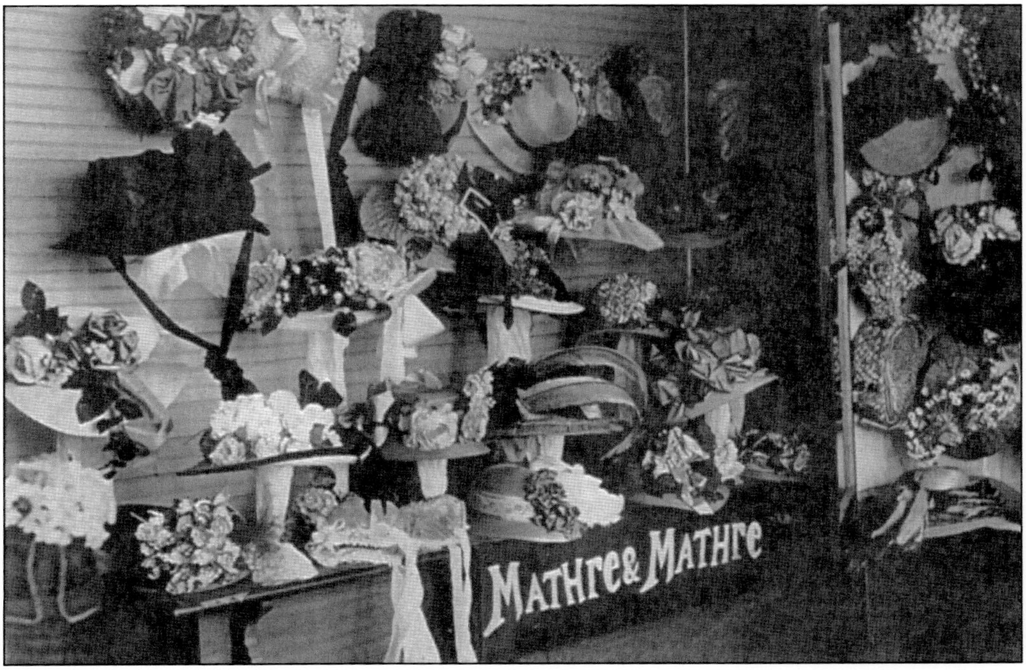

These millinery hats were produced by the Mathres for the women of Story City. Many of these hats were one-of-a-kind and carefully selected by the wearer for a number of occasions.

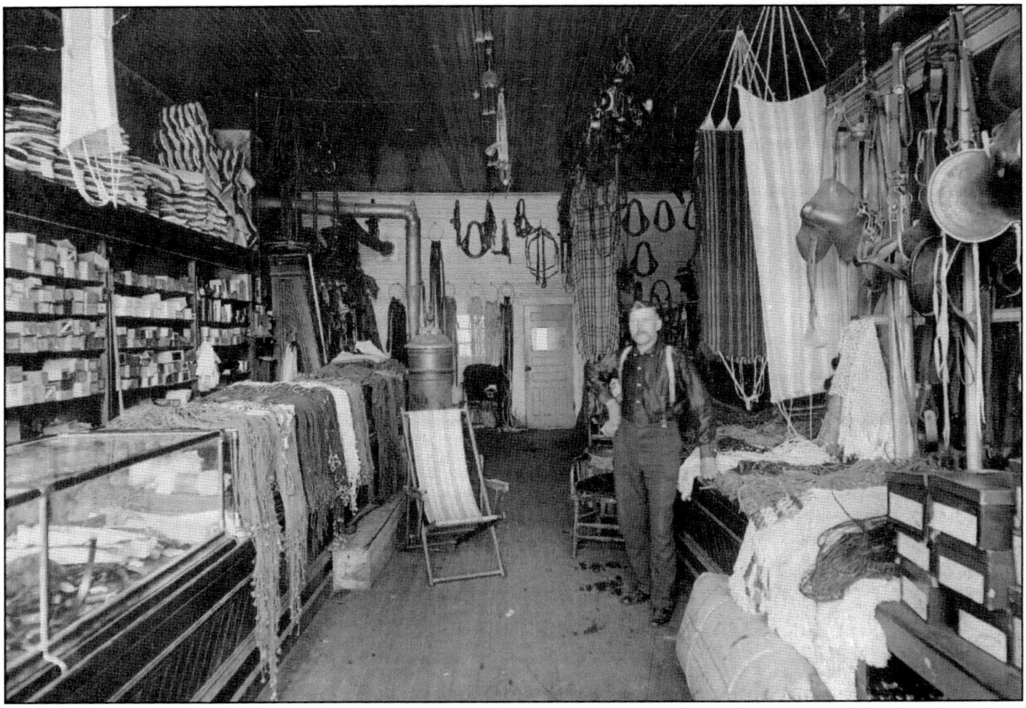

This interior view shows T.T. Holm's harness shop. Horse collars hang on the back wall and striped canvas hammocks are suspended from the ceiling. Slung across the counters are leather thong fly nets, which were placed on the backs of horses to discourage flies, an ingenious way of coping with biting insects in the days before chemical sprays.

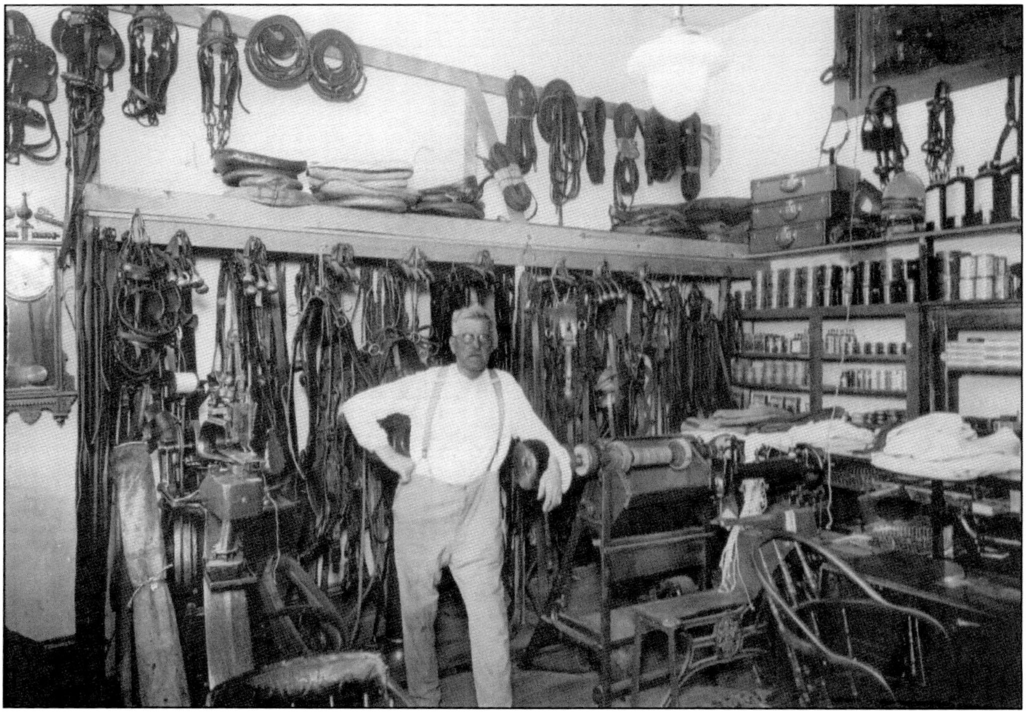

Holm's harness shop provided materials for farmers still using horses until the mid-1900s. This image shows a mix of technologies, with electric machinery alongside traditional leather harnesses.

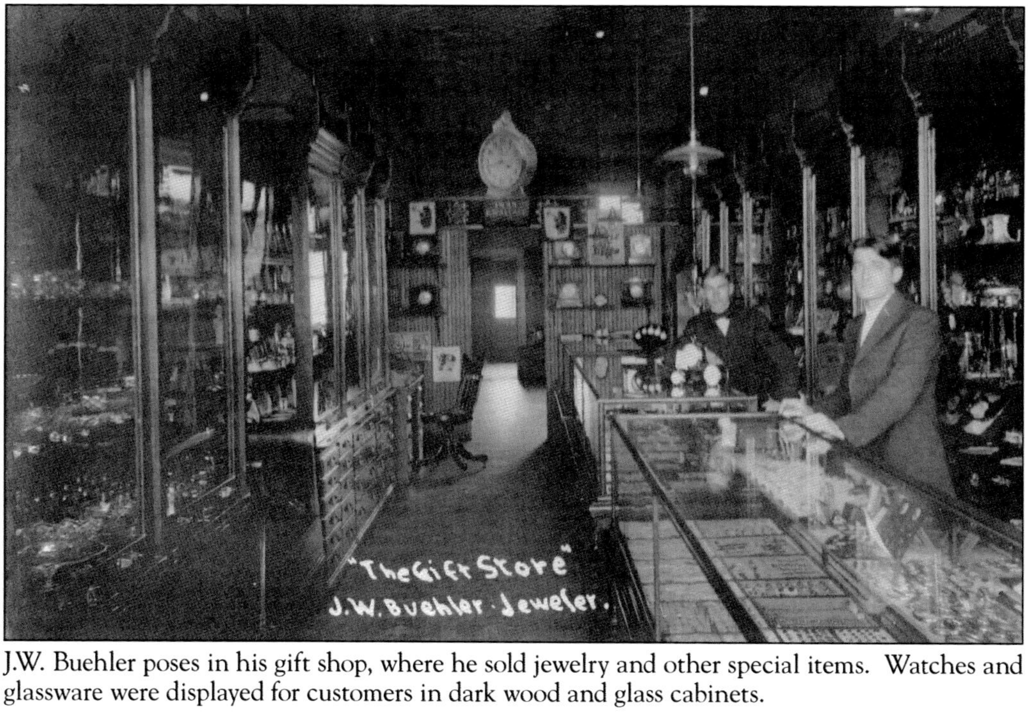

J.W. Buehler poses in his gift shop, where he sold jewelry and other special items. Watches and glassware were displayed for customers in dark wood and glass cabinets.

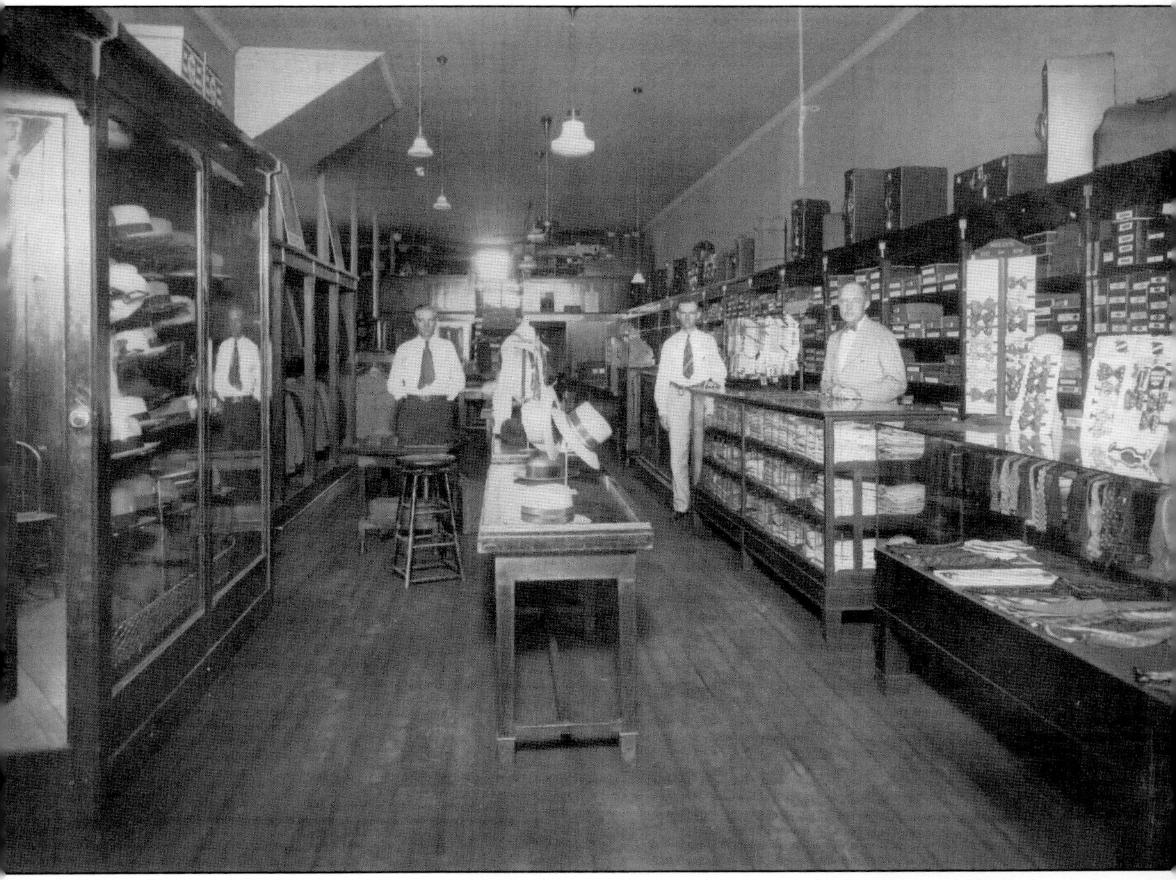

This photograph shows the interior of the Donhowe and Charlson clothing store. Well-dressed men shopped here for suits, shirts, and felt hats. The wooden balcony is still present in the store's former building, now an antique store.

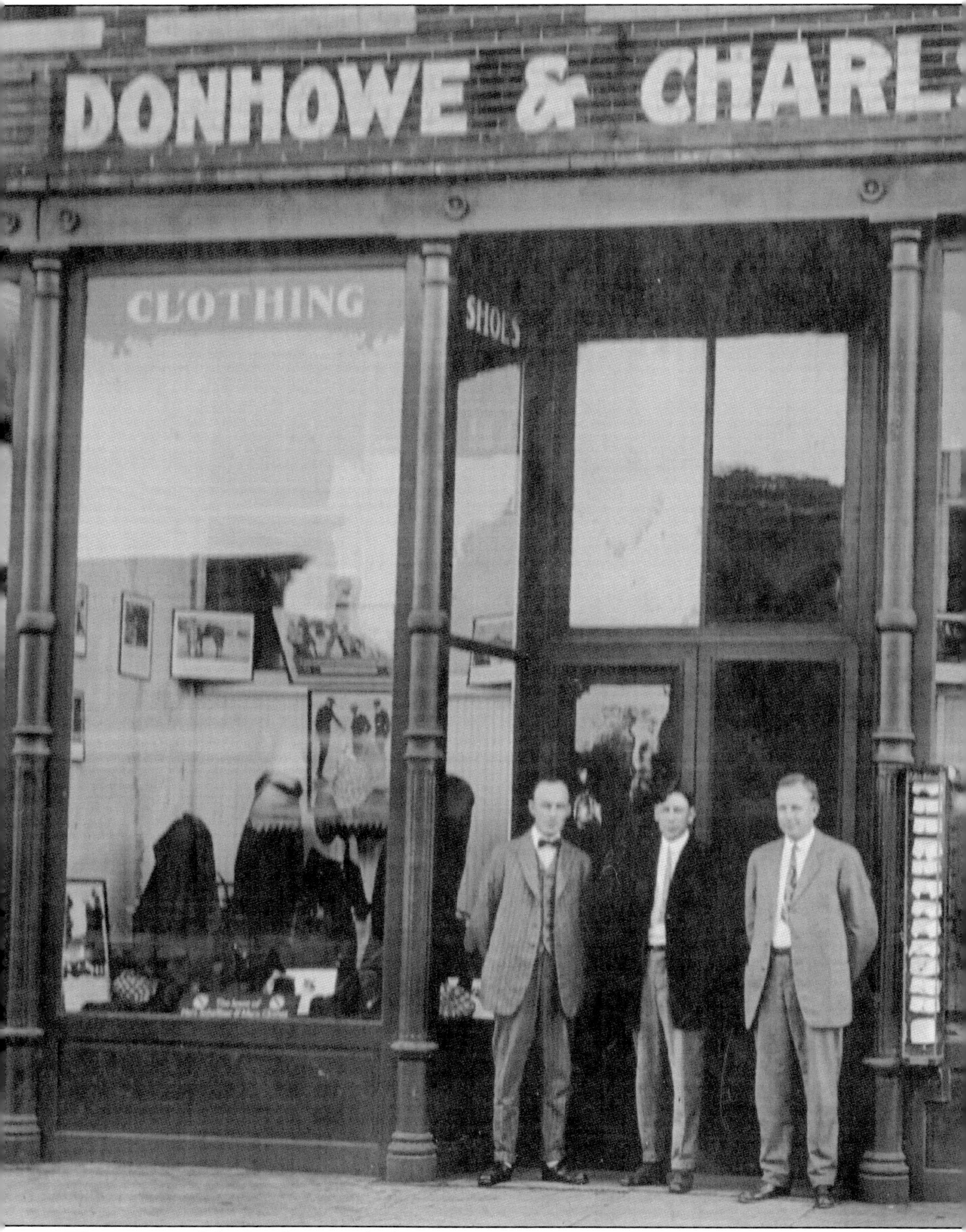

The exterior of the Dunhowe and Charlson clothing store featured large display windows and an advertising bench along the sidewalk. Peter Donhowe and Ed Charlson owned the business.

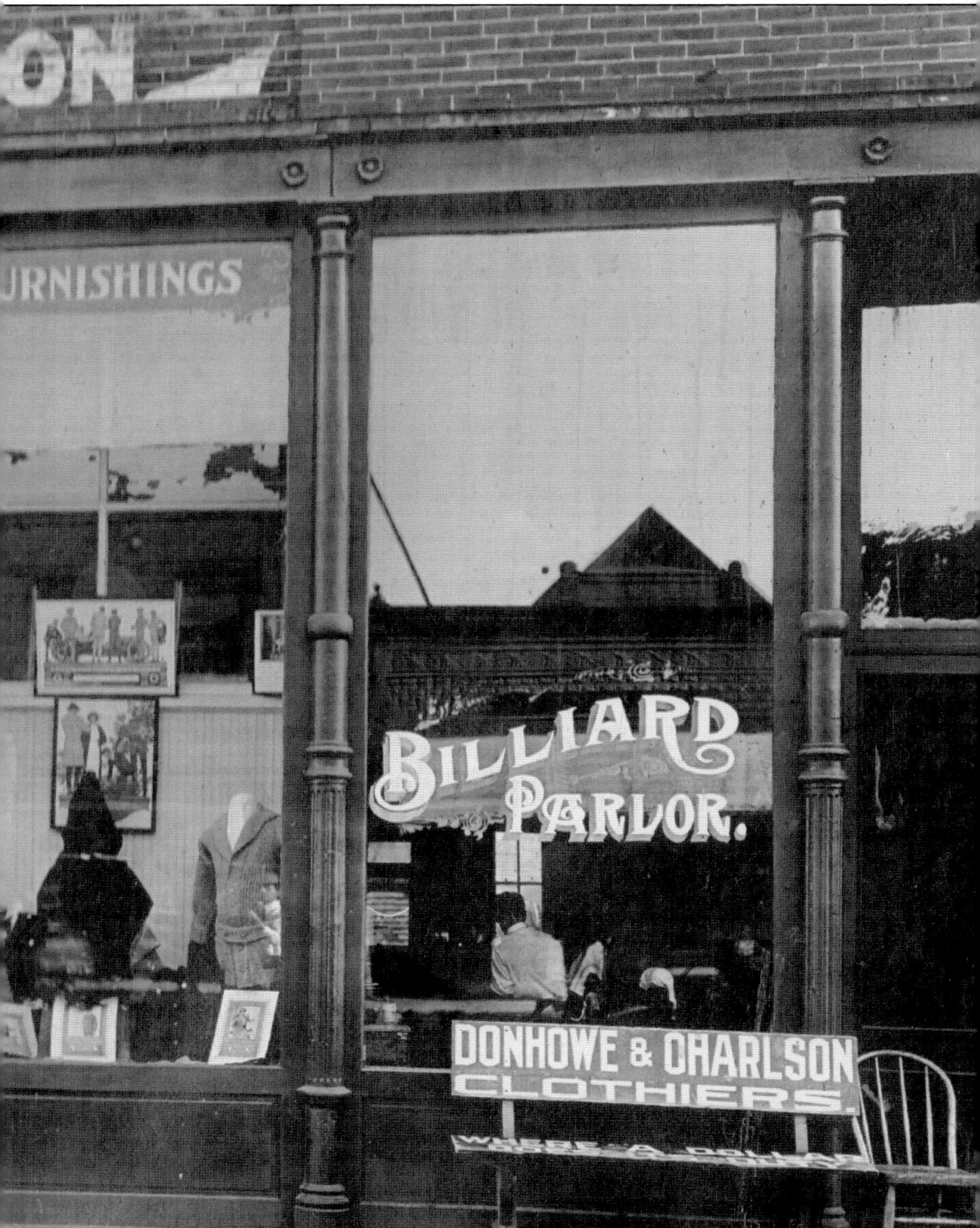

Arnold Johnson began working there as a teenager and eventually became the main salesman and the owner.

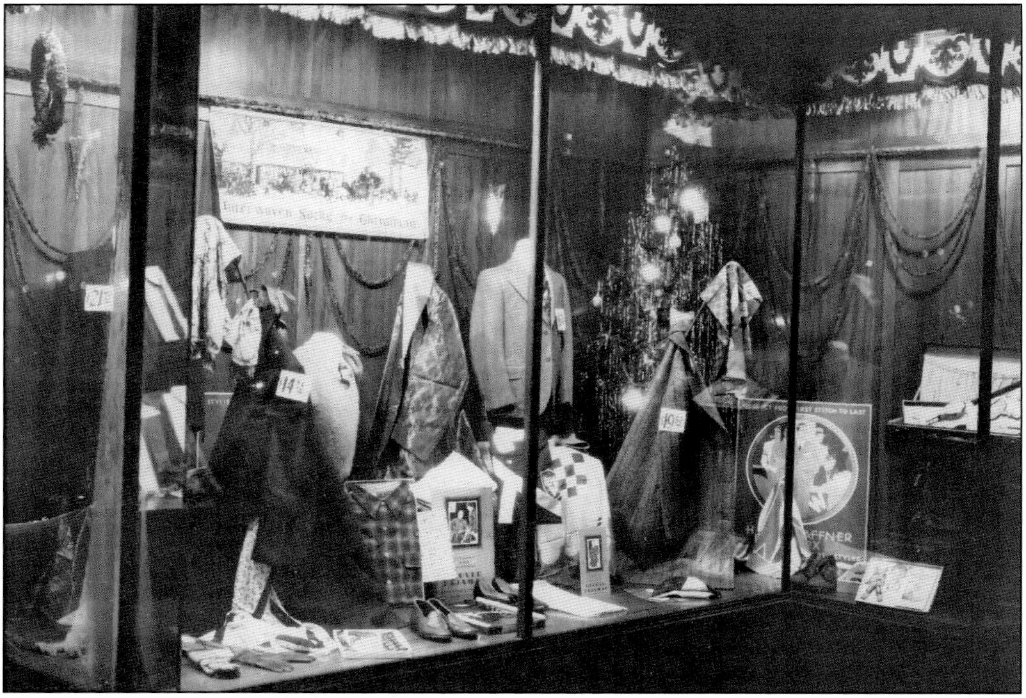

This display window along the sidewalk in front of Dunhowe and Charlson clothing store attracted customers. It was a popular venue for out-of-towners to visit and learn about what was taking place in the community.

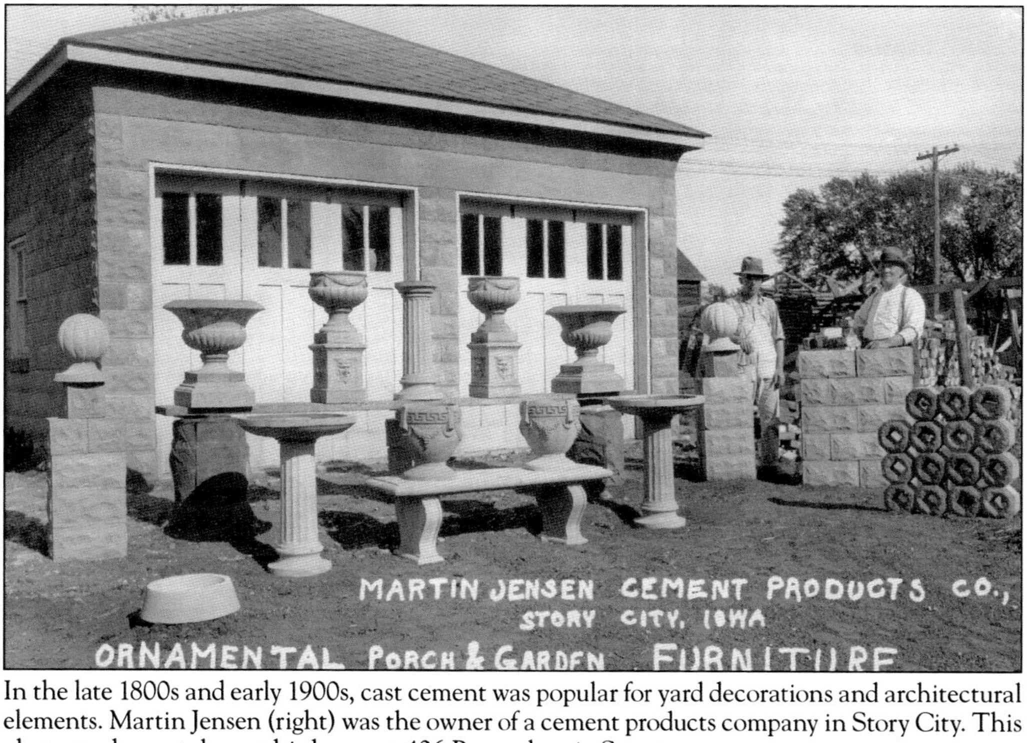

In the late 1800s and early 1900s, cast cement was popular for yard decorations and architectural elements. Martin Jensen (right) was the owner of a cement products company in Story City. This photograph was taken at his home at 406 Pennsylvania Street.

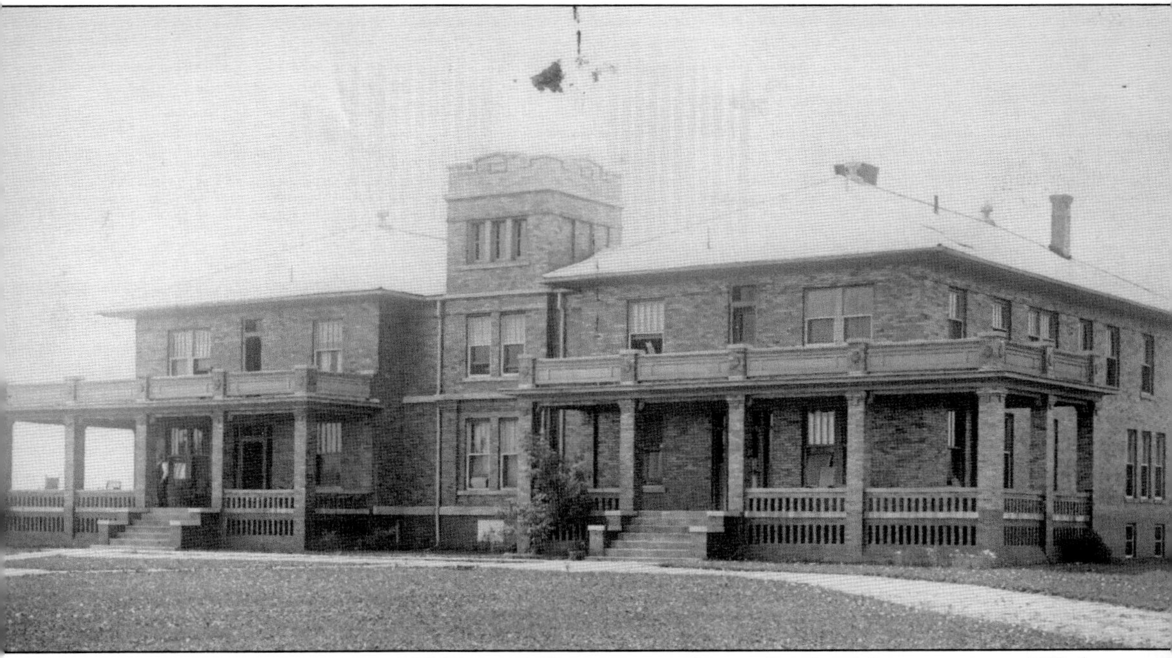

The Story City Sanitarium and Old Person's Home was on the south side of the community. While the historic brick building has long since been demolished, the operation became incorporated into Bethany Manor, a major employer in Story City today.

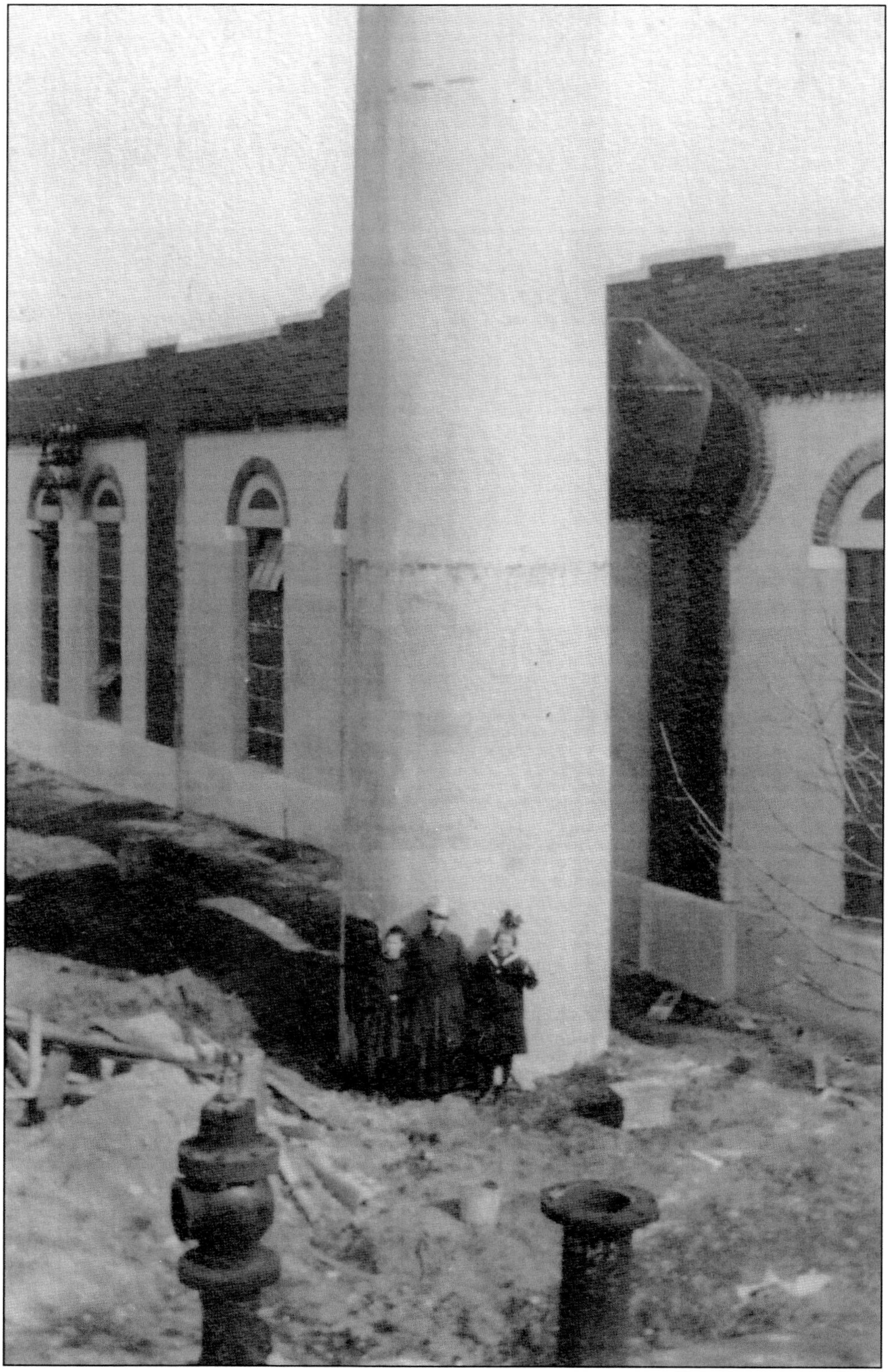

During construction of the Story City power plant, a few community residents posed for a snapshot dwarfed below the towering smokestack of the building.

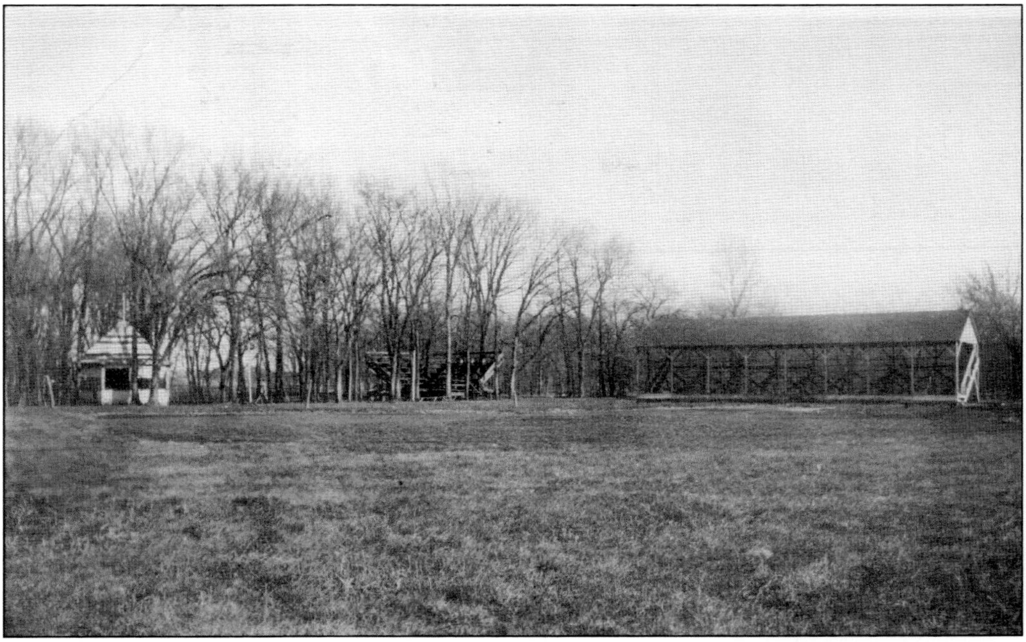

Baseball games and other community events took place in the open space in front of this grandstand in the Story City park around 1900.

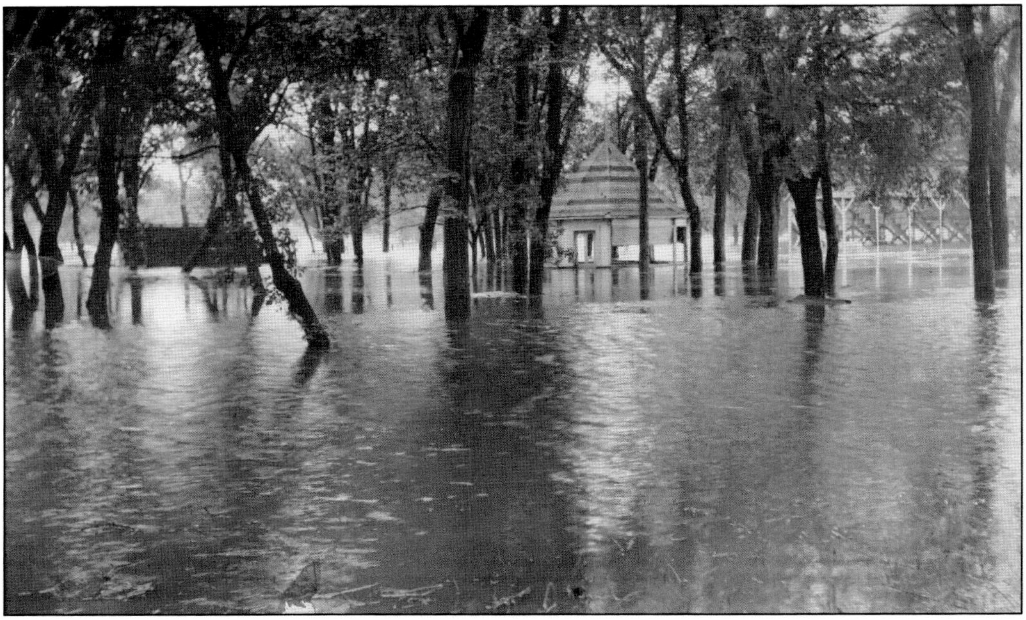

The city park is on bottom ground along the Skunk River, which is prone to flooding after the spring thaw or summer rains.

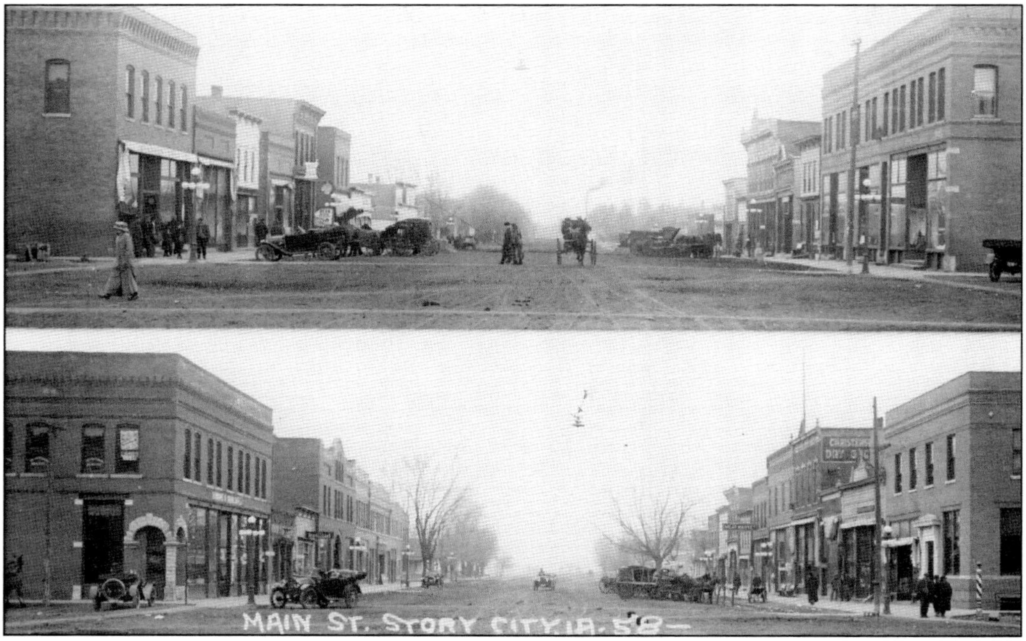

This historical postcard faces west (above) and east (below) from the same location along Broad Street. A light is strung on a cable between two poles in the air above the intersection.

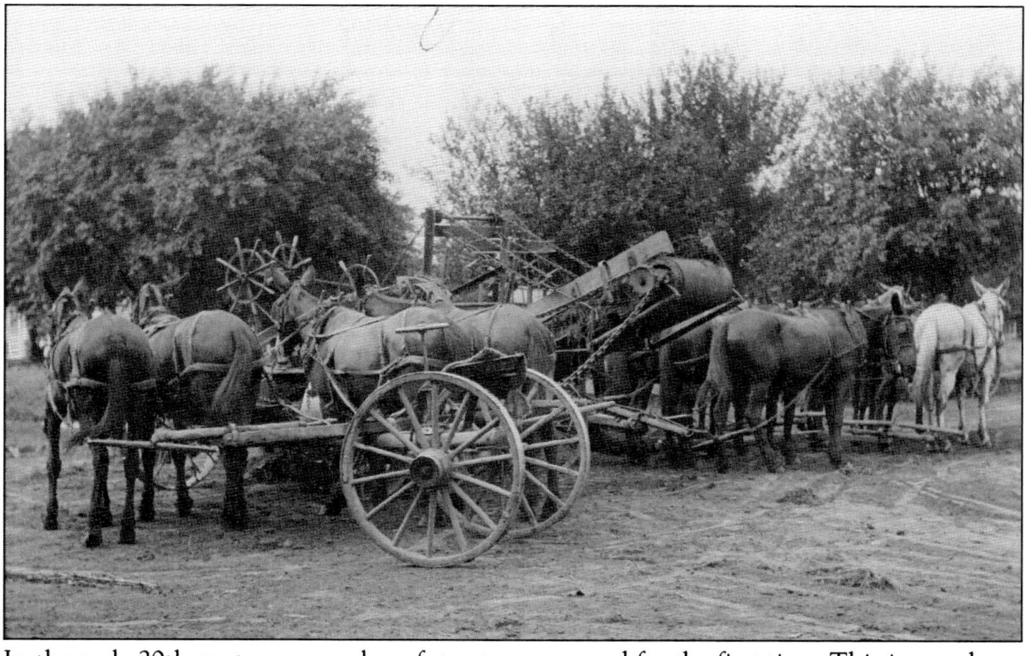
In the early 20th century, a number of streets were paved for the first time. This image shows some of the equipment used for the operation.

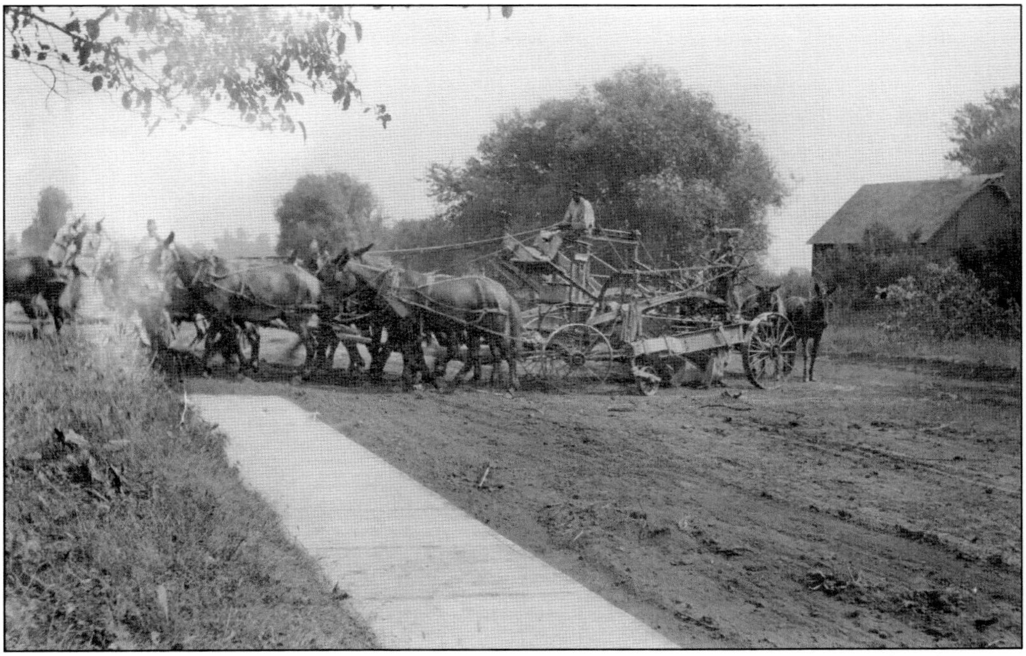

A tremendous amount of power was required to move earth and grade streets, and mule teams were utilized to fill the need. Teams of mules were likely rotated to pull this equipment once or twice each day during the grading process.

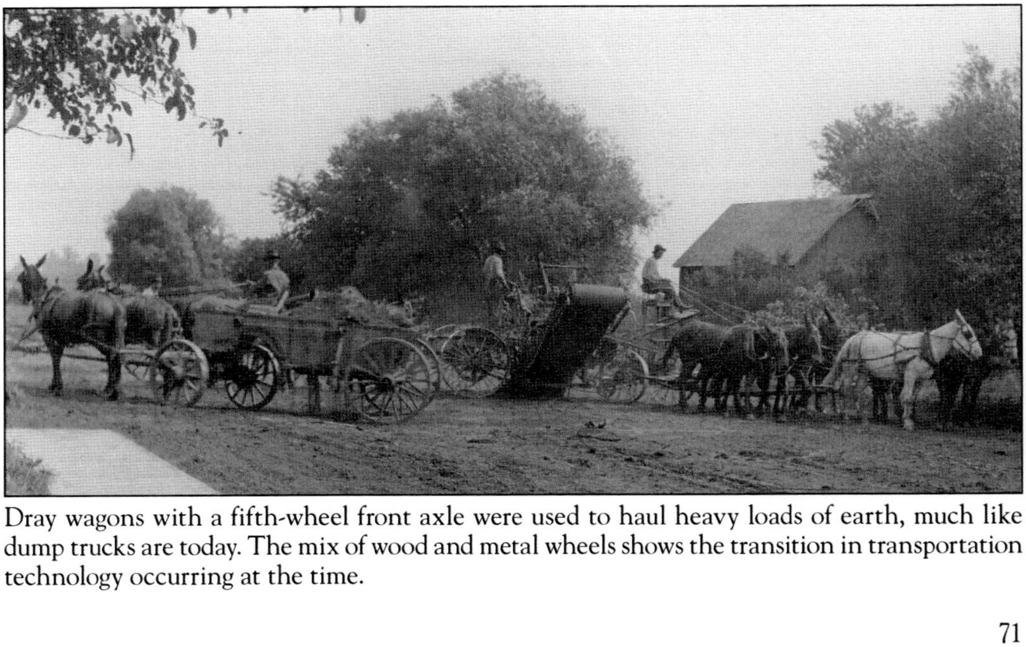

Dray wagons with a fifth-wheel front axle were used to haul heavy loads of earth, much like dump trucks are today. The mix of wood and metal wheels shows the transition in transportation technology occurring at the time.

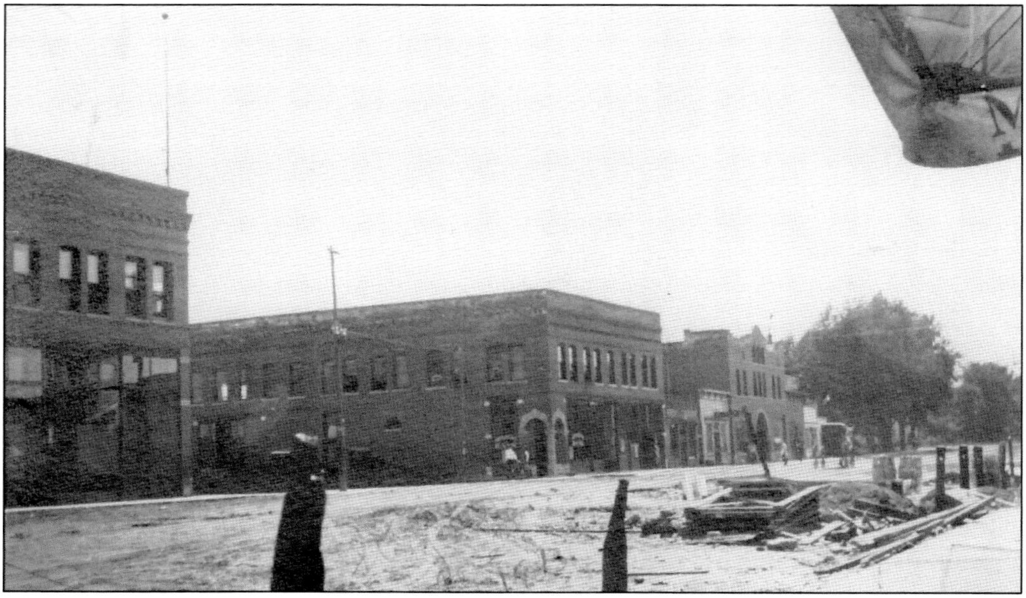

These wooden hitching posts along Broad Street are prepared for removal for brick paving. Buggy horses were replaced by cars fairly quickly, but draft horses were retained on many farms for agricultural work for decades later.

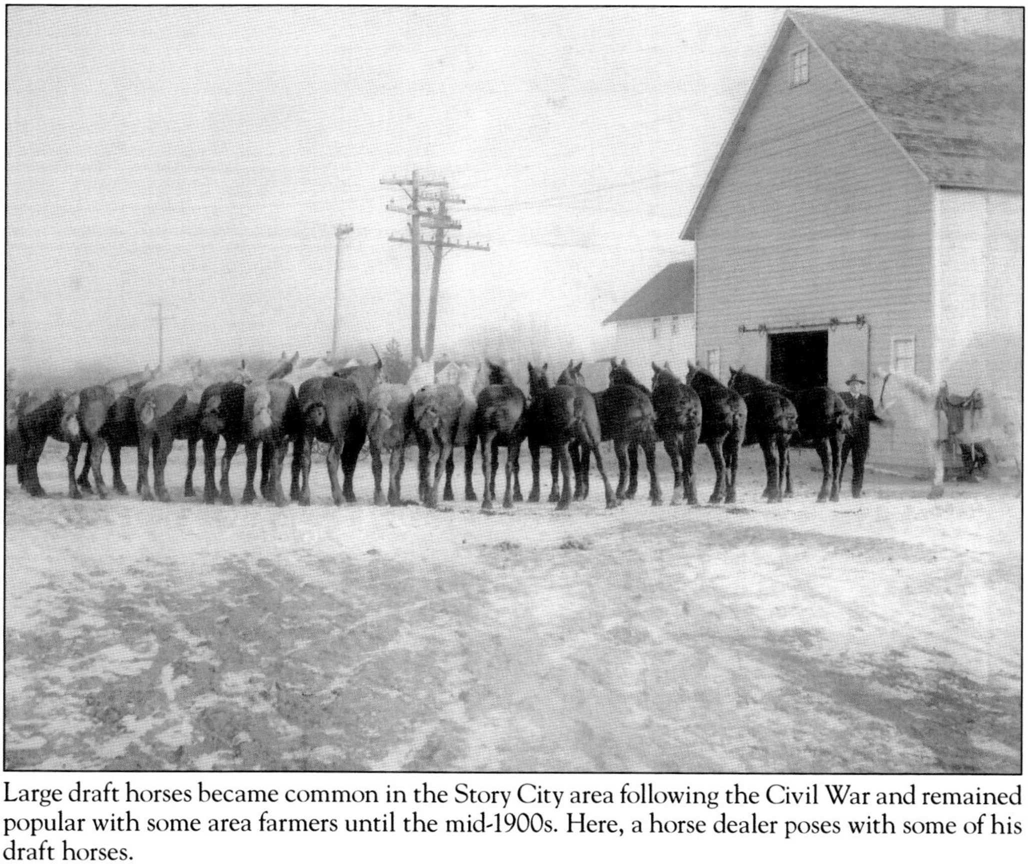

Large draft horses became common in the Story City area following the Civil War and remained popular with some area farmers until the mid-1900s. Here, a horse dealer poses with some of his draft horses.

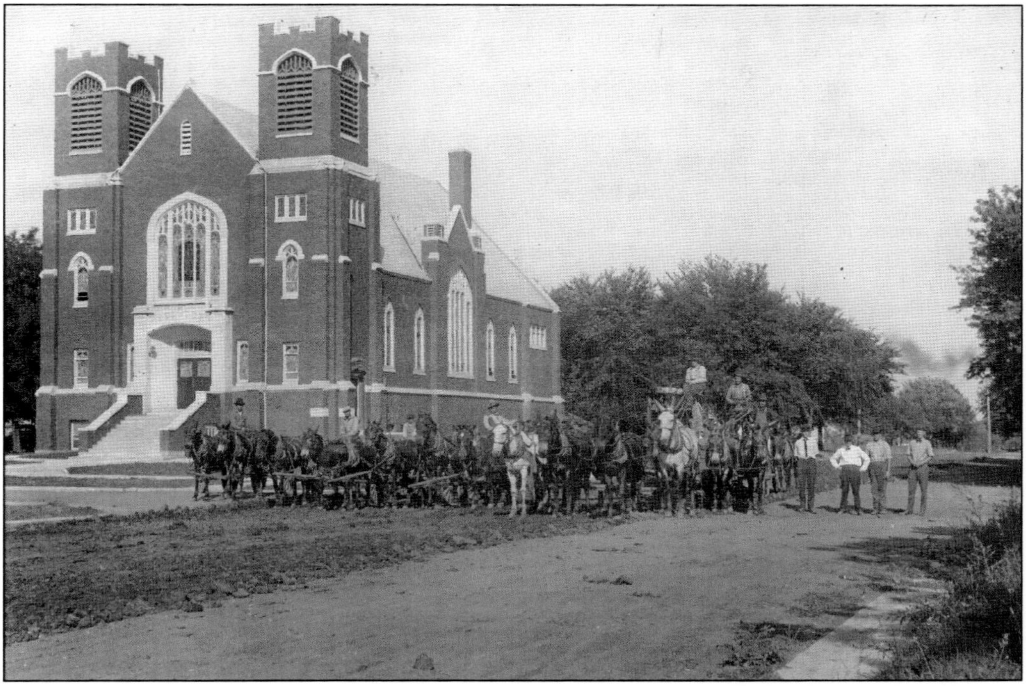

Road crews grade Broad Street in front of Immanuel Lutheran Church to prepare for the laying of brick. In recent years, some of these historic bricks have been salvaged and placed in walkways around one of the Story City Historical Society's exhibit buildings.

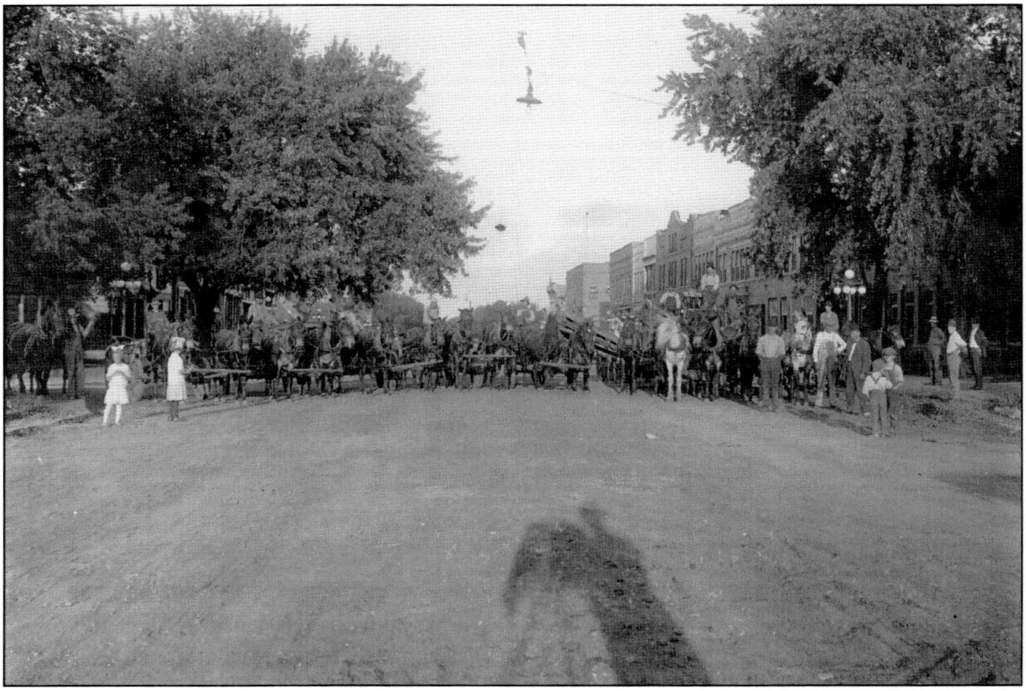

A resurfacing crew works along Broad Street on the west end of the business district, near where the Wells Fargo building is today. An electric streetlight is suspended above the tree-lined intersection.

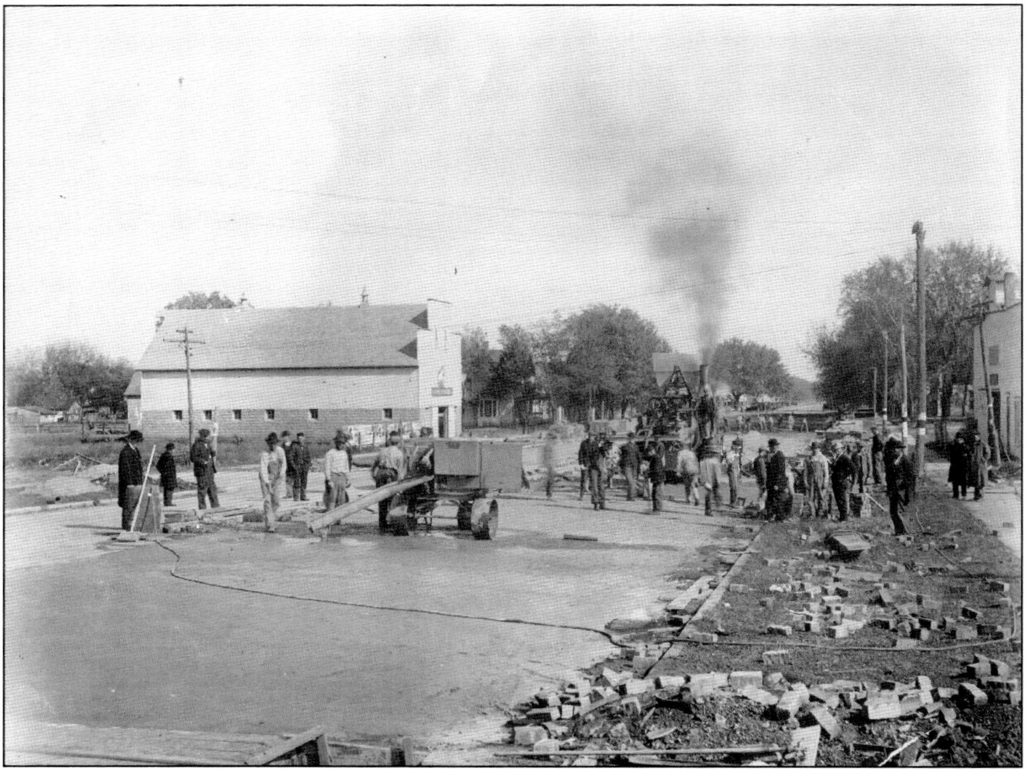

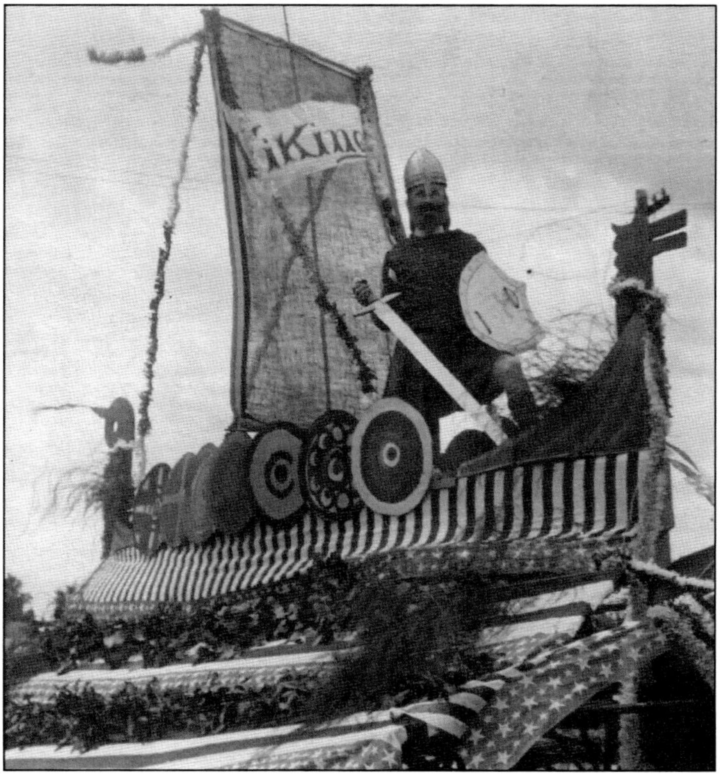

In 1918, Broad Street was paved from the Chicago Northwestern Railroad line to the east end of the business district. The Johnson Auction Barn is on the left.

Story City has a rich Scandinavian heritage, as seen in this image of parade float. A local citizen dressed as a Viking stands in a reproduction boat above a sea of American flags.

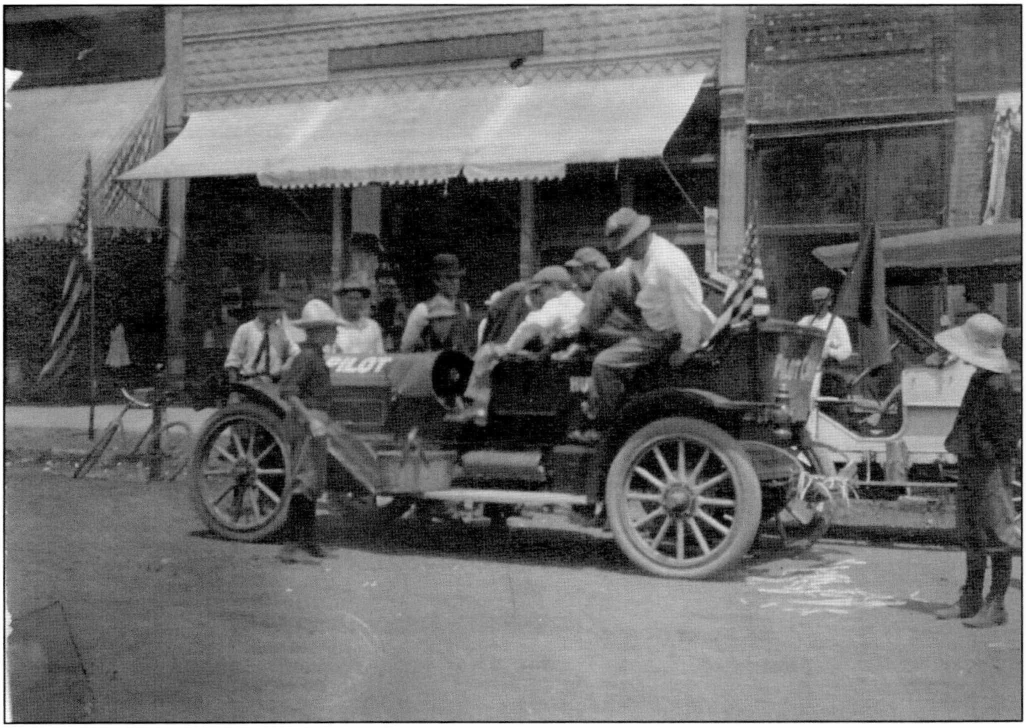

This pilot car was likely for local parade stops in the Fourth of July parade along Broad Street.

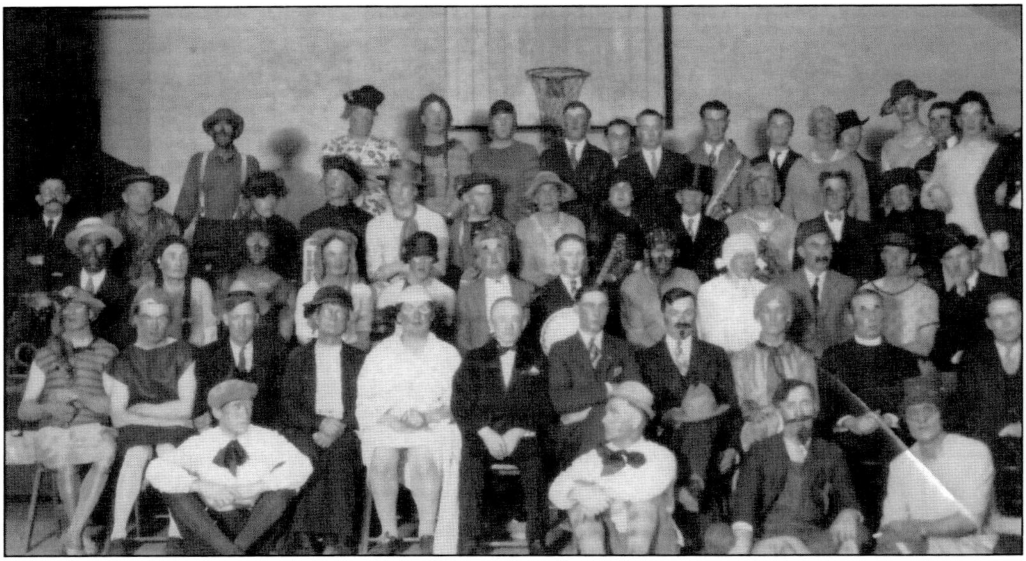

A theater production poses in the Story City High School gymnasium. For this play, both men and women dressed as the opposite sex, which is quite noticeable upon close examination of the image.

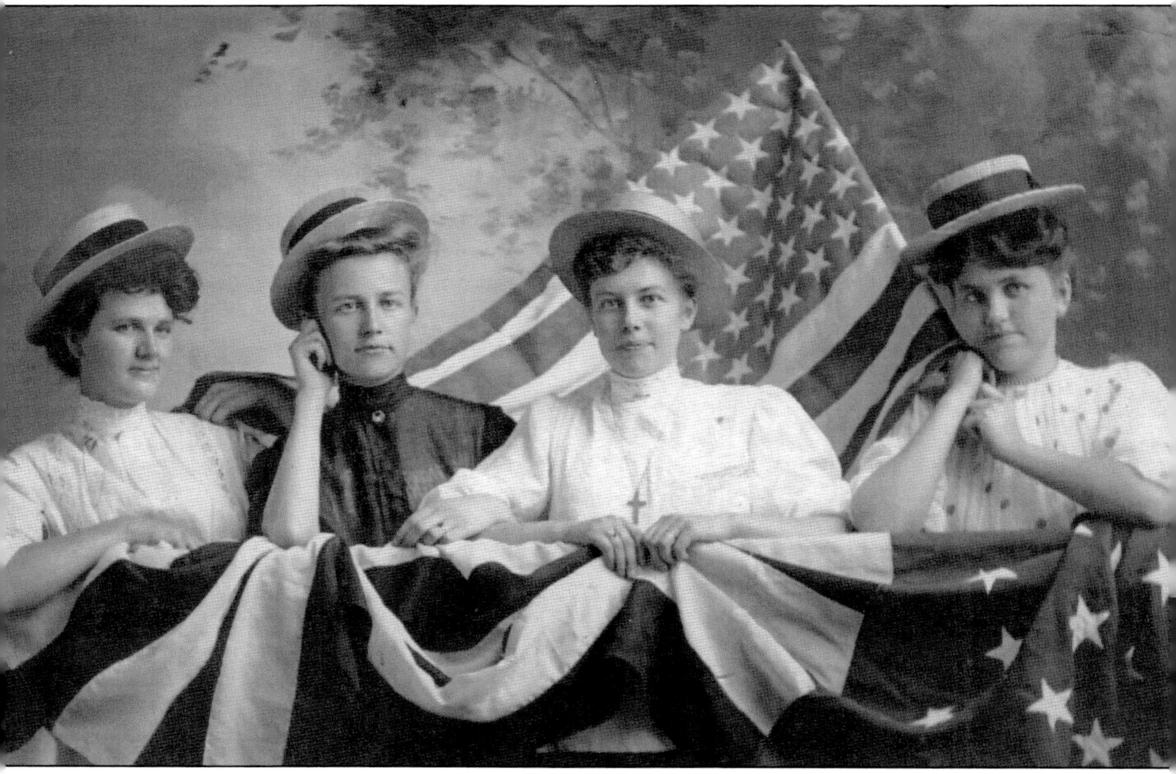

In this image humorously titled "The Old Maids," Story City women pose in patriotic fashion for the camera. In the rear is a painted backdrop of a nature scene, a common feature of photography studios.

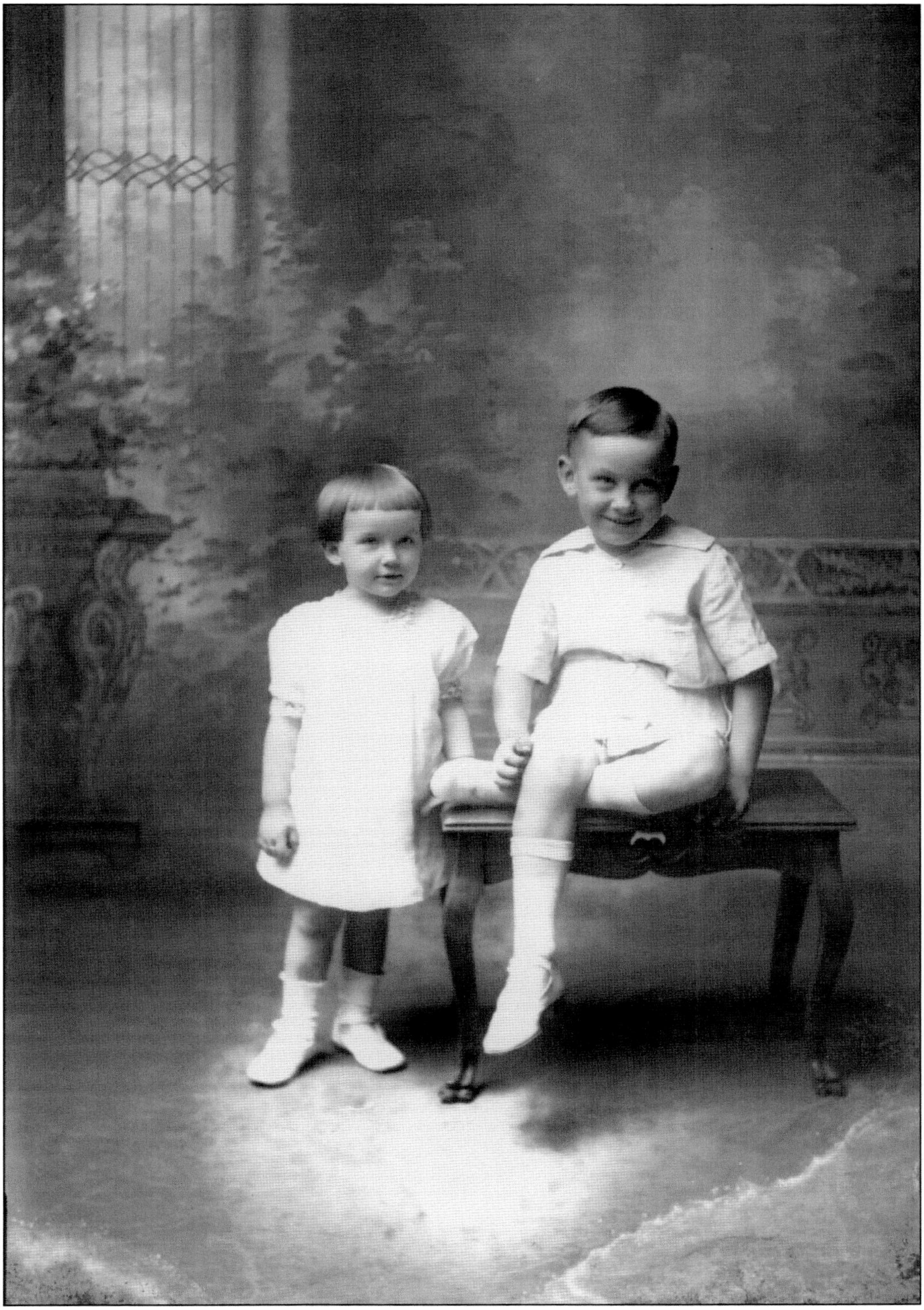

Two-year-old Fran Kinne poses for the camera in a Story City photography studio with her brother, Chuck, who was five at the time. Fran would go on to earn her Ph.D. in music and become the first female president of Jacksonville University in Jacksonville, Florida.

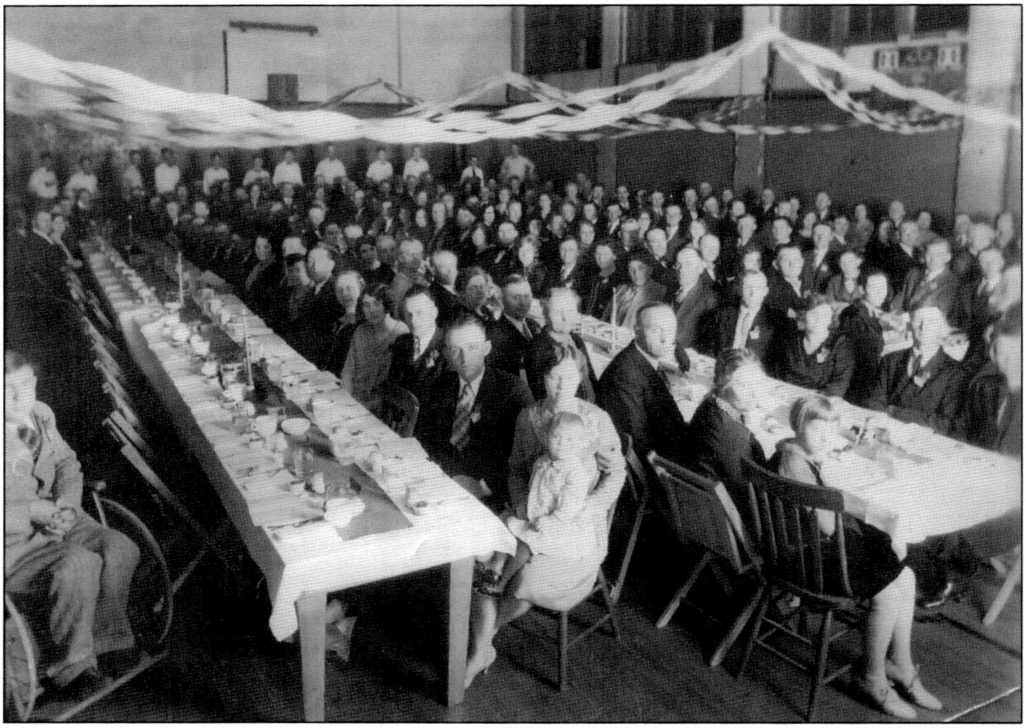

This businessmen's banquet was in the Story City High School gymnasium in the early 1900s. An early basketball hoop is in the background behind the paper streamers.

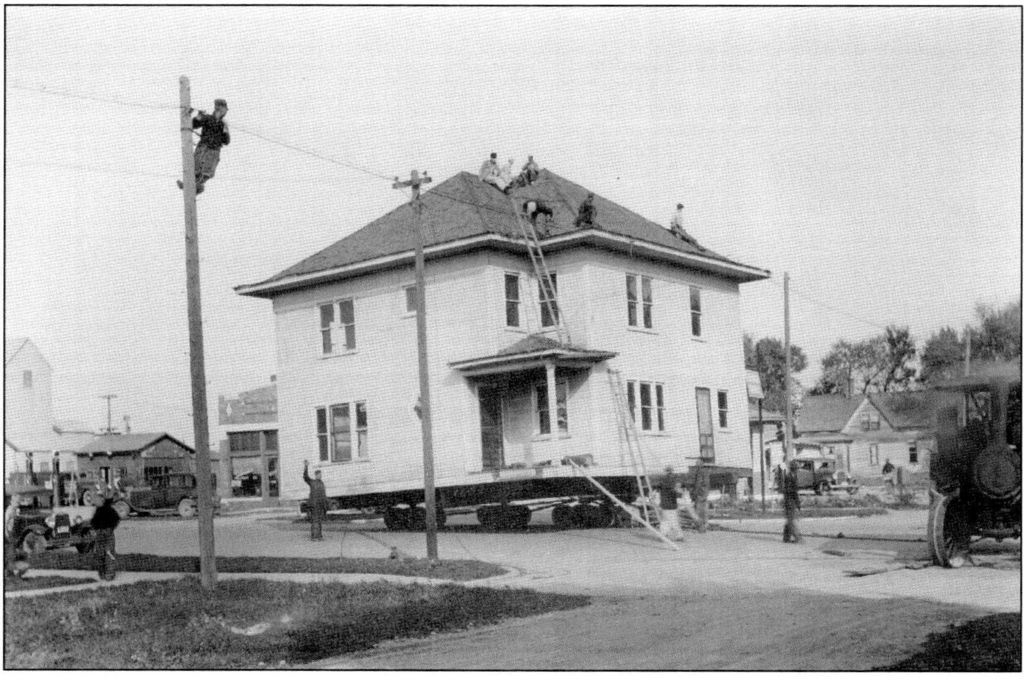

Historically, moving houses was not all that uncommon in central Iowa. This house in Story City is being moved south on Pennsylvania Street before it turns right on Washington Street. A steam engine is on hand to assist with pulling the heavy load through town.

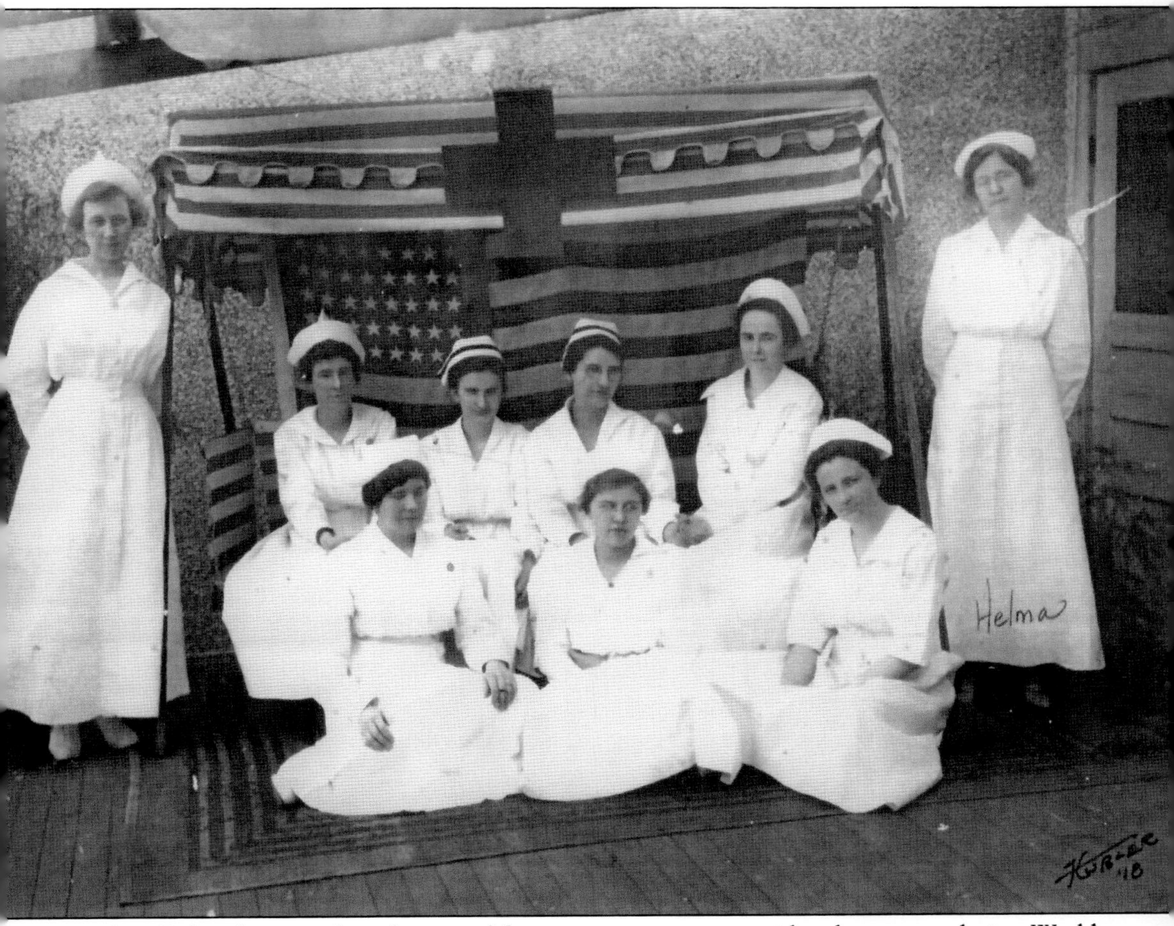

Helma Dale, who served in the armed forces as a nurse, poses with other nurses during World War I. Nurses were invaluable in treating soldiers exposed to mustard gas, artillery, and early machine guns.

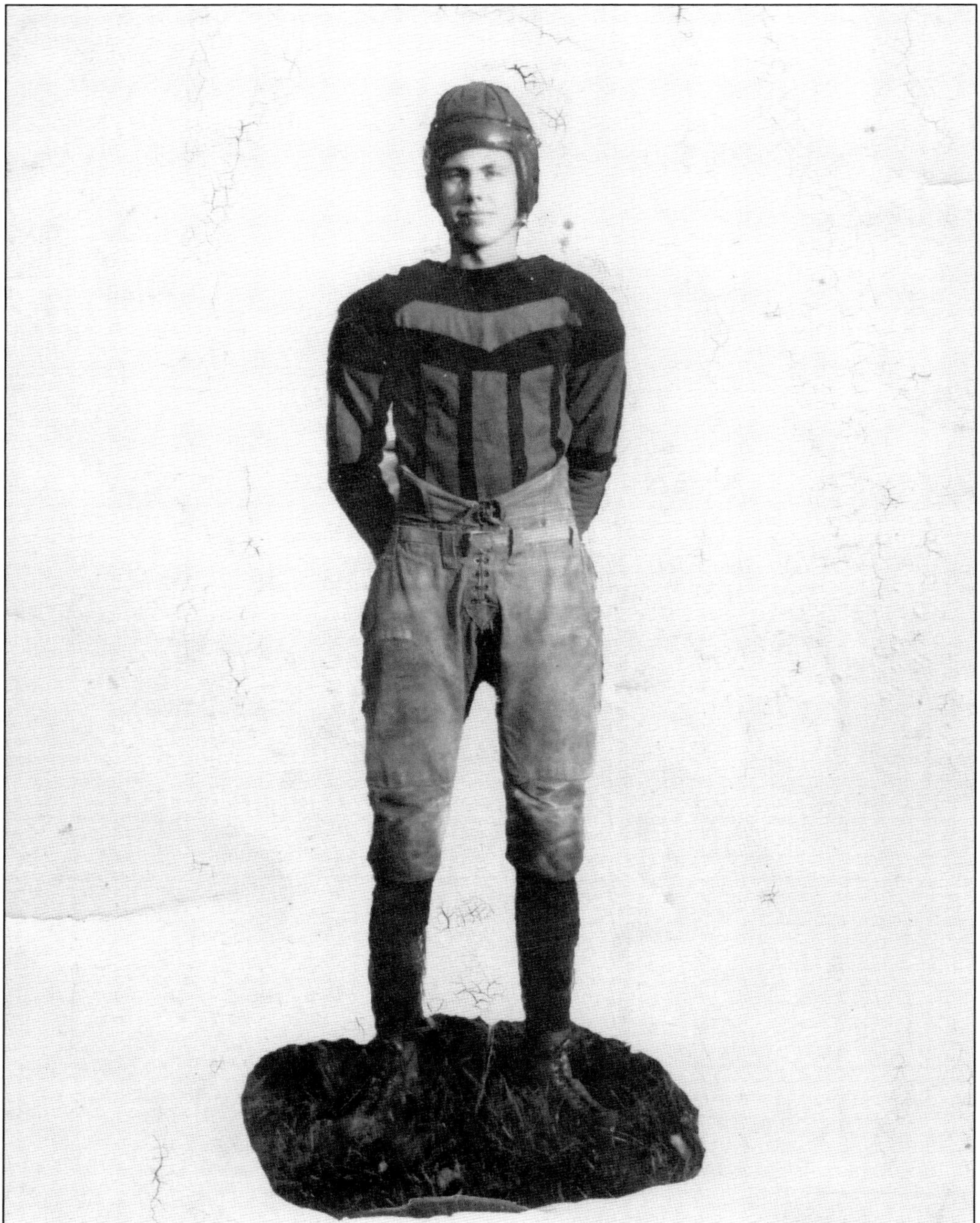

Irving Wierson posed for this photograph in his football uniform during the fall of 1931. A little more than a decade later, he was fighting in Italy during World War II.

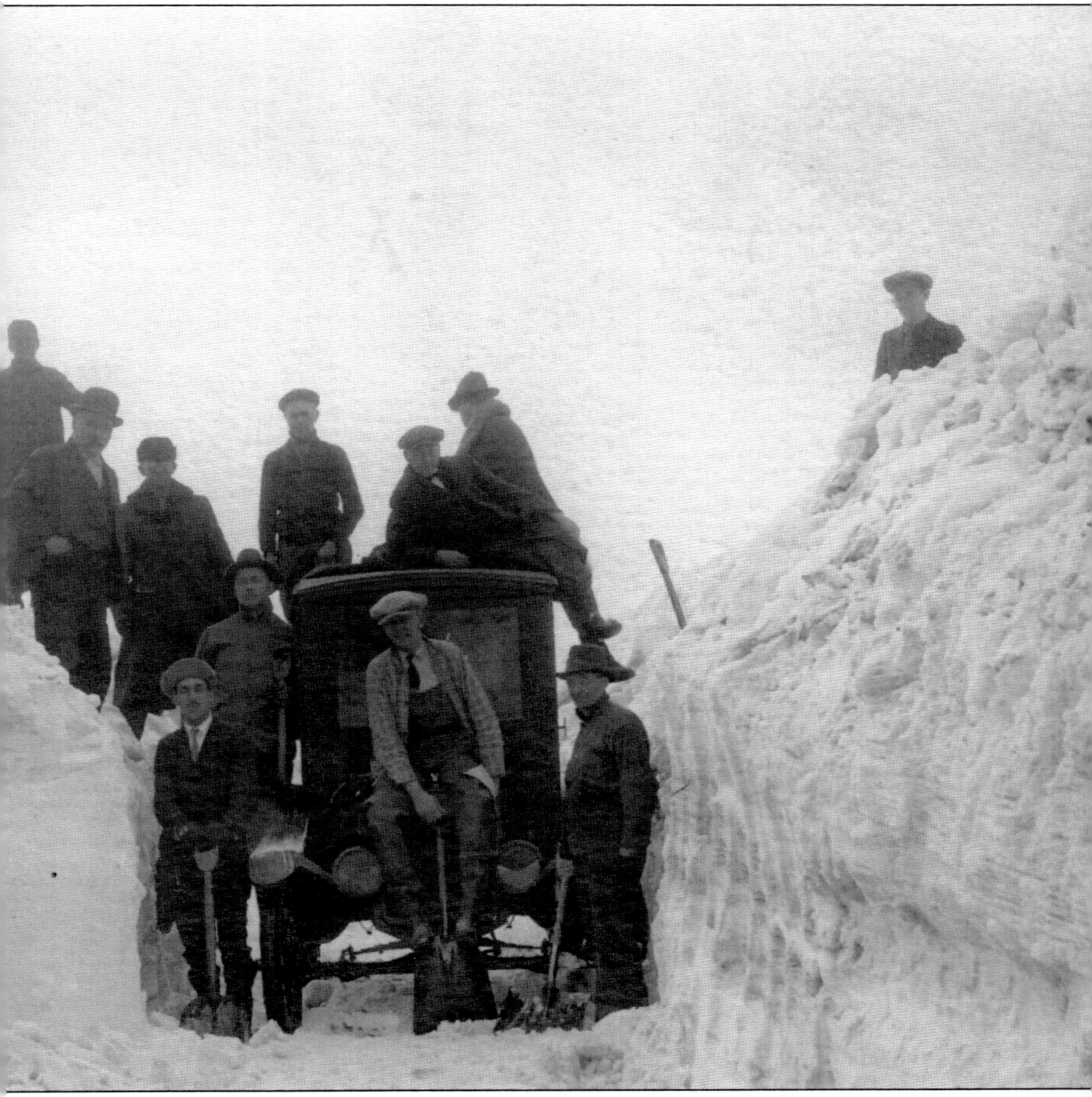

This 1923 image shows Story City businessmen digging through a snowdrift on the outskirts of town following a late spring blizzard. Significant snowstorms could have a serious impact on the surrounding countryside as drifts needed to be cleared by hand in many cases.

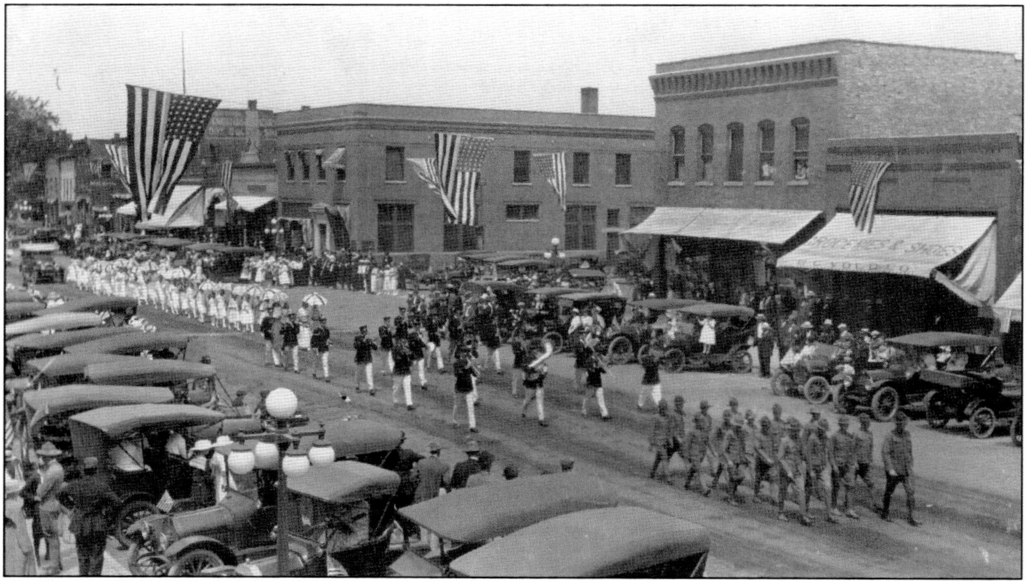

This Fourth of July parade shows an early Story City Boy Scout troop wearing World War I–era uniforms and marching in the front of the community's band. The Boy Scout movement became very popular in America in the early 1900s.

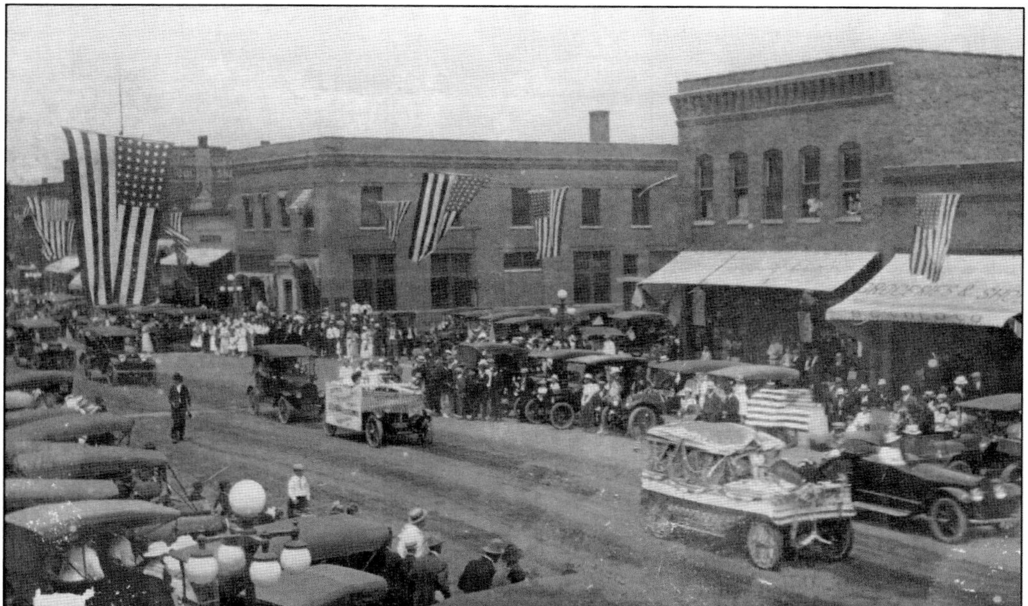

Story City residents were creative in transforming their cars and tractors into floats for the annual Fourth of July parade. American flags suspended upon wires wave in the breeze.

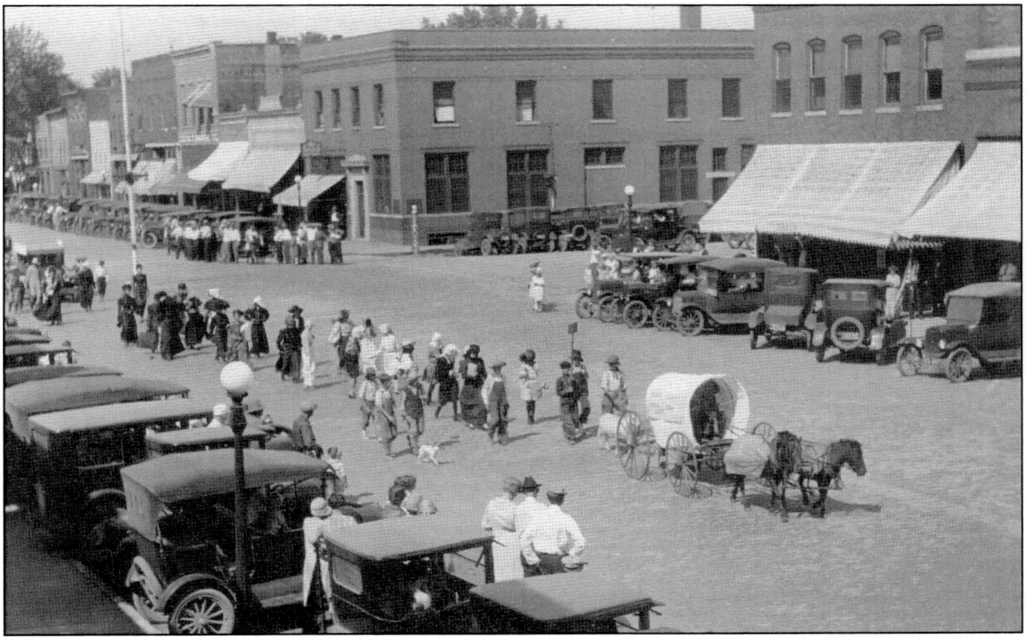

In the early 1900s, barbecue parades were an annual event in Story City. Here, a child drives a team of ponies while his classmates follow in historical costume.

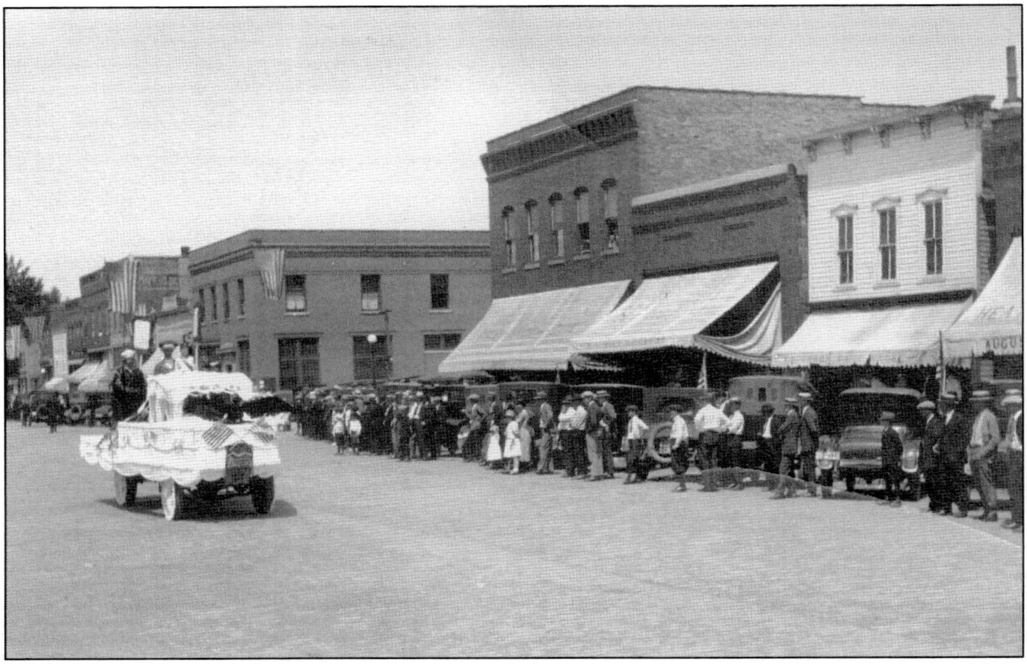

This image looks westward along Broad Street at an early-1900s Fourth of July parade. Servicemen stand in the back of a festooned pickup truck.

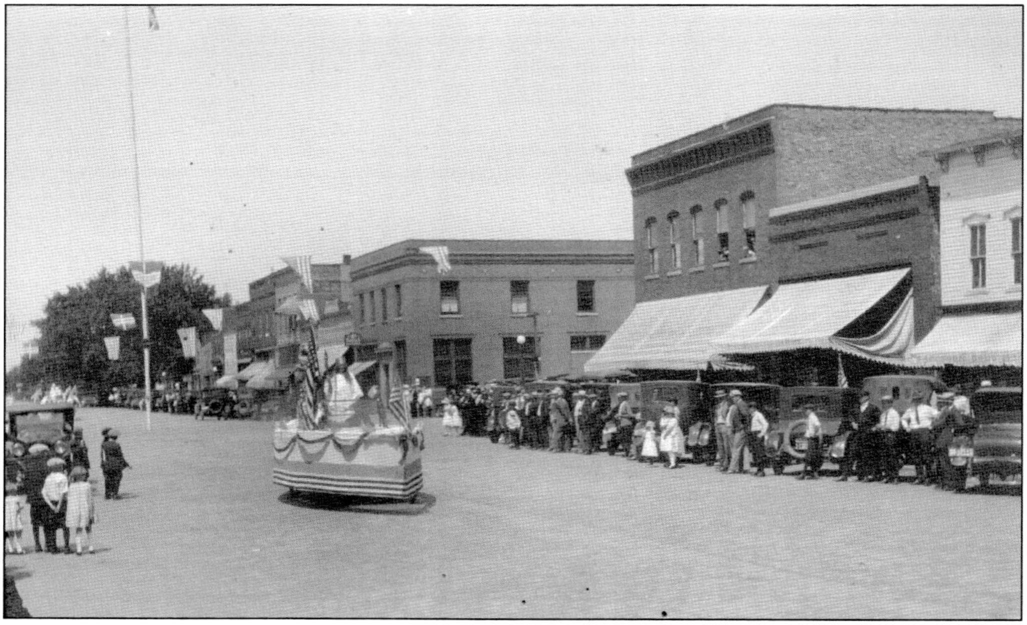

This unique float is in front of a large flagpole standing in the middle of Broad Street at its intersection with Pennsylvania Street.

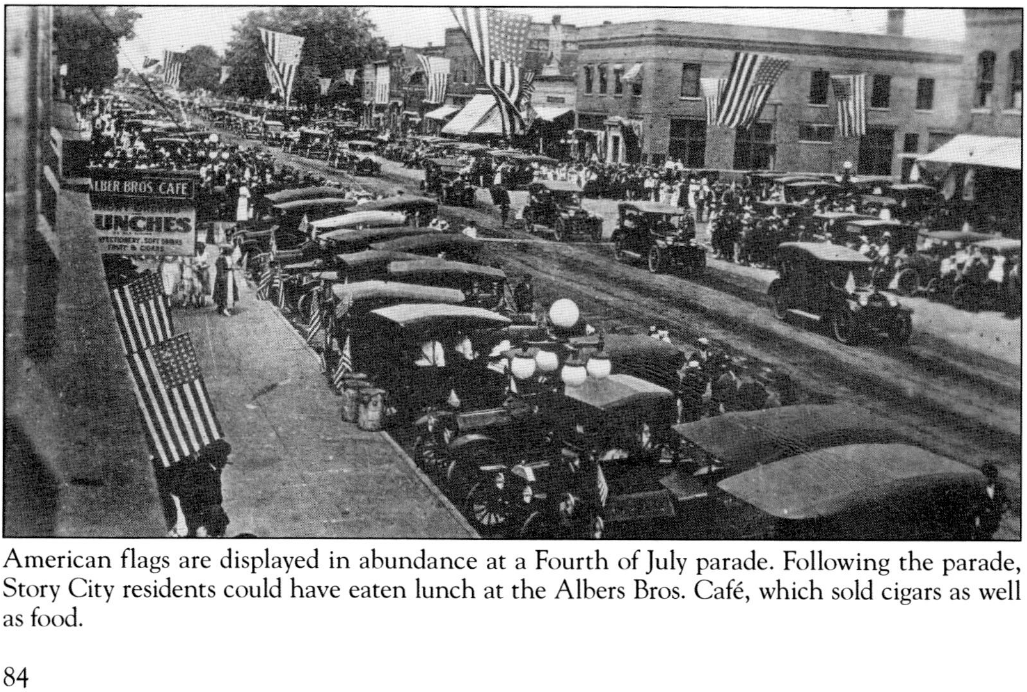

American flags are displayed in abundance at a Fourth of July parade. Following the parade, Story City residents could have eaten lunch at the Albers Bros. Café, which sold cigars as well as food.

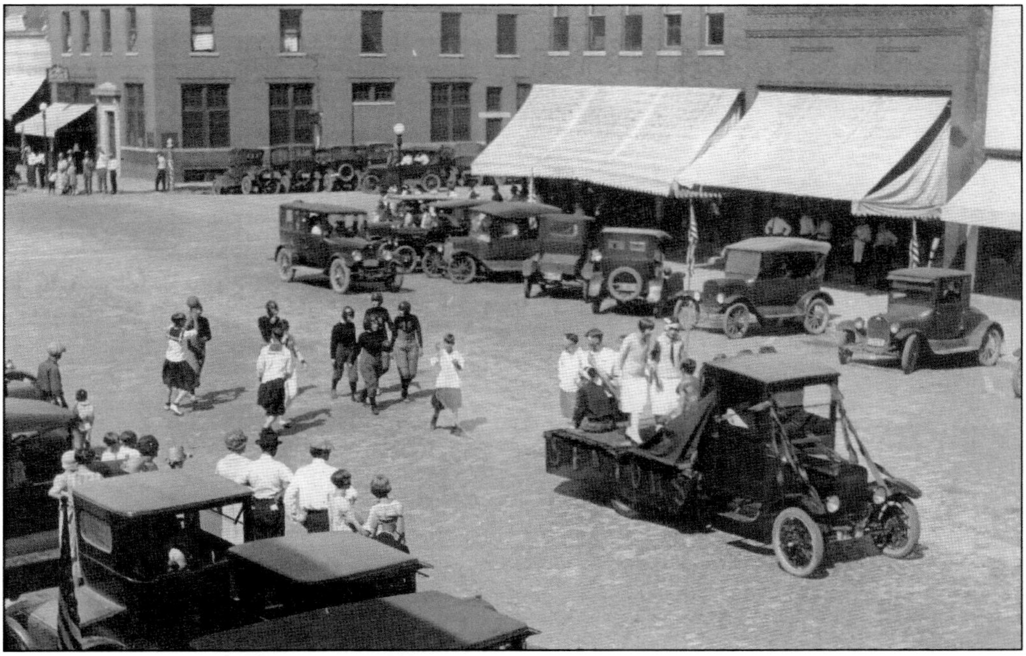

Story City High School football players walk down Broad Street in a homecoming parade. The truck is labeled "seniors" along the side.

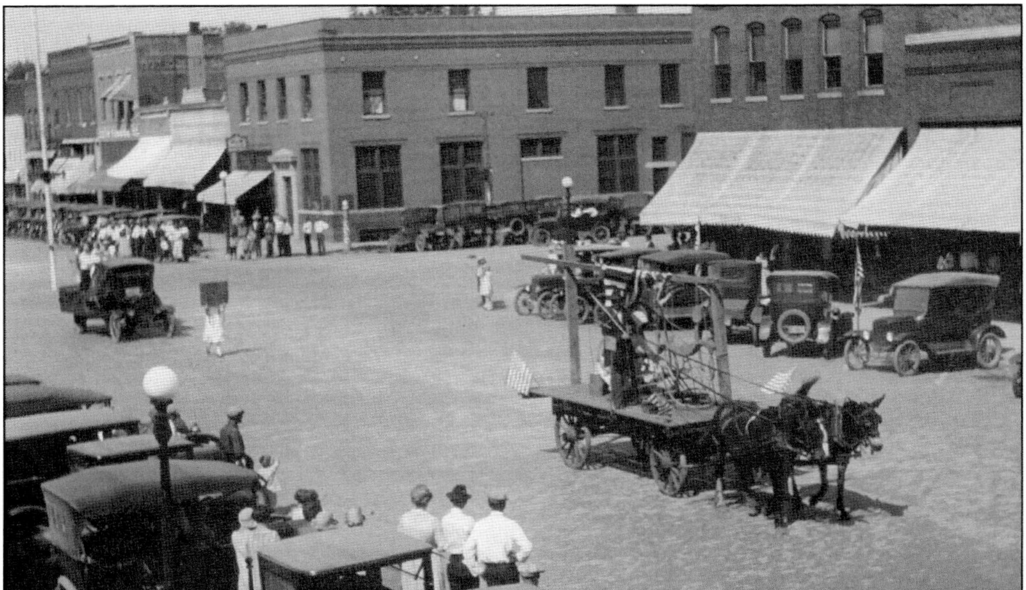

This float, pulled by horses and showing pioneer artifacts, was a creative way to share an aspect of the community's heritage. Standing on a horse-drawn hayrack, an ox bow and other historical items are displayed for parade watchers.

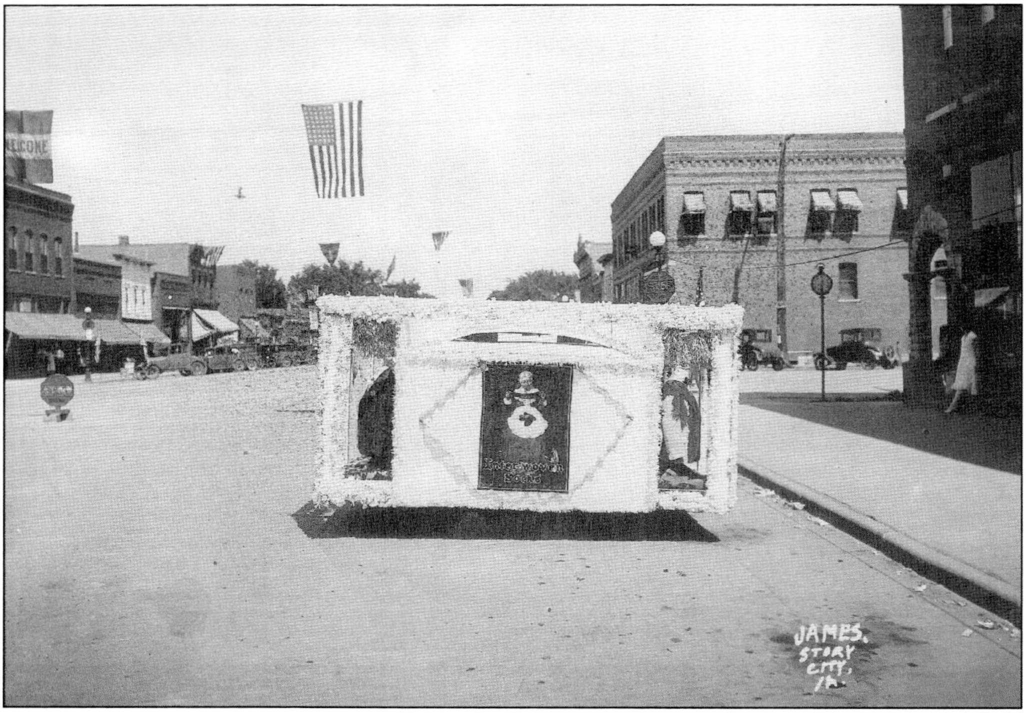

The Charlson clothes shop sponsored this parade float advertising interwoven socks. This photograph was taken in front of the Charlson building as the float passed.

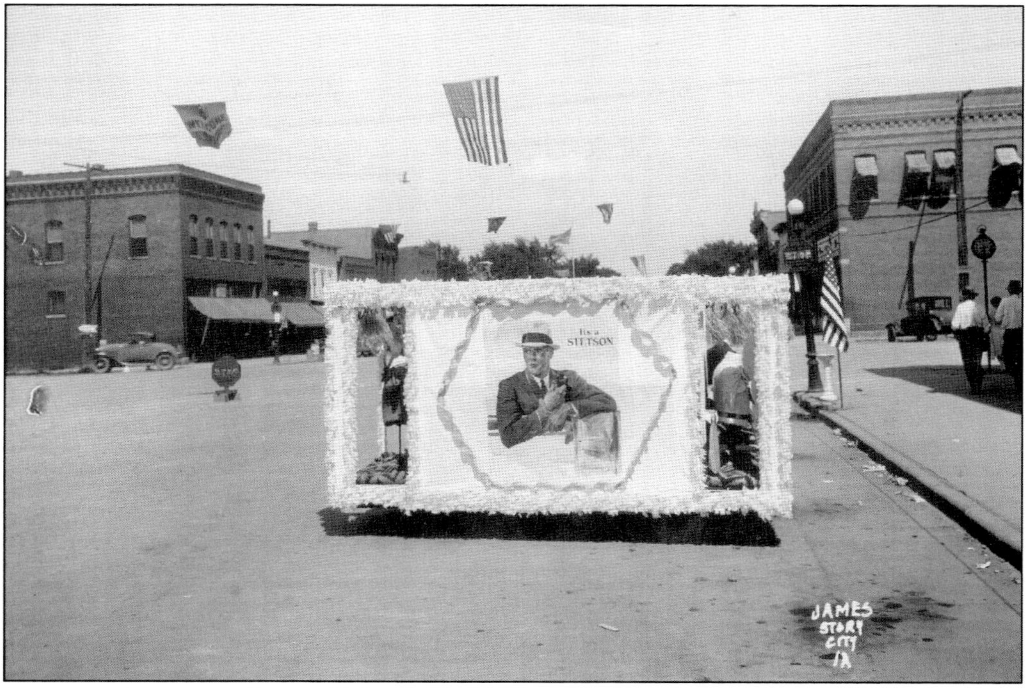

In an age when men still wore felt hats, this Charlson clothes shop float advertises Stenson Hats. Felt hats were worn by all classes of men in Story City, and when they went out of shape due to wear, Charlson's could re-steam and re-form them on wooden blocks to bring them back to new.

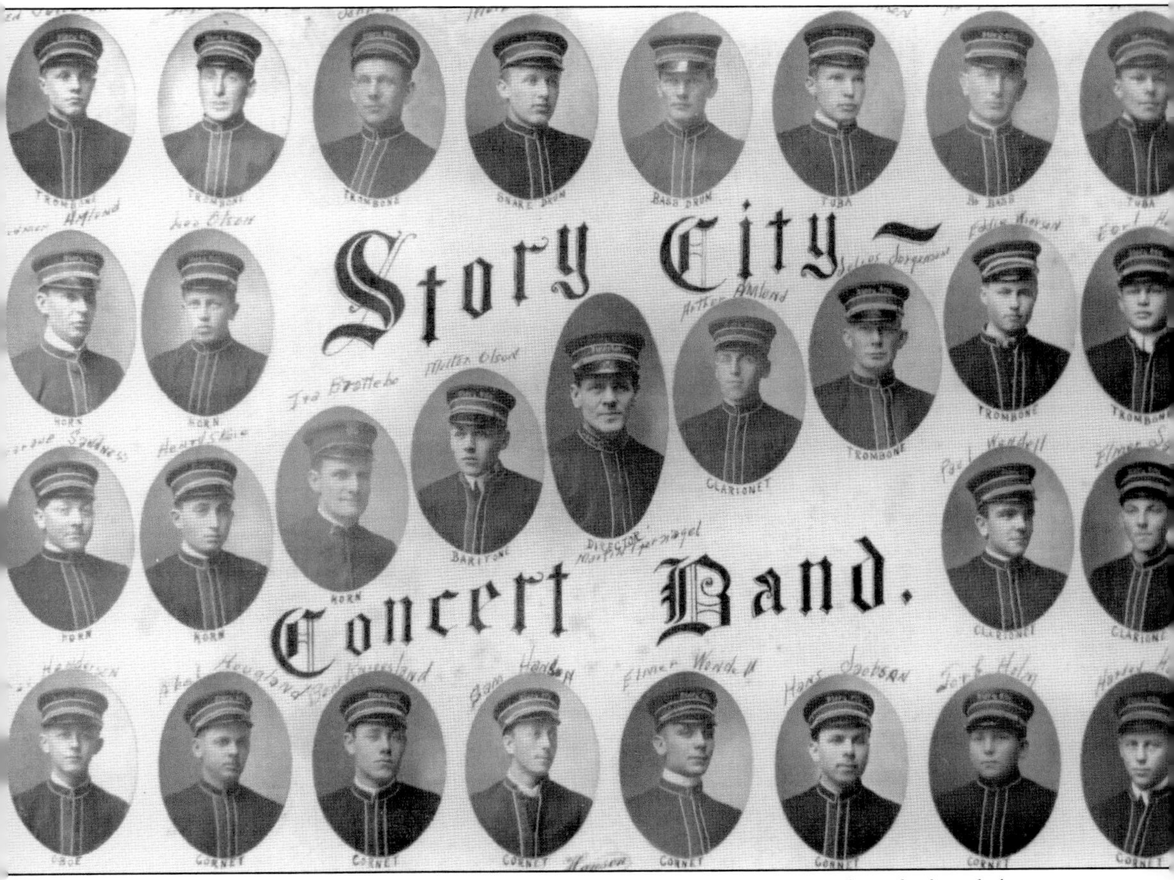

The Story City Concert Band is seen here around 1900. Each man is identified with his name above his portrait and the instrument he played below.

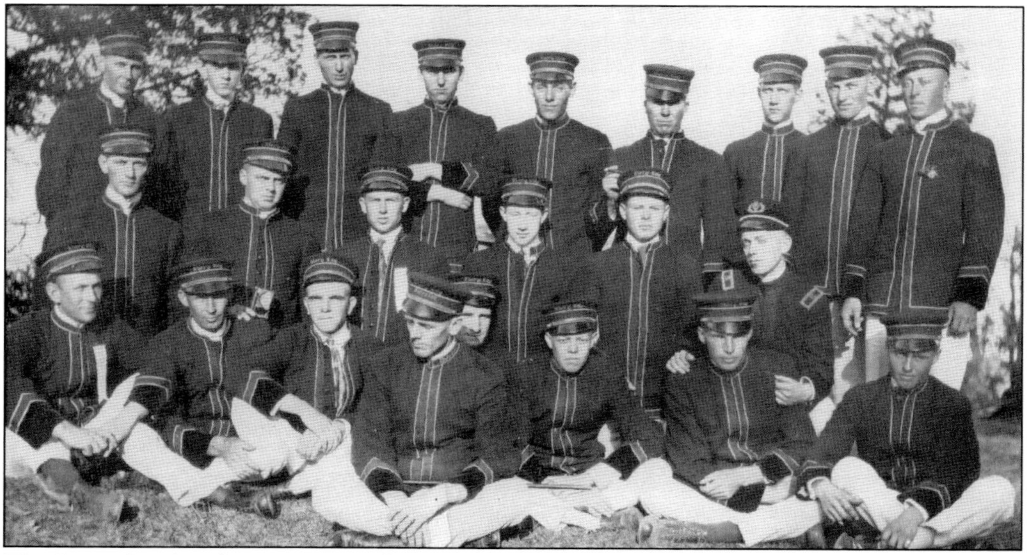

The Story City band was very popular in the community in the early 20th century but many of the band members had to leave the band briefly to serve their country in World War I. Their concerts were common in the City Park.

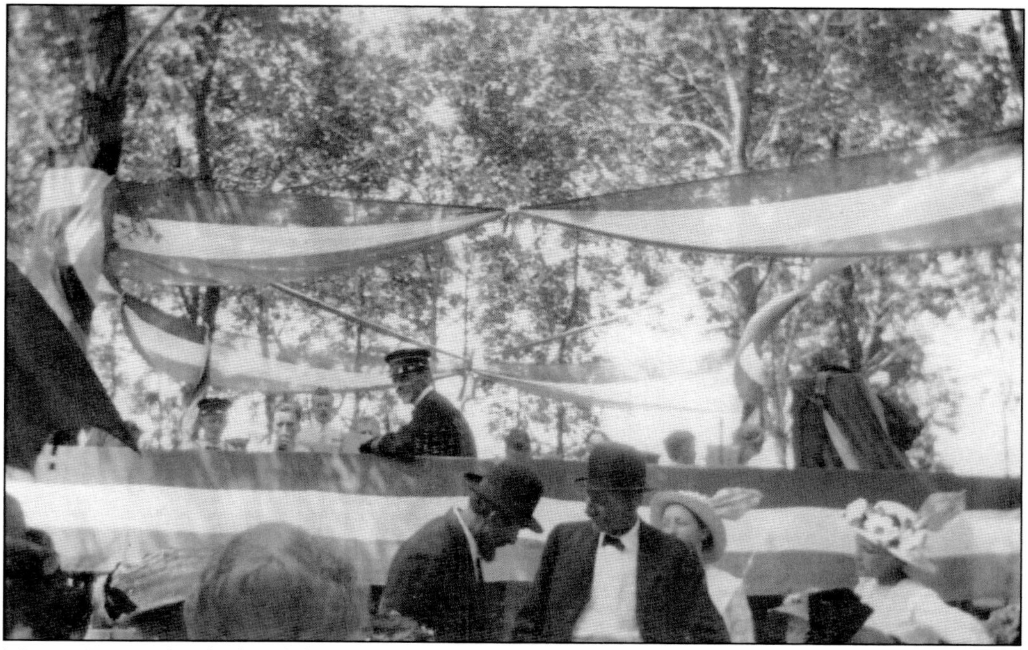

Martin Tjernagle, the band director, is seen here in a patriotic celebration. The women's millinery made hats stand out against the red, white, and blue banners.

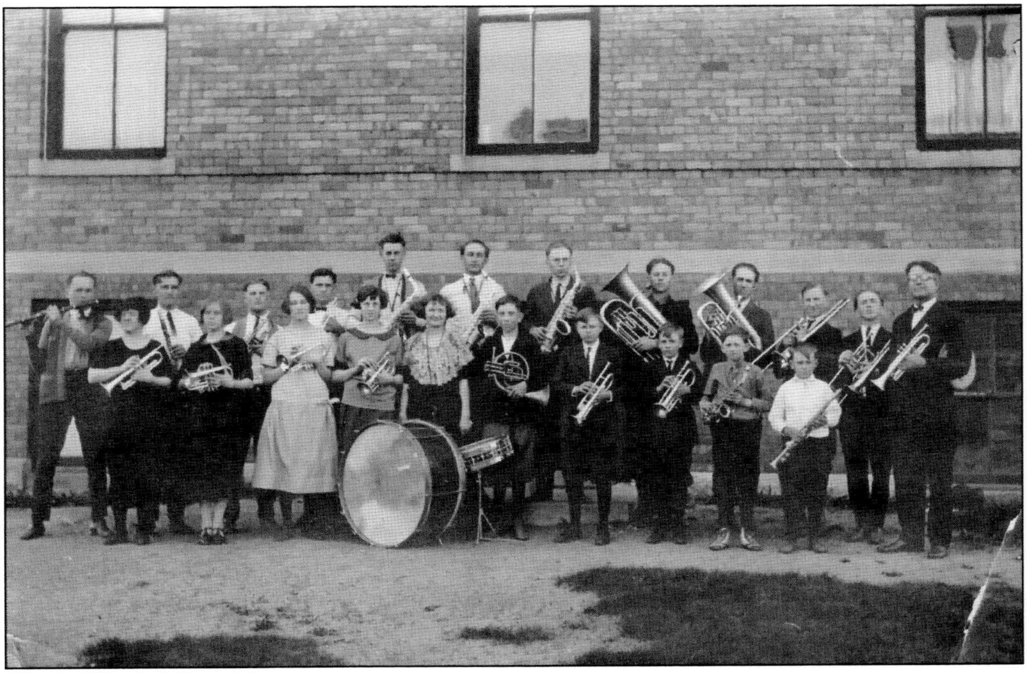

The Story City High School band poses outside of the school.

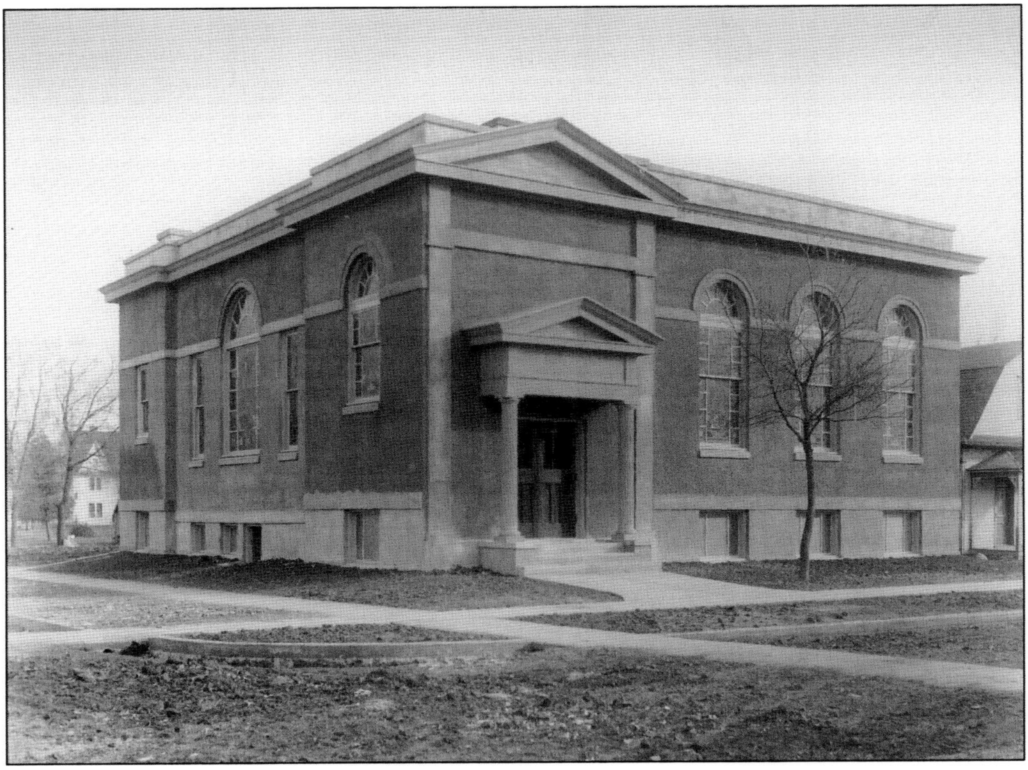

The newly constructed Grace Evangelical Church is seen here in 1914.

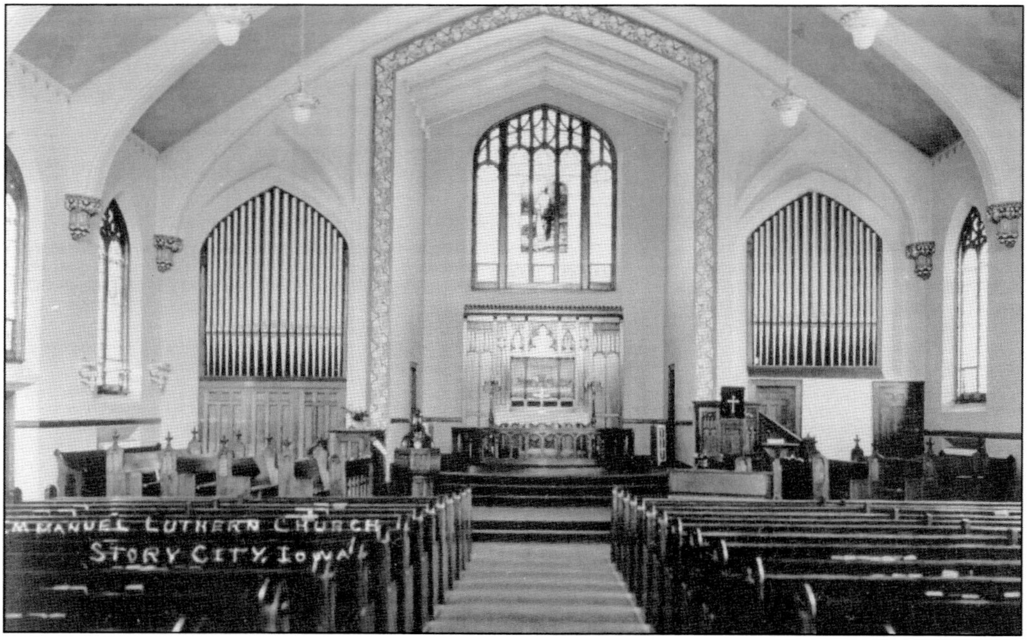

This photograph shows the interior of the brick Immanuel Lutheran Church in Story City along Broad and Lafayette Streets and shows the workmanship that went into constructing the sanctuary. Electric lights hang down to provide light for evening services when the sun could not shine through the beautiful stained glass windows.

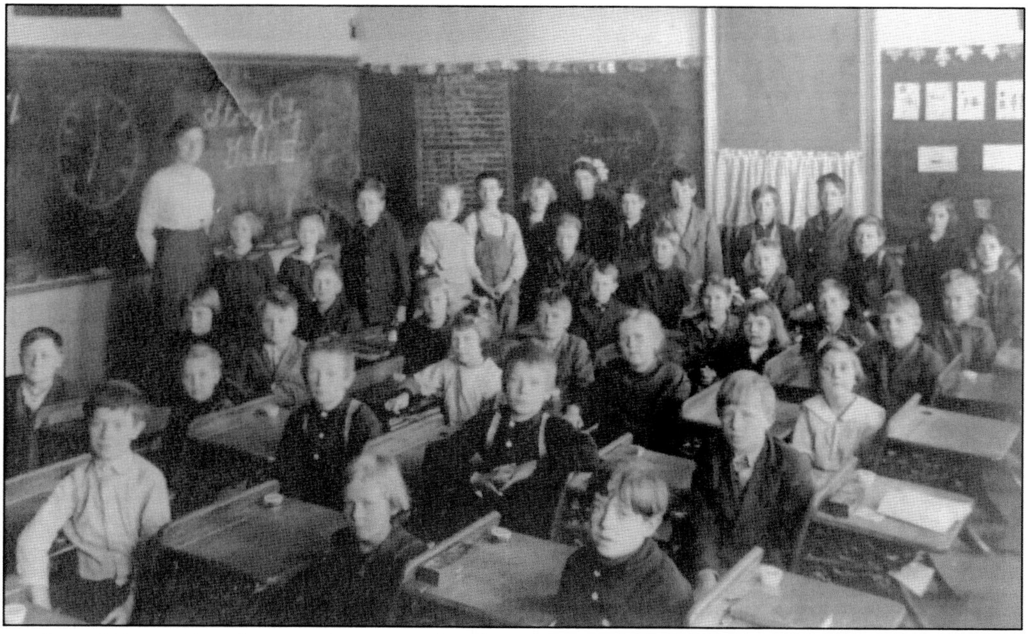

A class of Story City third graders poses for the camera in their classroom. Each desk had a hole in the upper right corner for an ink well, for use in learning cursive penmanship with nib pens.

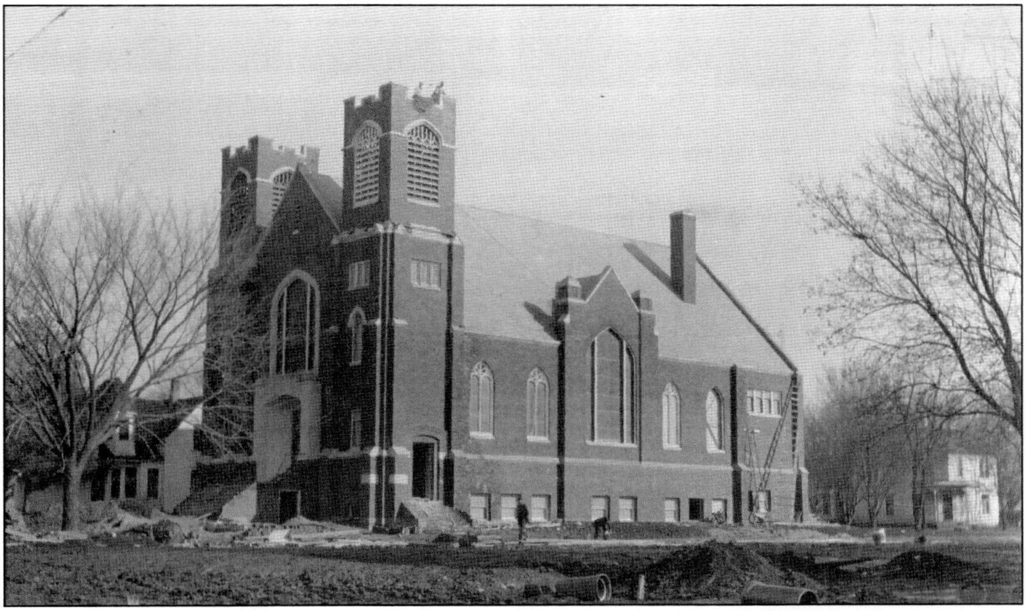

Debris abounds in this photograph of construction work on Immanuel Lutheran Church. Homes that have since been removed from around the church can be seen here.

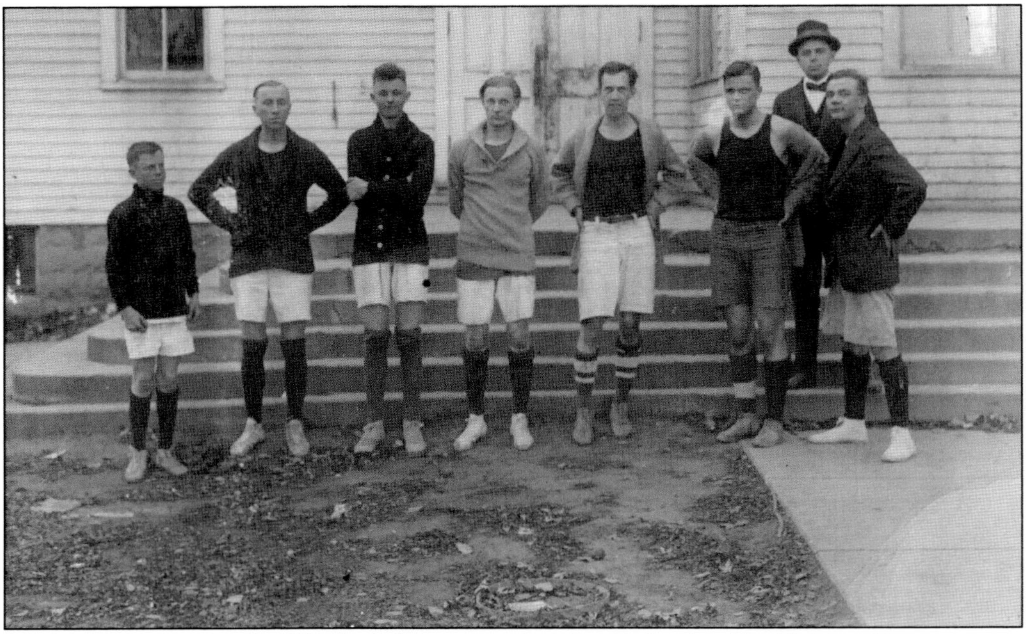

The Story City High School basketball team stands in front of a school building in the community of Colo while there for a game in 1915.

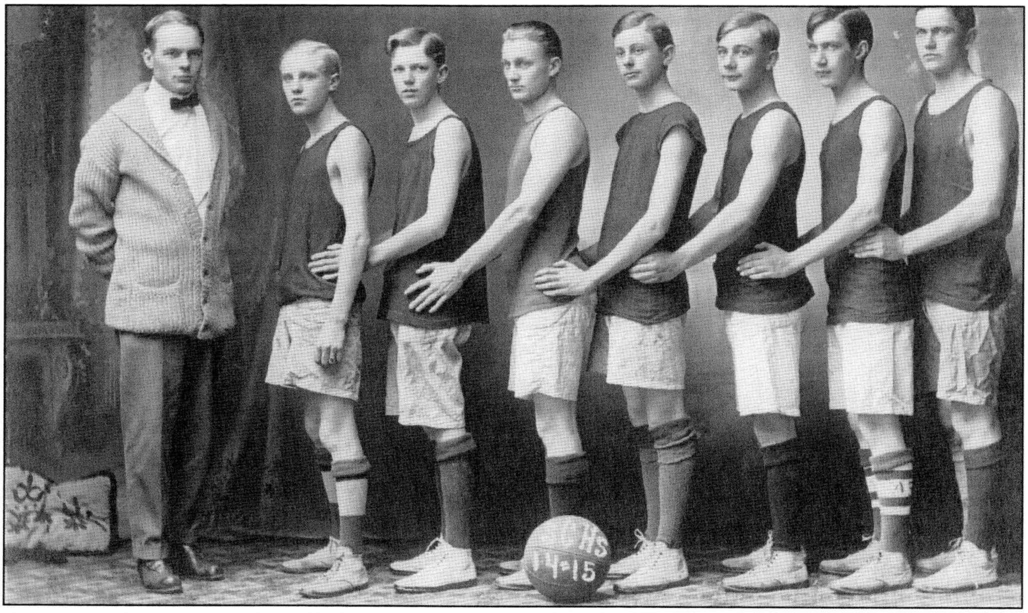

The 1914–1915 Story City High School basketball team, coached by Edgar Hervig, poses in a local photographer's studio. Long-sleeved sweaters and high socks contrast distinctly with modern-day uniforms.

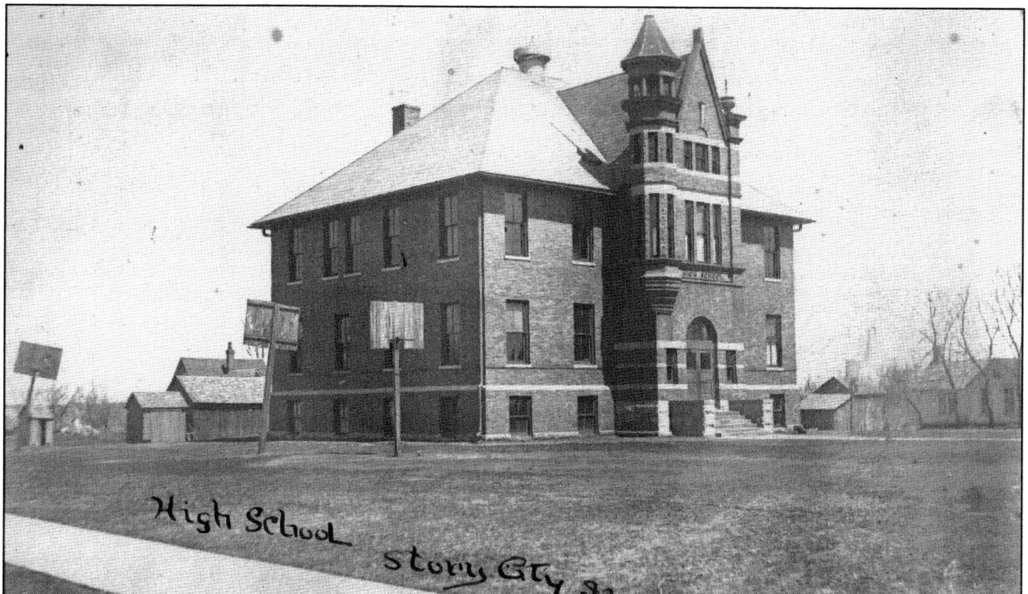

This pre-1911 photograph of the Story City High School shows the primitive early basketball courts. An outhouse can be seen in the background, near the home behind the school.

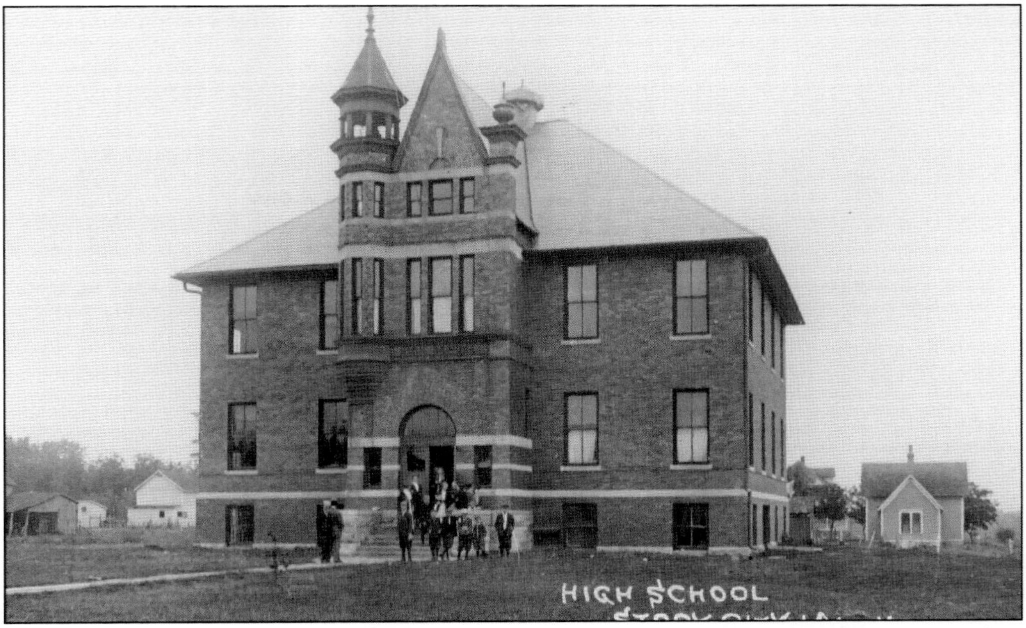

This photograph shows the architectural details of Story City High School and the surrounding neighborhood. To the left is a carriage house, which provided a place to store hay, oats, a carriage, and a horse or two.

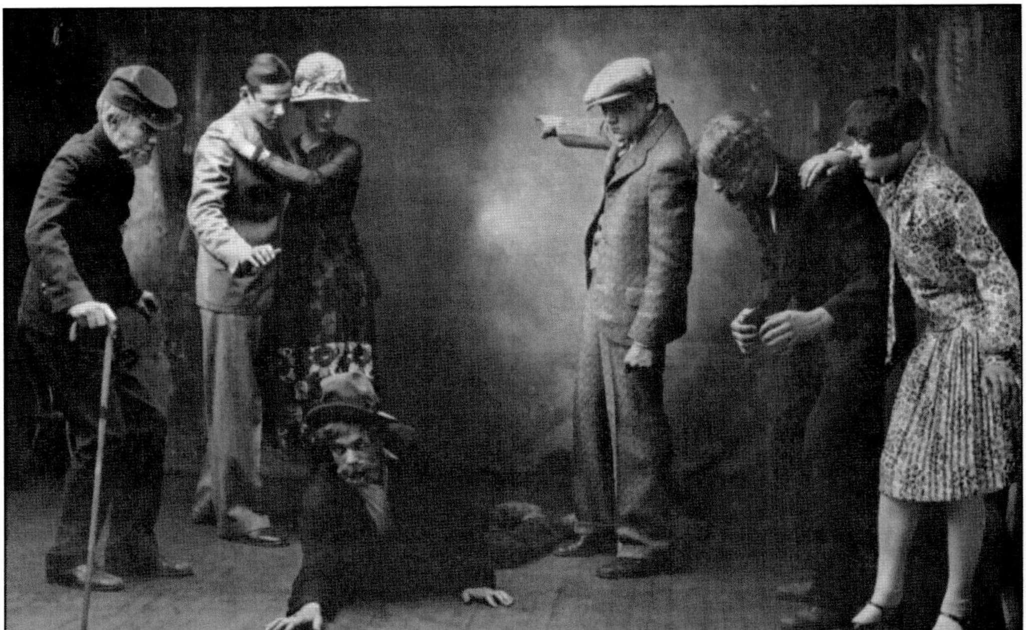

In 1928, the Story City High School's junior class presented the play *The Copperhead*. Even though it was decades after the war, Clarence Hove (left) wears an original Civil War cap.

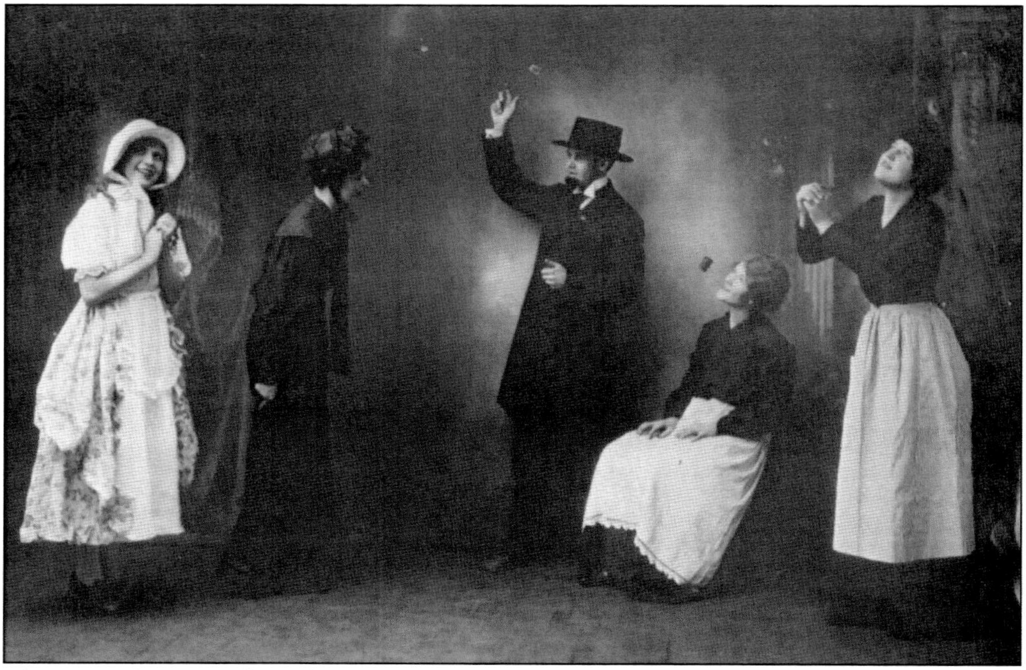

This is another scene from the 1928 Story City High School junior class play, *The Copperhead*. A close look shows the pipe Julia Elwell is pretending to smoke.

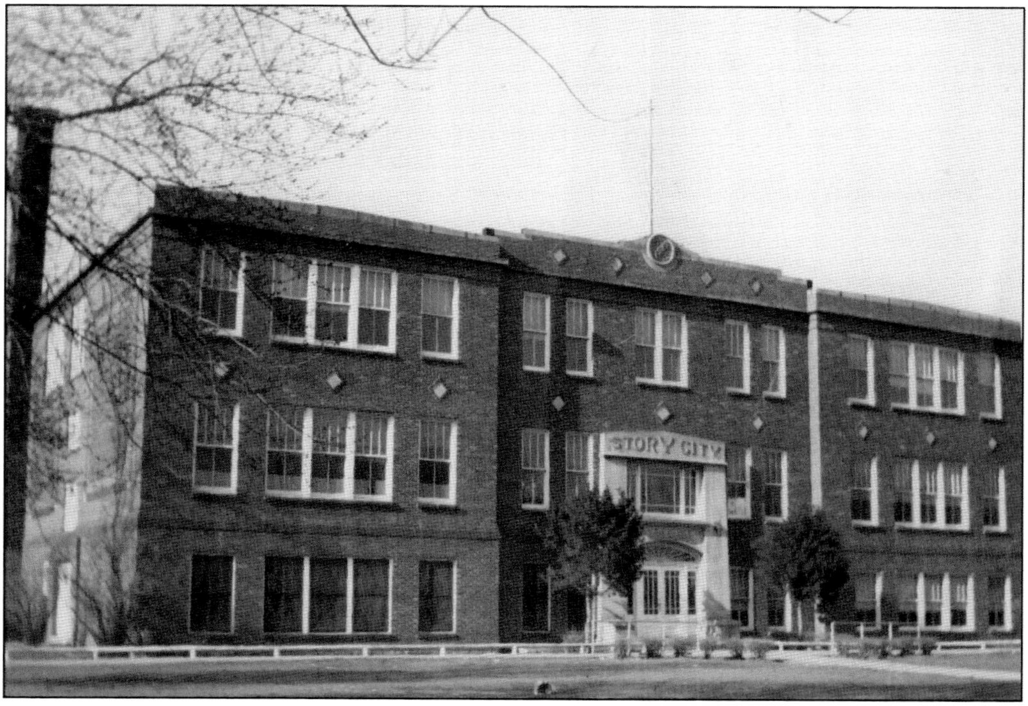

The 1919 Story City "Upper Level" school was located close to the 1905 school building site. Architecturally, this building had many similarities to other central Iowa schools of the period.

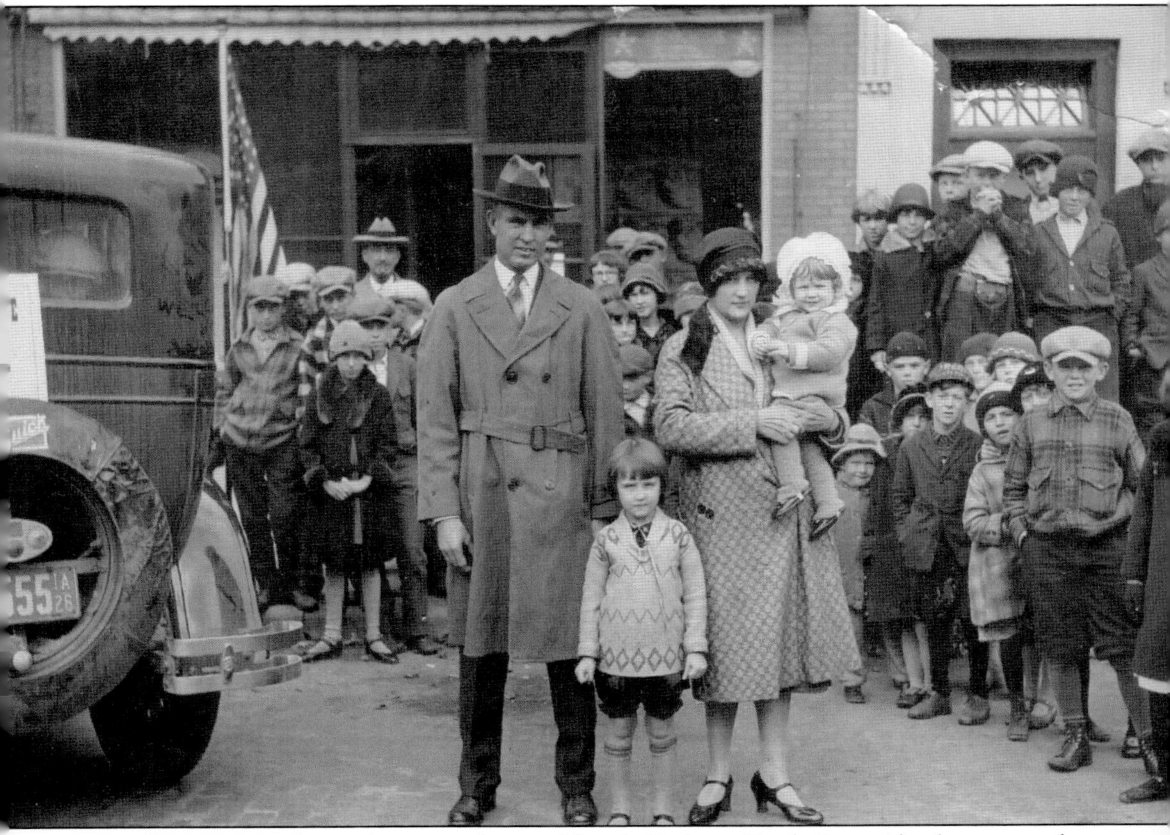

Schoolboys gathered to welcome professional baseball player Hank Severeid, who returned to his hometown of Story City with his wife, Del, and their two children in 1926. In the back seat of the car to the left are Harris and Charles Hill.

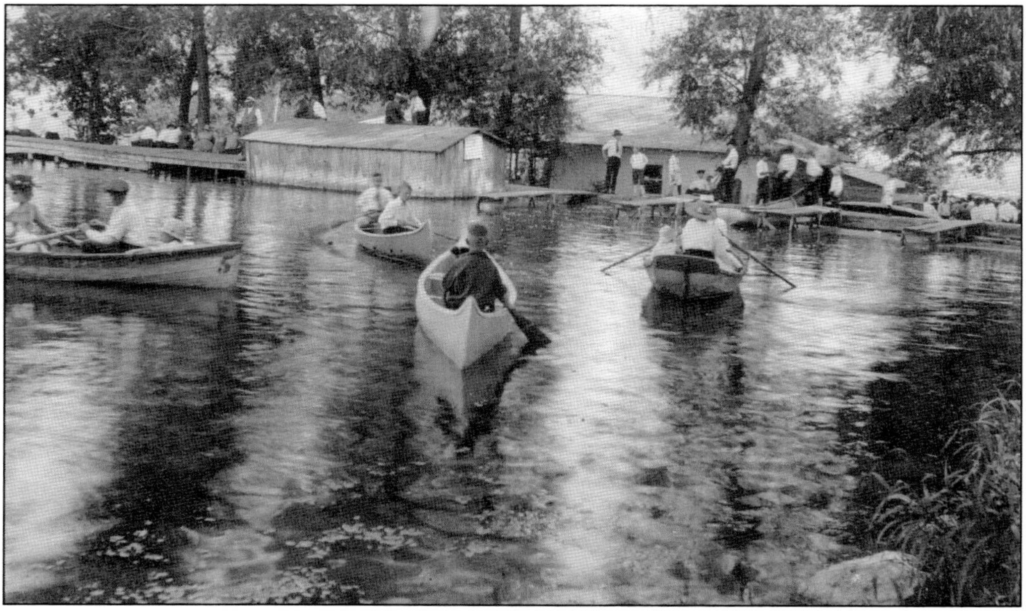

Visitors to Lake Comar enjoy canoeing and rowing on the boathouse corner of the manmade lake. Fed by five artesian wells, this vacation spot was popular from the early 20th century through World War II.

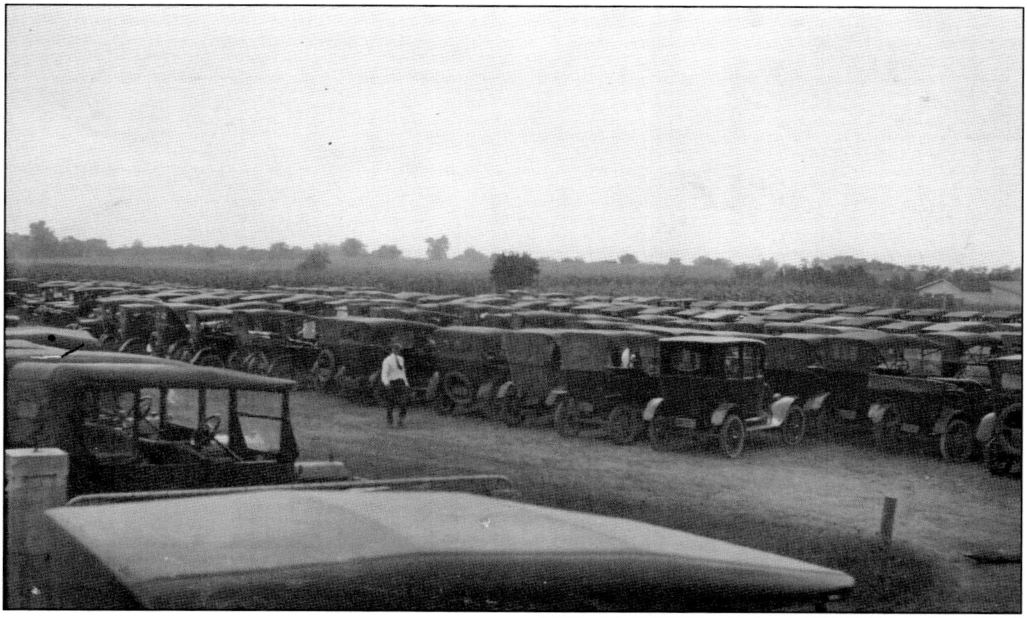

Lake Comar was a popular summer vacation venue for north central Iowans, attracting thousands of people at times. Adding to its popularity were contests to win free automobiles.

Floyd, Don, and Francis Langland poke their heads above water at Lake Comar. Remnants of the summer vacation spot that made Story City a resort town are still south of town. The dry lakebeds and surrounding timber stand out against a sea of cornfields.

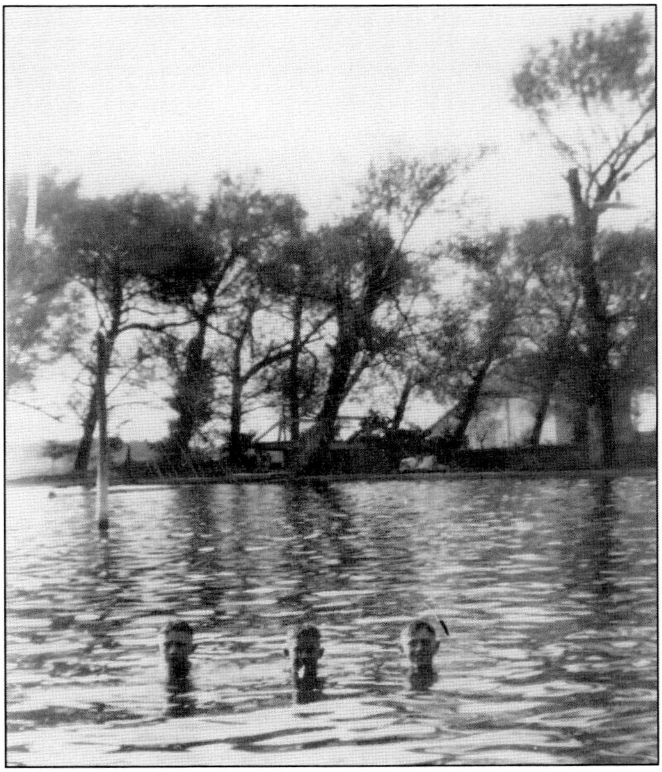

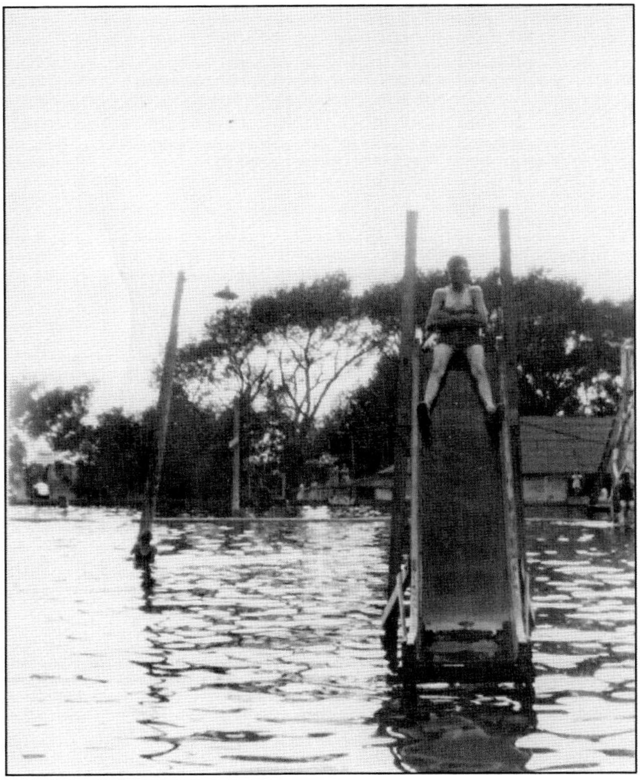

One of the attractions at Lake Comar was the waterslides. There was also a golf course, an airstrip, an entertainment stage, and a boathouse.

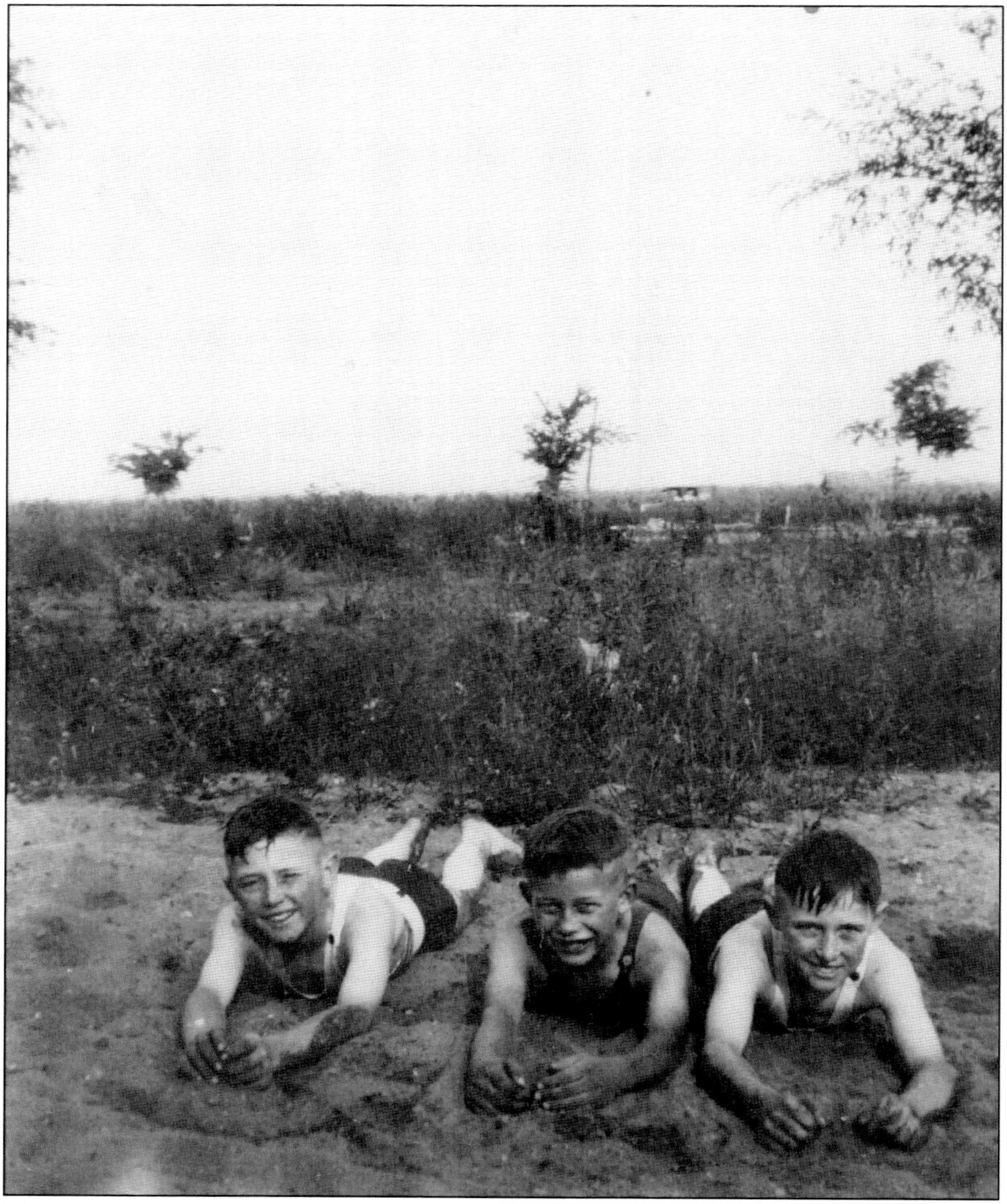

The Langland boys enjoy the Lake Comar beach. Over the years, the lake underwent a number of changes until it closed in the years following World War II.

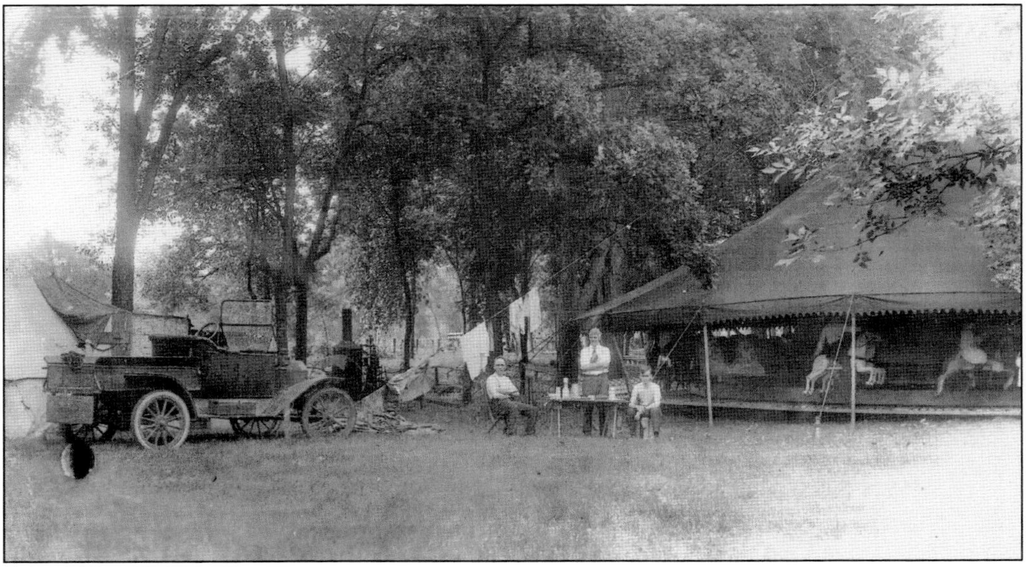

Laundry dries on a tent rope outside of a carousel in the Story City area. The operators temporarily lived in the tent next to the amusement ride. Today, Story City has a restored 1913 carousel that visitors to the community can ride.

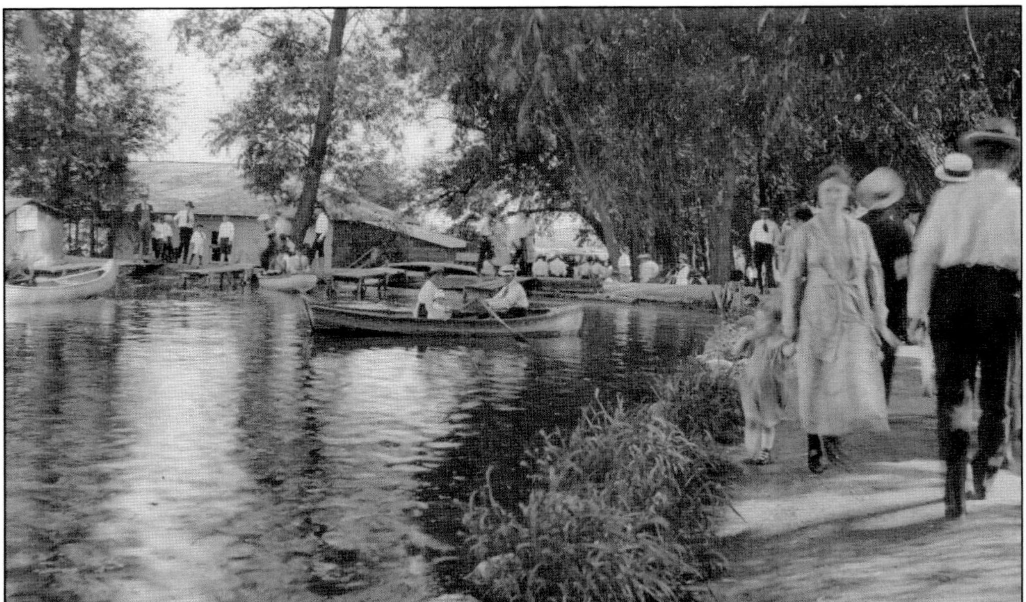

Lake Comar visitors walk along the path leading to the boathouse. There were two connected manmade lakes at Lake Comar. Supplied by cold freshwater from an artesian well, the lake was a popular vacation venue.

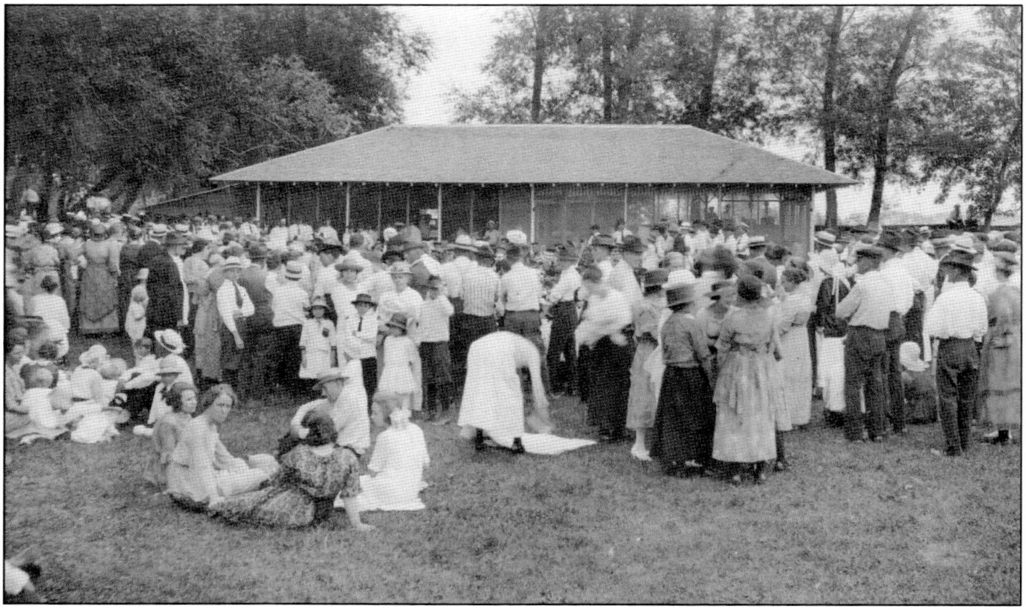

This photograph shows a gathering at a Lake Comar shelter house. Summer clothing in the early 20th century consisted of long-sleeved shirts, straw or felt hats, and long dresses.

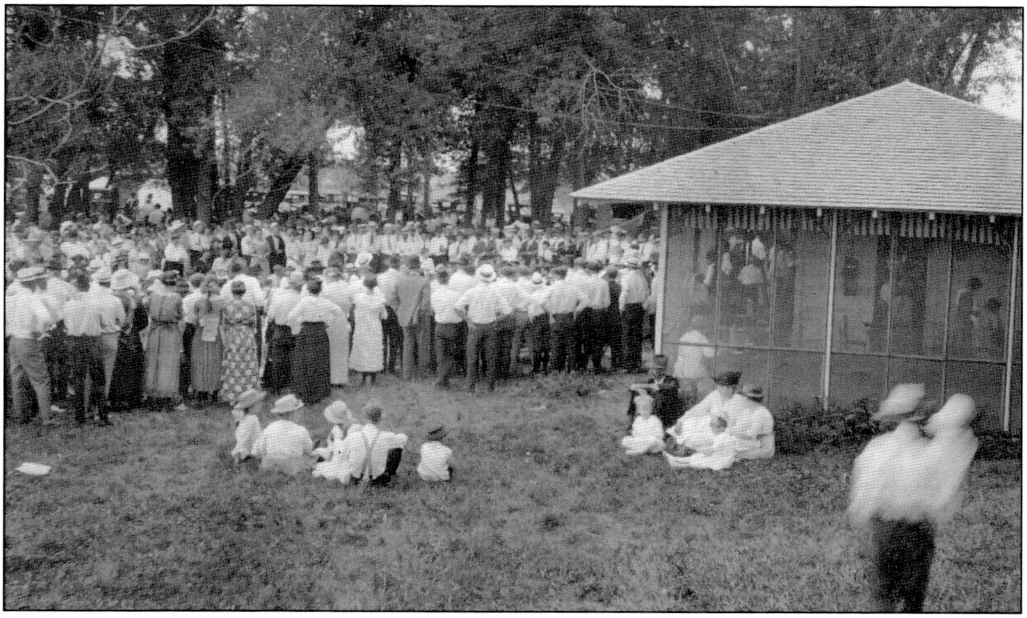

This is another view of a Lake Comar building. As wire screening became economical, it was commonly used to make porches insect-proof in the days before bug spray.

Four

The Greatest Generation

Many historians write that the American youth who went through the trials of the Great Depression, the struggle of World War II, and applied their work ethic to make our nation successful in the postwar years are the "Greatest Generation." It is a difficult claim to refute. In the depths of the great economic depression of the 1930s, people in Story City found ways to cope and defy the adversity confronting them and the rest of the nation.

Despite economic challenges, the community of Story City remained progressive and made efforts towards installing improvements. A great deal of work was conducted on the city parks, including a Works Progress Administration (WPA) project to construct a suspension bridge across the Skunk River in the South Park. The beautiful stonework will stand for centuries as a tribute to those who built it at such an important time in our nation's history.

Following the economic hardship of the Great Depression, Story City residents were drawn into World War II following the attack at Pearl Harbor. Men and women from the community served in the Pacific, North Africa, Italy, France, Germany, and on the home front. In 1942, *Life* magazine came to the area and ran a story on twin brothers who were joining the Navy, placing the community in the glow of the national spotlight. On the home front, there was war rationing, Red Cross knitting, and scrap drives to support the efforts of the large number of residents serving overseas, 20 of whom would never return home.

During World War II, Lake Comar tilled up its golf courses to provide additional farmland and more farmers began utilizing tractors and other progressive agricultural technology to make up for the shortage of labor in the workforce.

Following the war, the generation that saved the world from the Axis powers came home to Story City, bringing their work ethic and thrift to the farms and businesses of the area to guide the community through the rest of the century.

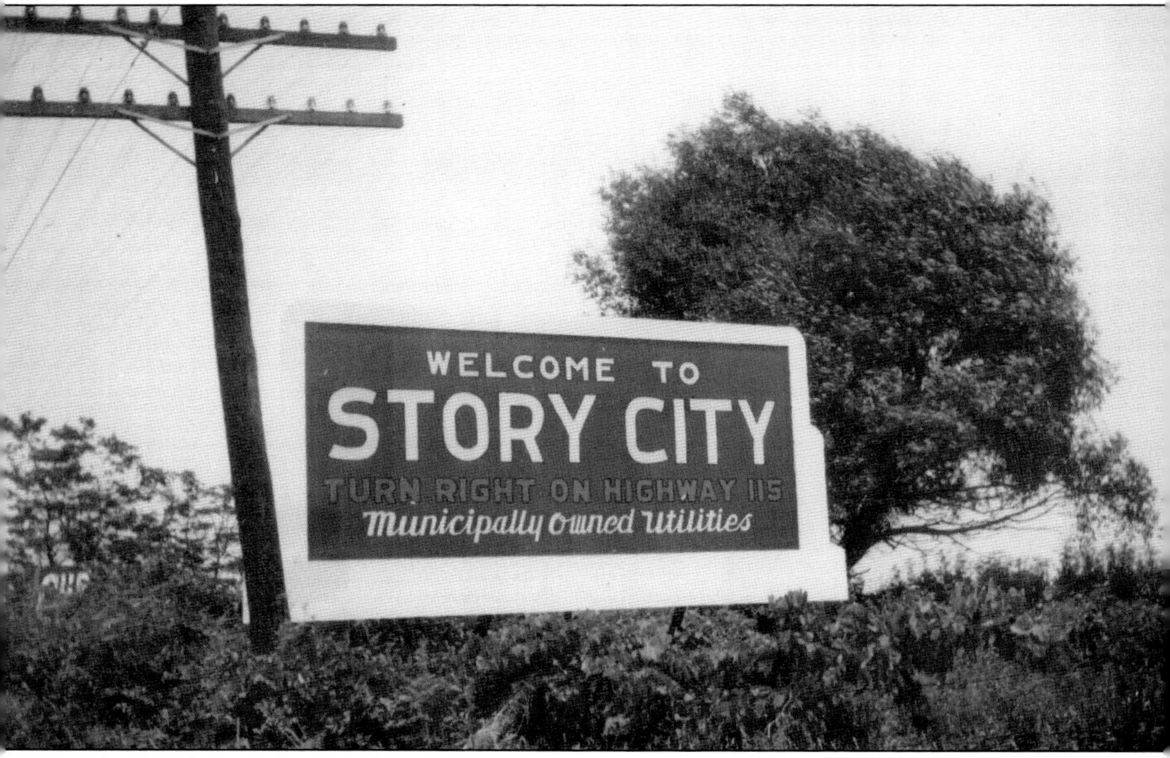

This hand-painted sign welcomed visitors to Story City in the mid-1900s. It showed the pride that the community had in municipally owned utilities.

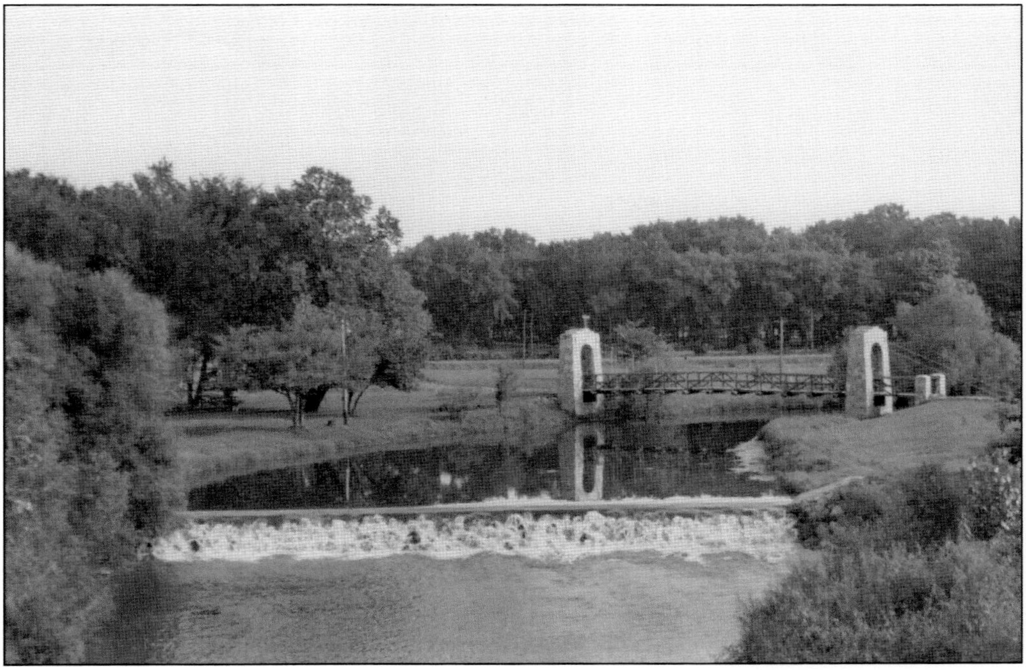

This suspension bridge was constructed as a WPA project along the Skunk River. The bridge is still present in the city park and visitors to the community can walk across it to picnic under shade trees.

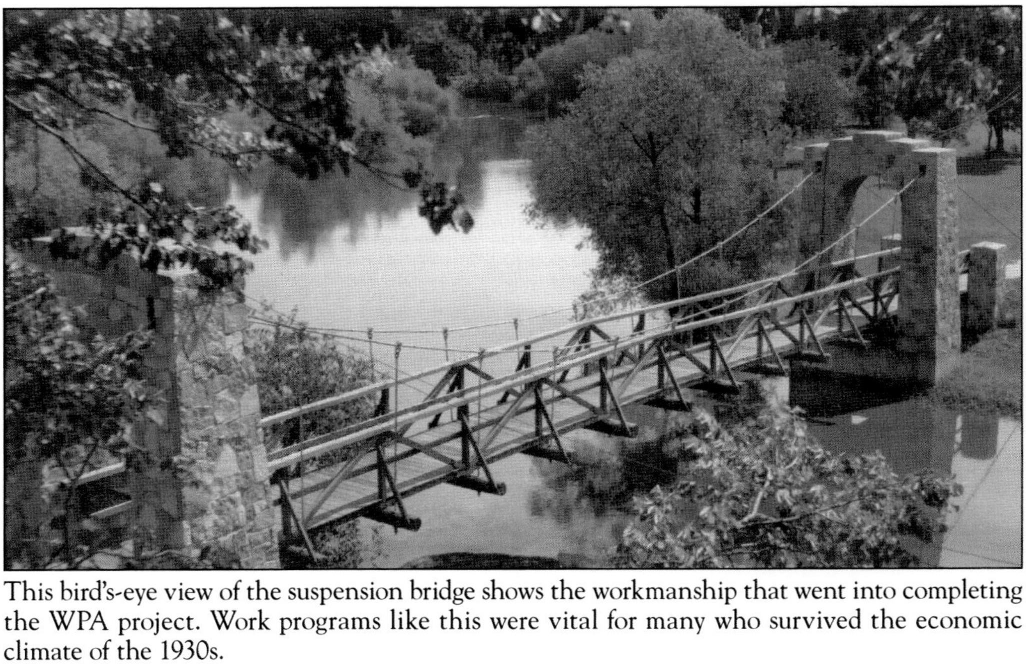

This bird's-eye view of the suspension bridge shows the workmanship that went into completing the WPA project. Work programs like this were vital for many who survived the economic climate of the 1930s.

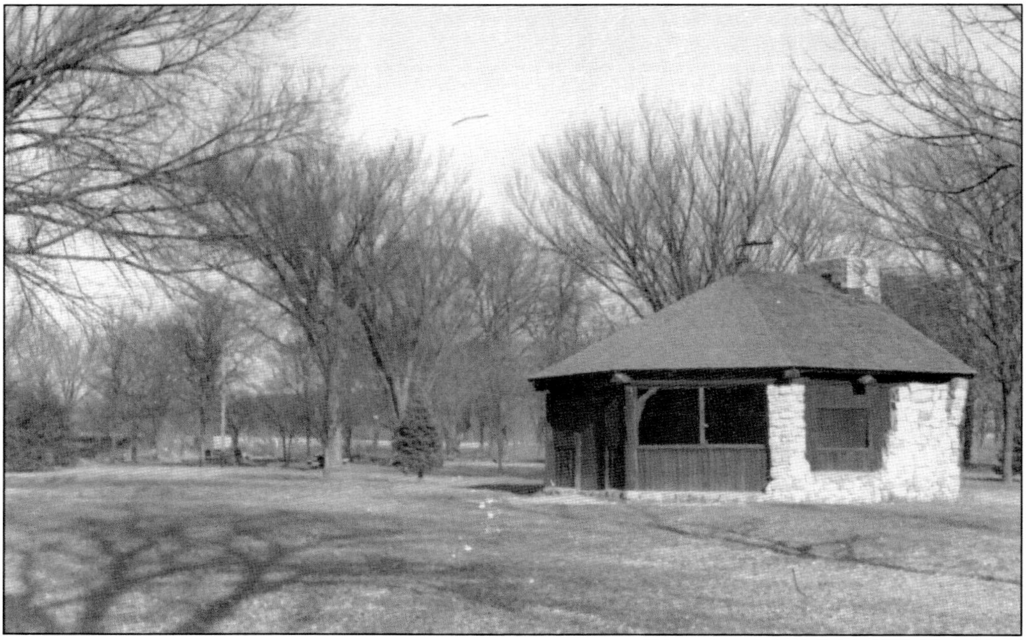

This stone shelter house was constructed by WPA workers and stands only a short distance from the swinging suspension bridge across the Skunk River. Still standing today, the building is situated in a beautiful clearing and can be rented.

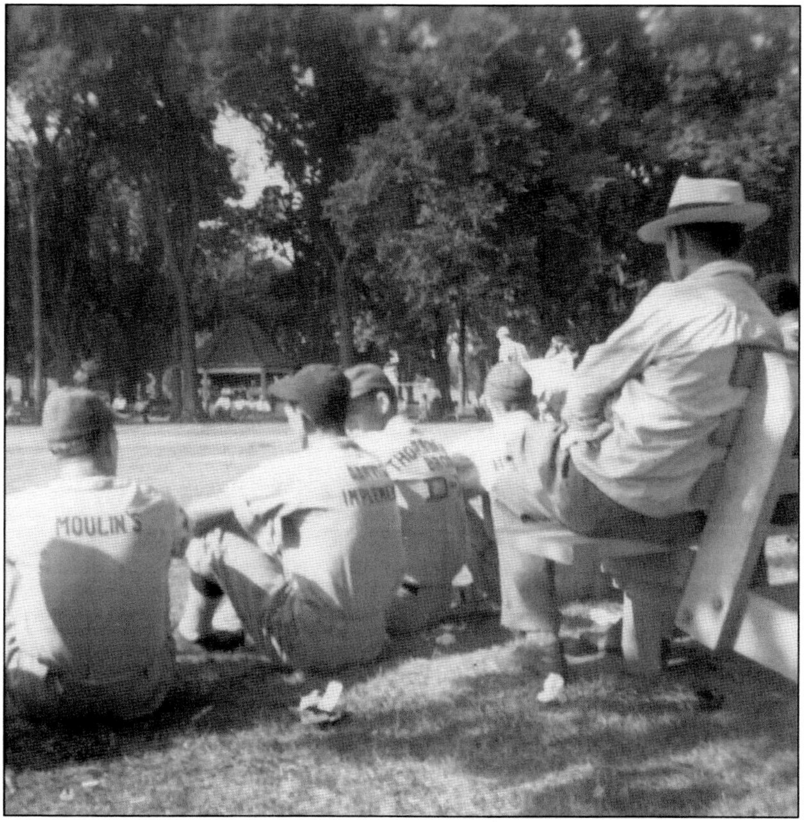

These baseball players at City Park have the names of sponsoring businesses on the backs of their jerseys.

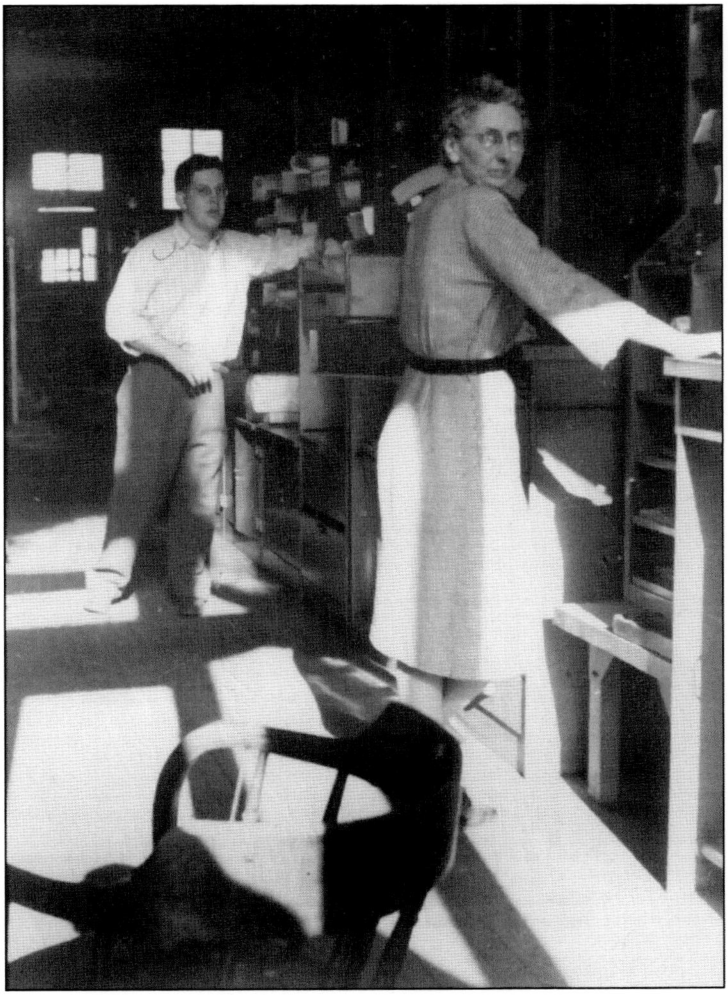

Workers take a break in the back room of a Story City business. The "captain's chair" in the foreground was a common piece of business furniture in central Iowa in the 1800s and continued to be utilized in professional environments through the early 1900s.

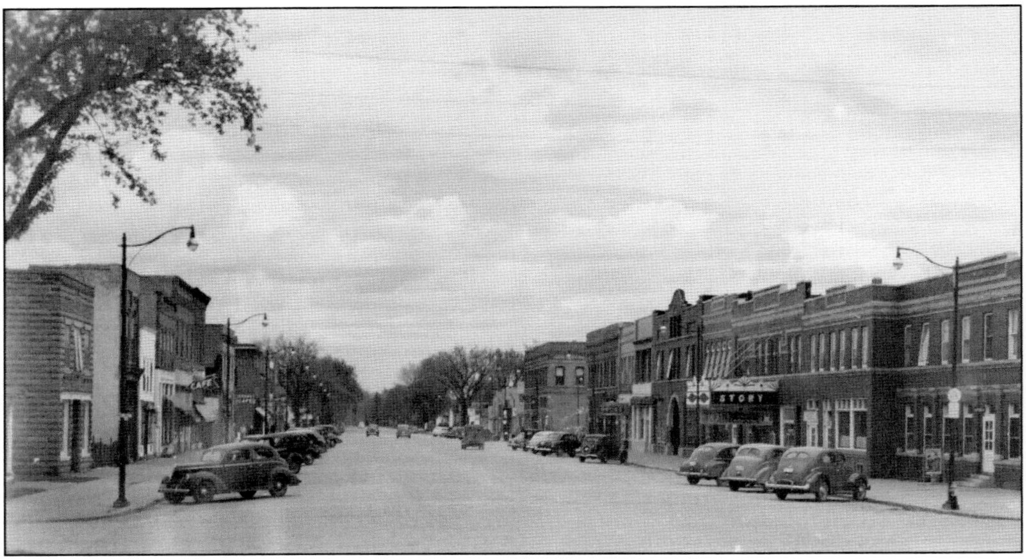

This image, looking east along Broad Street, shows the marquee of the Story City Theater and Opera House, which is still in use today. Built in 1913 during the age of silent movies, this is the region's oldest operating theater. A variety of historical and well-known films were shown at the theater over the decades.

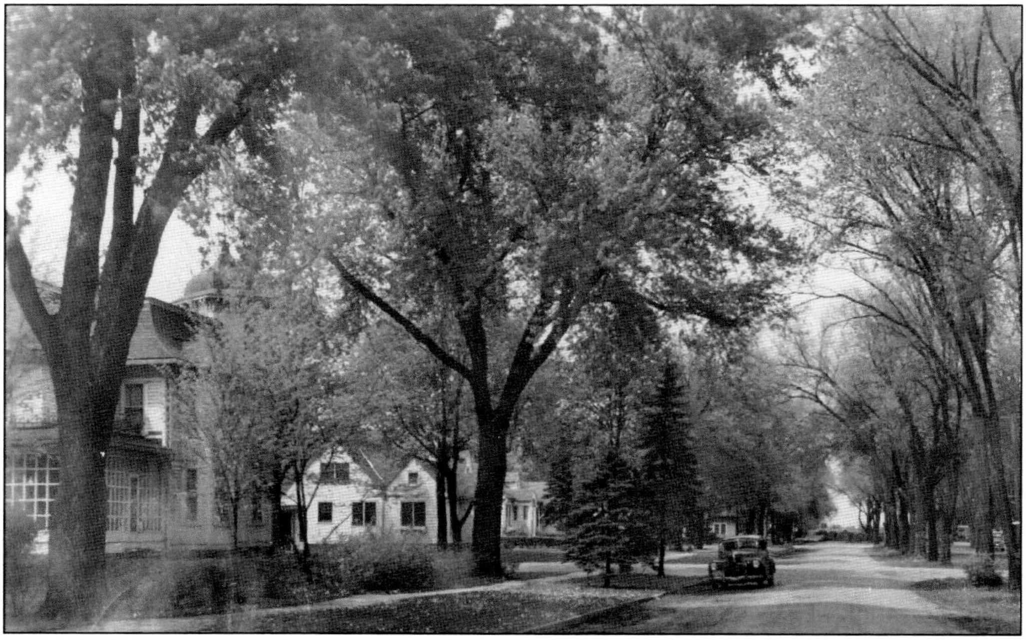

Large shade trees provided a great deal of beauty along residential streets in Story City. Today, shade trees still line the streets of Story City thanks to the hard work of community members in maintaining and replanting urban forestry. This photograph was taken a few blocks south of Broad Street and looks northward at Park Street.

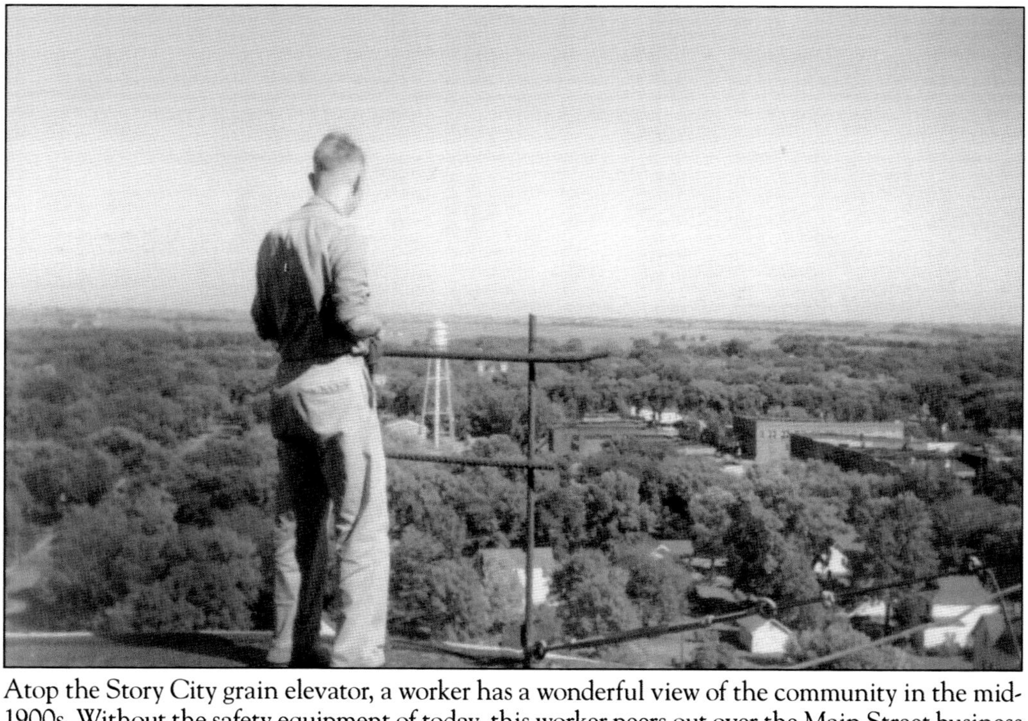

Atop the Story City grain elevator, a worker has a wonderful view of the community in the mid-1900s. Without the safety equipment of today, this worker peers out over the Main Street business district. In the distance, there is a contrast between the rapidly growing urban tree cover and the fields on the former prairie.

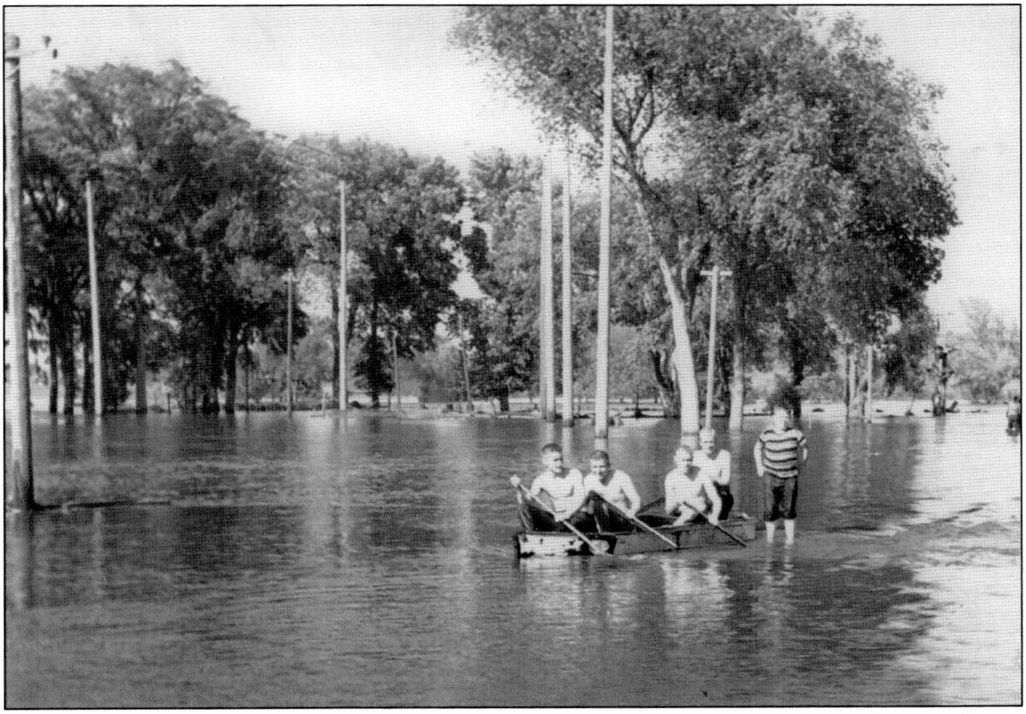

Throughout Story City's history, the Skunk River has flooded after heavy rains. This significant flood occurred on June 10, 1954. These boys play in the floodwaters covering one of the main routes out of the community.

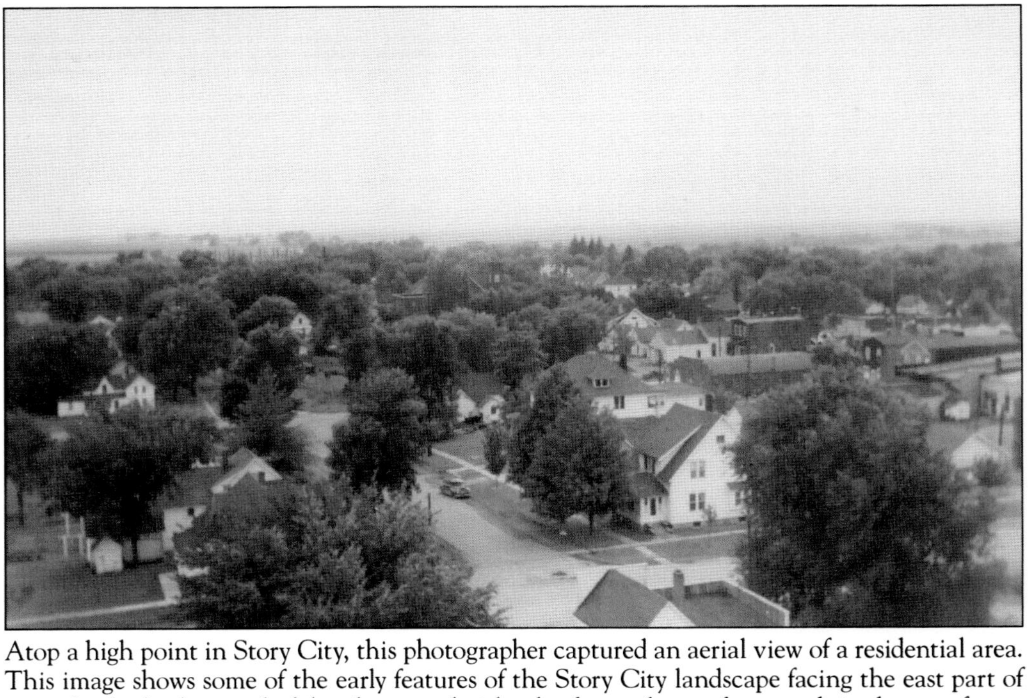

Atop a high point in Story City, this photographer captured an aerial view of a residential area. This image shows some of the early features of the Story City landscape facing the east part of town. In the background of the photograph, islands of trees denote farmsteads in the sea of corn and soybeans.

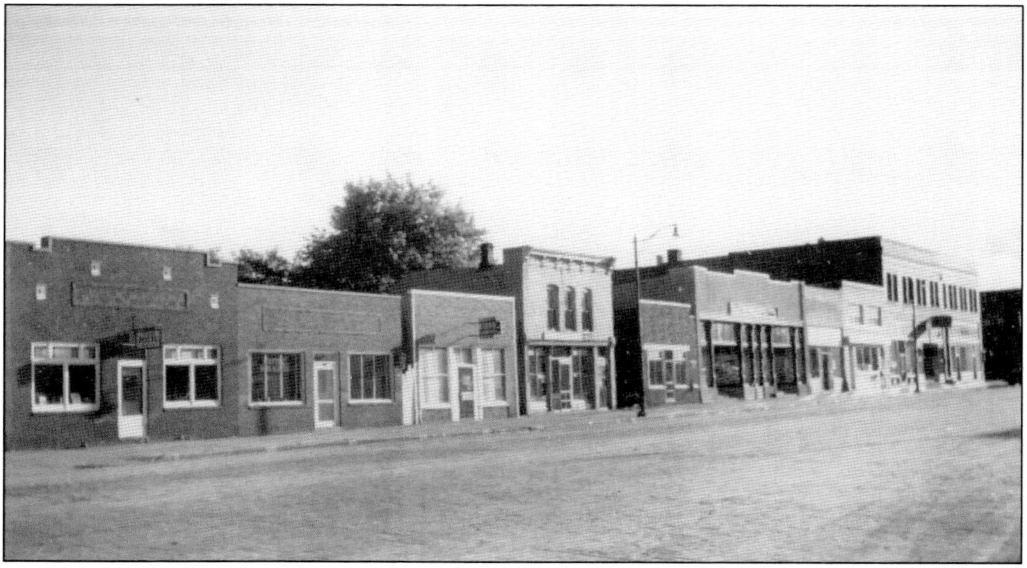

A variety of architectural styles were incorporated into the construction and renovation of brick commercial buildings along Broad Street. Many of these buildings are still in existence but with updated commercial facades. This view shows the south side of Broad Street.

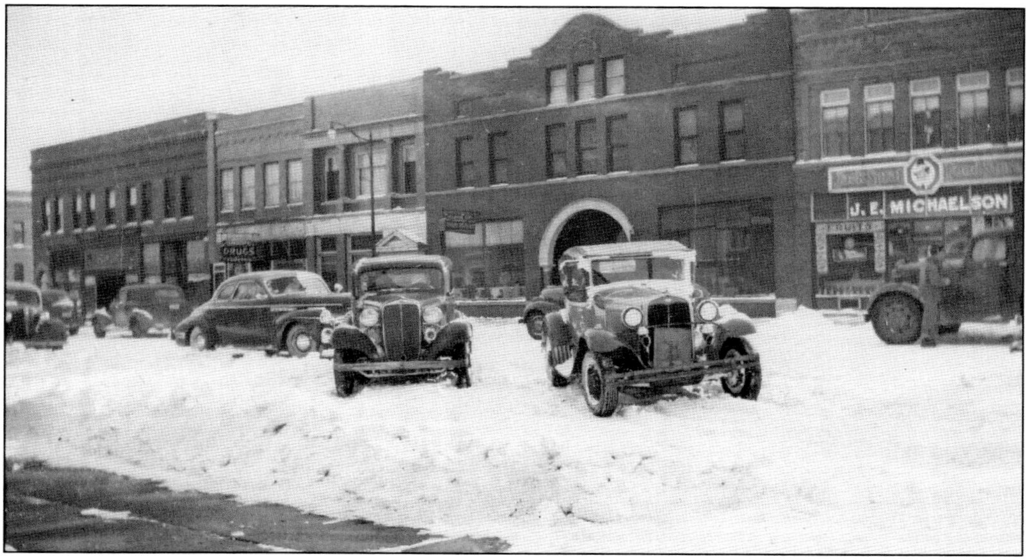

Iowa winters can be harsh and great difficulty was had removing snow from the busy streets of Story City. Seen here is the south side of Broad Street with the Charlson building to the far left.

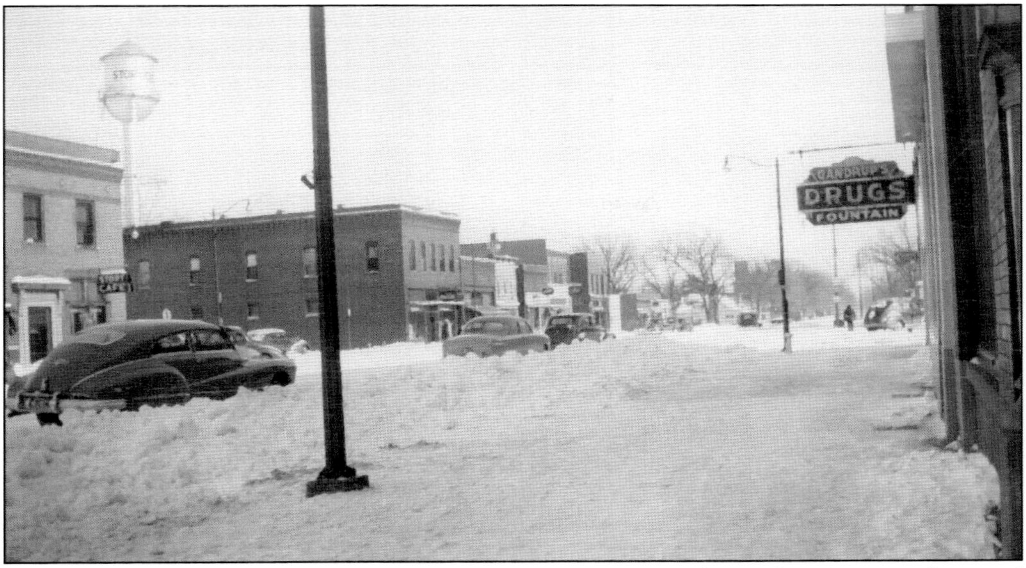

This image looks northeast, showing the signs for the Story Café—where Alley's Pizza is today—and Gandrup's Drugs and Fountain across the street. The silhouette of Immanuel Lutheran Church is in the background.

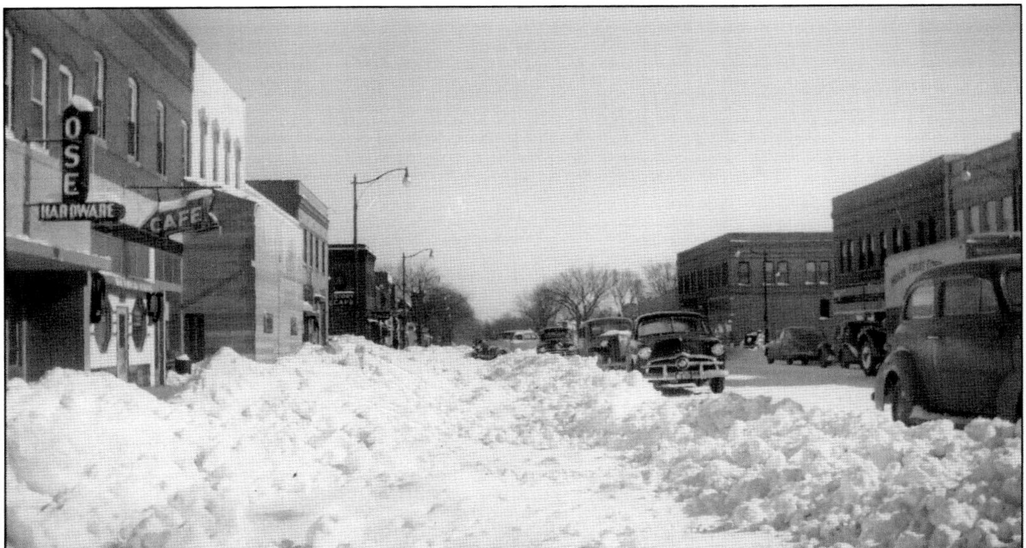

Looking east along Broad Street, the sign for Ose Hardware stands out against the snowy background. Historically, advertising was often seen on the storefronts of the businesses down the street. To the right is the mid-1900s renovation of the Charlson storefront.

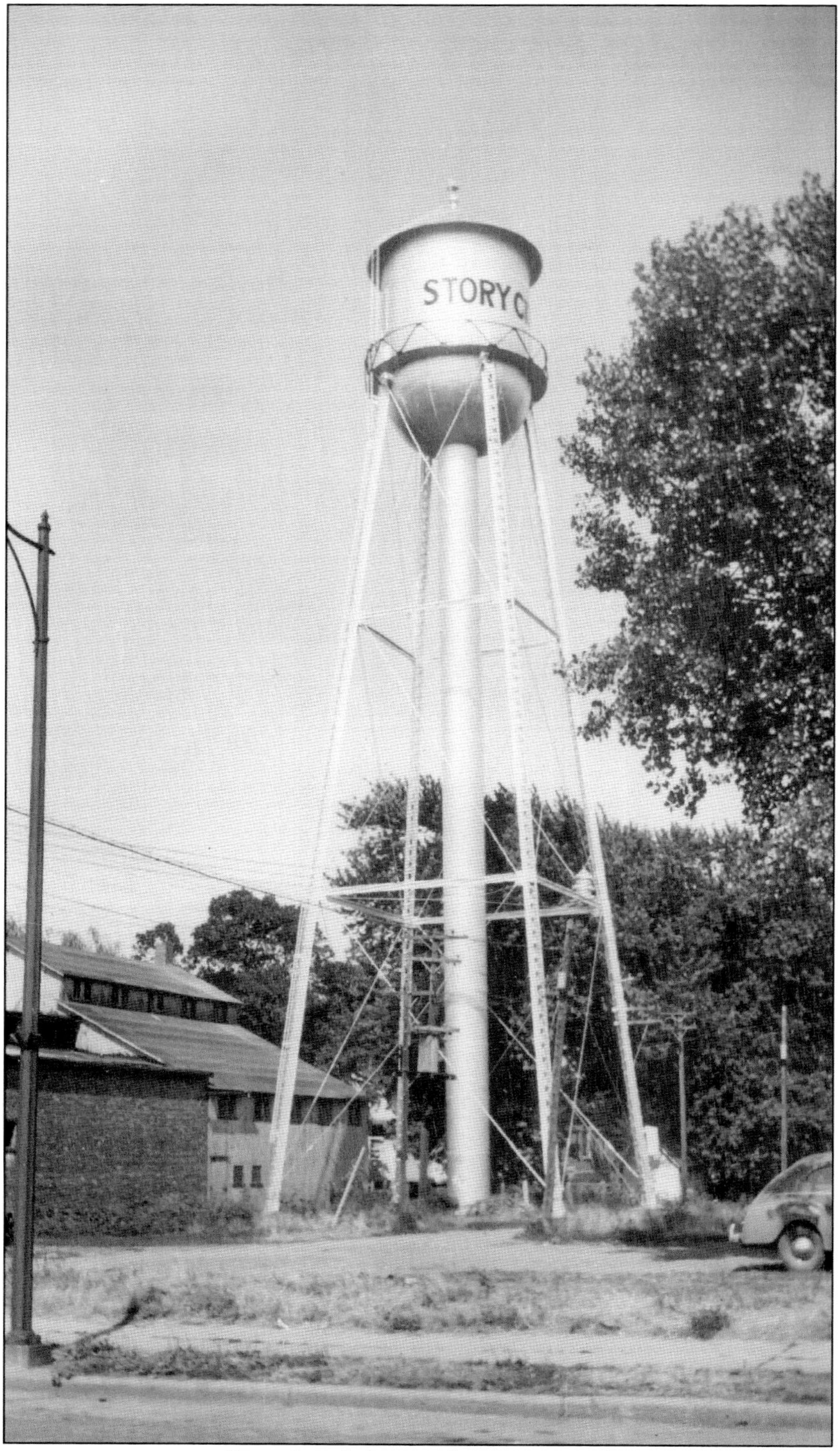

A metal water tower eventually replaced the wooden one, providing a more modern means to store water for the community. In the lower left are some commercial buildings and to the right is a dusty car, which has no doubt been traversing the gravel roads of the Story City area.

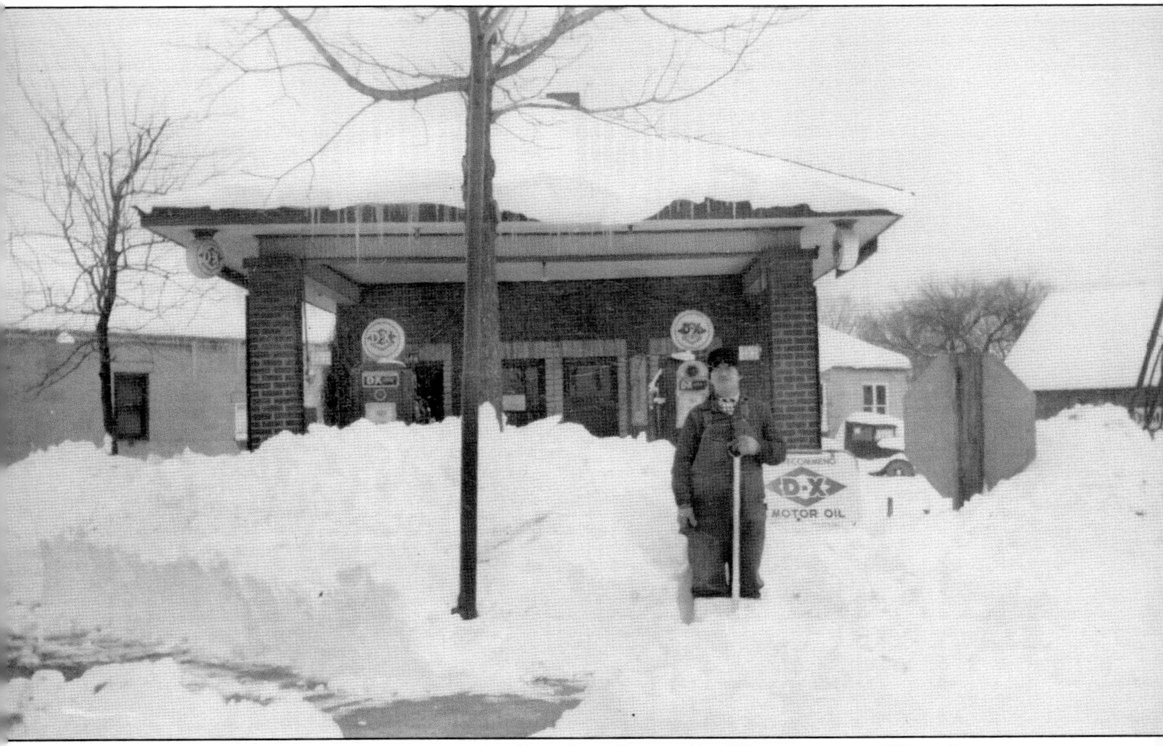

A resident of Story City scoops snow by hand in front of a filling station. The glass reservoir gas pumps, oil signs, and brick architecture are all details that early travelers through Story City would have experienced while visiting a filling station. Today, such gas stations have given way to self-service convenience stores.

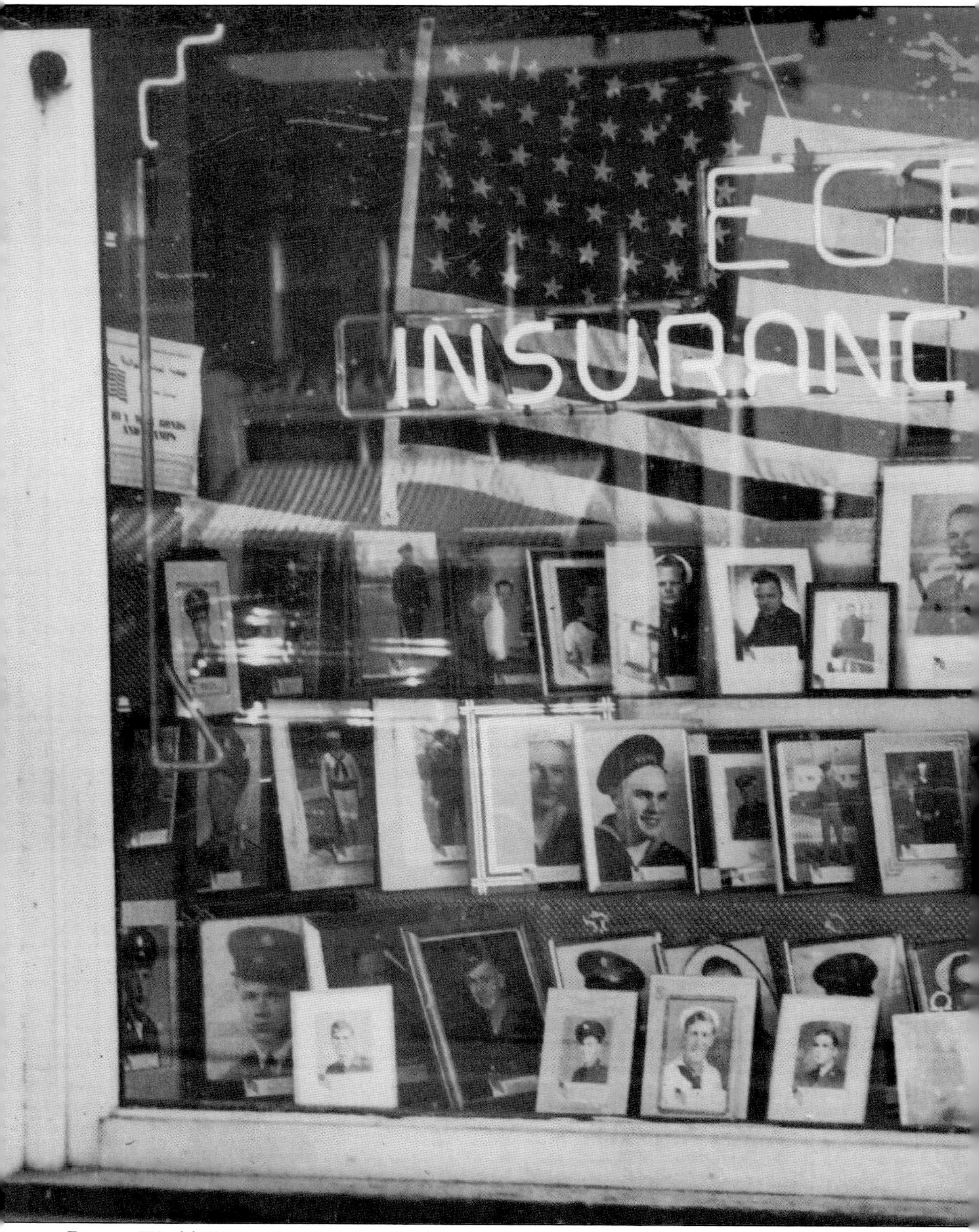

During World War II, Ivar Egenes displayed portraits of local servicemen and women in the front window of his insurance business. A large poster of General McArthur hangs to the right

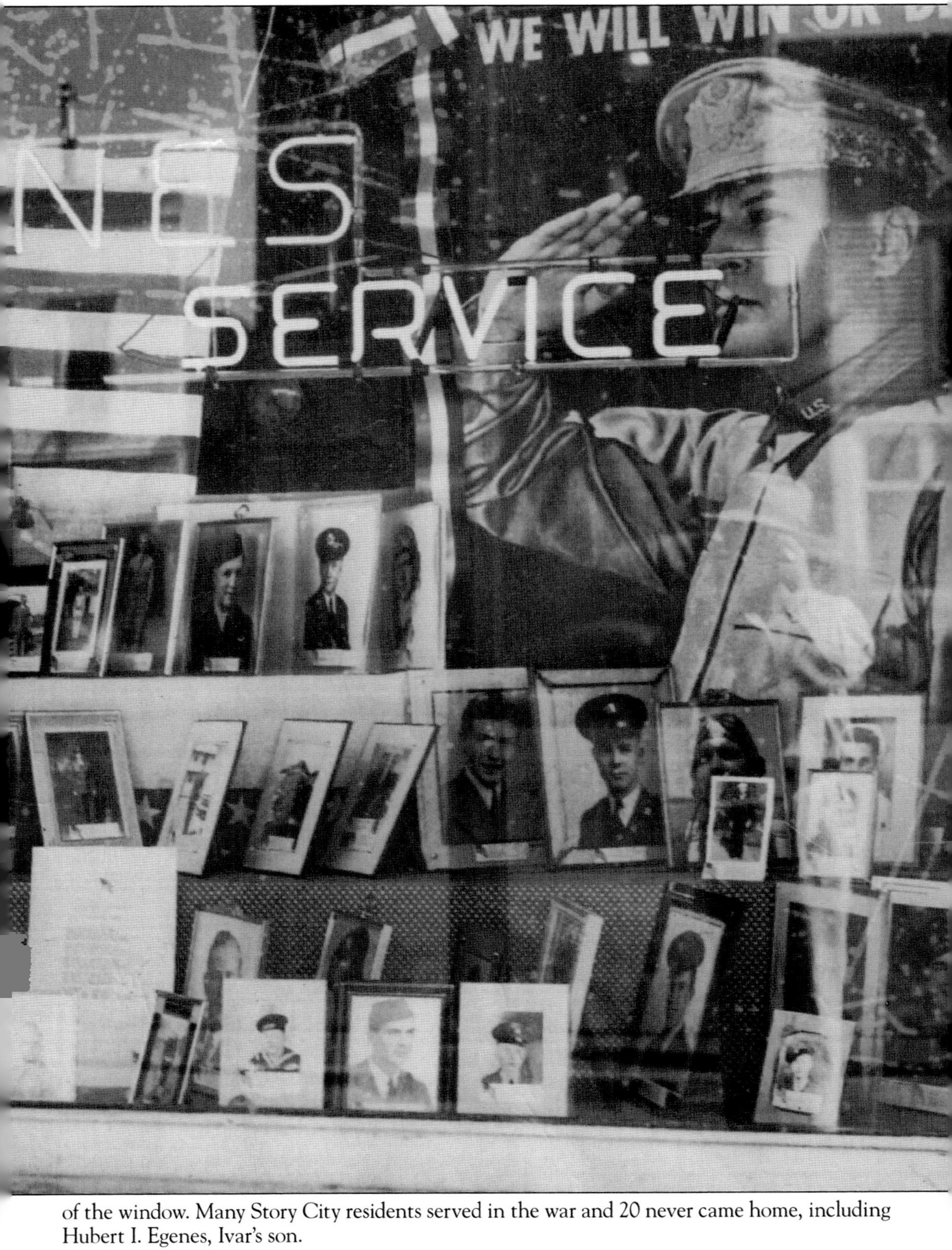

of the window. Many Story City residents served in the war and 20 never came home, including Hubert I. Egenes, Ivar's son.

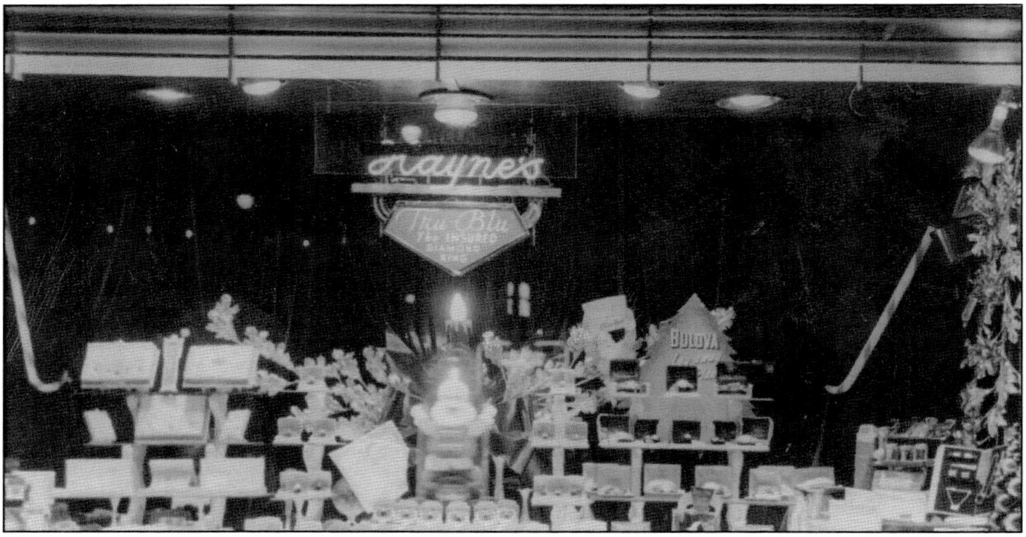

The display window of Haynes Jewelry Store was lit up with this neon sign. Candy canes and greenery helped to attract Christmas shoppers. Historically, there was stronger reliance on the Main Street district for holiday retail purchases than there is today.

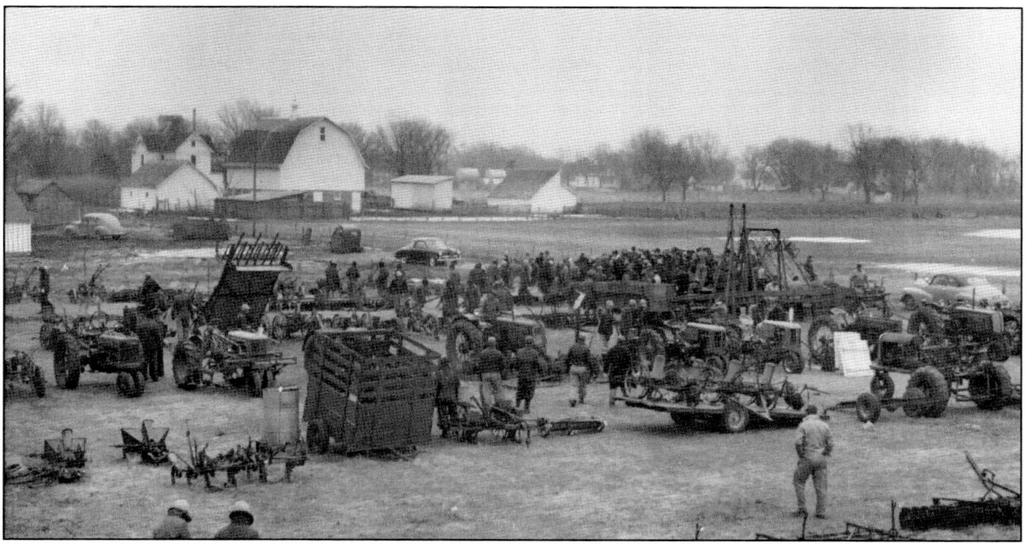

Agricultural implements are placed on display for a 1949 farm auction. This photograph was taken in the final period of the agricultural transition from horse-drawn equipment to tractor-powered implements, with both shown in the display.

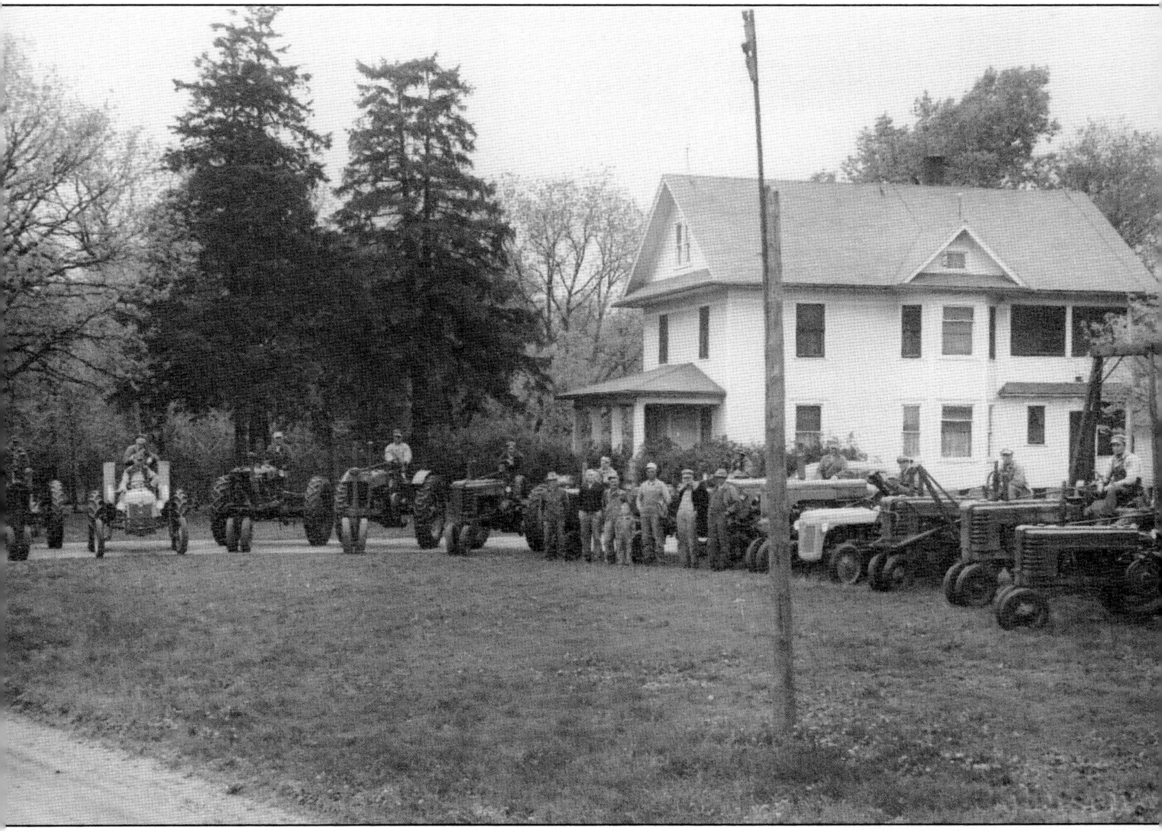

A variety of tractors of different manufacture are parked in the front yard of this farm. This could be the result of an auction or an early local tractor club showing off their passion. In the background is a fairly typical early-20th-century Story City farmhouse.

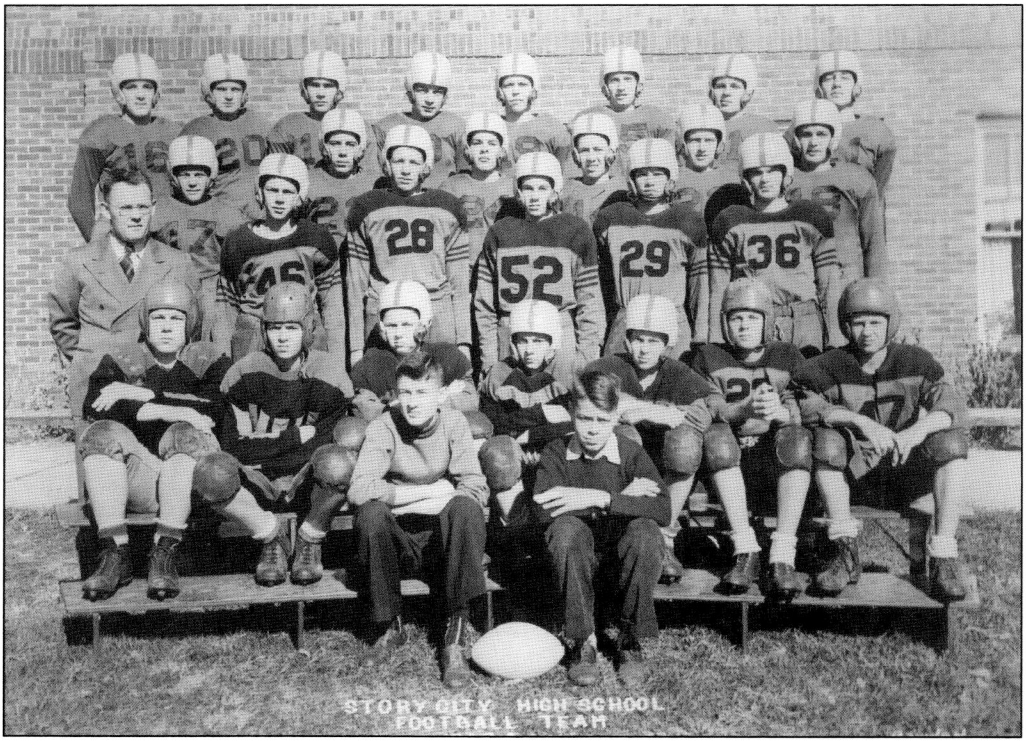

The Story City High School football team poses for a team photograph in the fall of 1943 during World War II. With the war lasting another two years, many of these boys would end up serving their country in Europe, Italy, and the Pacific. Wartime rationing of resources may have contributed to the mix of leather helmet styles and the variance in jerseys.

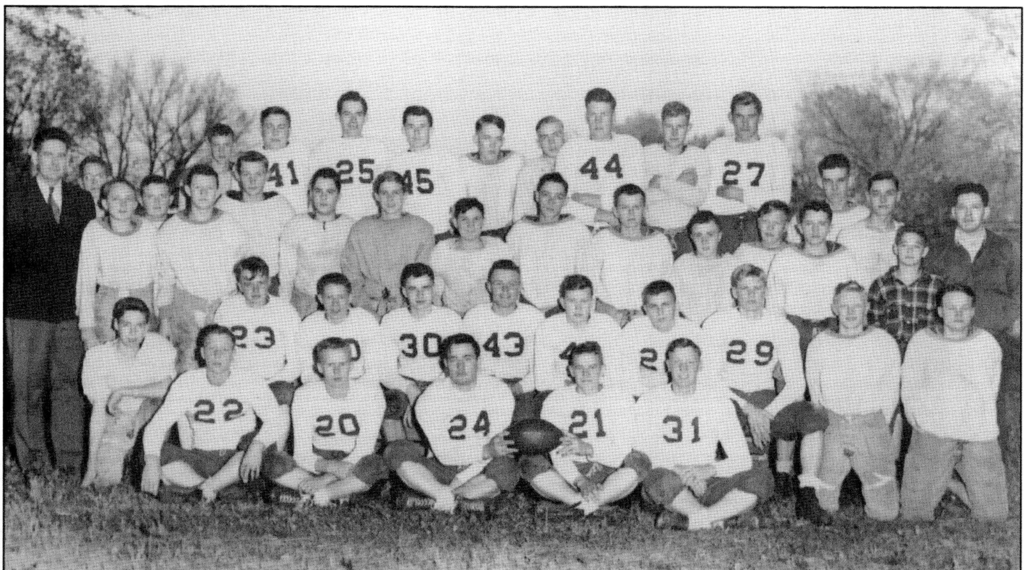

The Story City High School football team is seen here in 1945, only months after Germany surrendered to Allied forces. Possibly only days or weeks before this photograph was taken, Japan surrendered after atomic bombs were dropped on Hiroshima and Nagasaki.

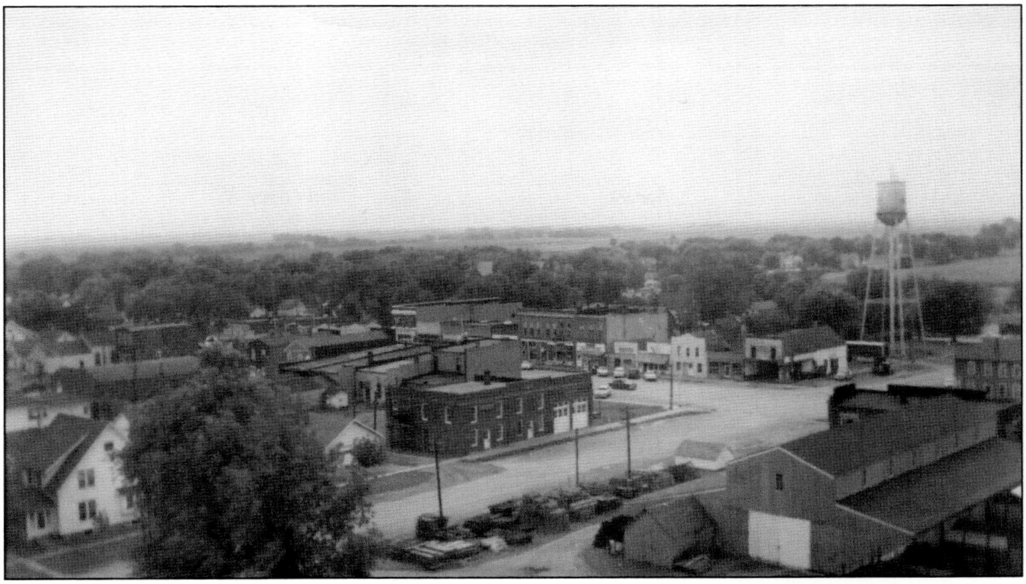

This bird's-eye view of Story City shows the variety of historical commercial architecture in the community's business district. Much of the construction in this area occurred over decades, with wooden buildings eventually giving way to brick storefronts.

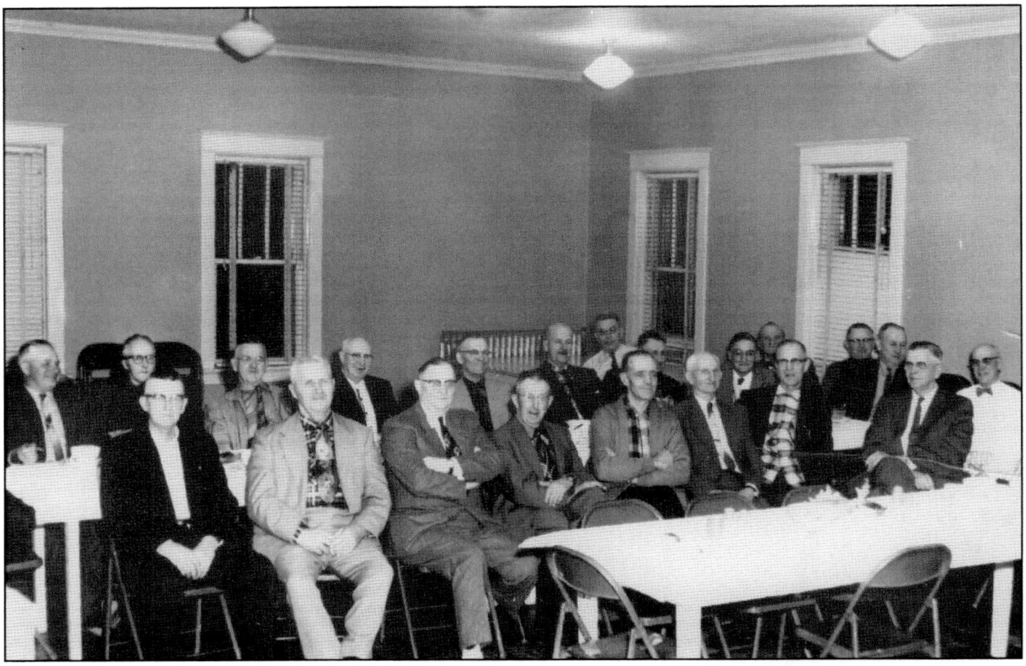

This group of men poses for the camera in Story City in the early 1900s. The image is dated by the style of window sashes and the woodwork.

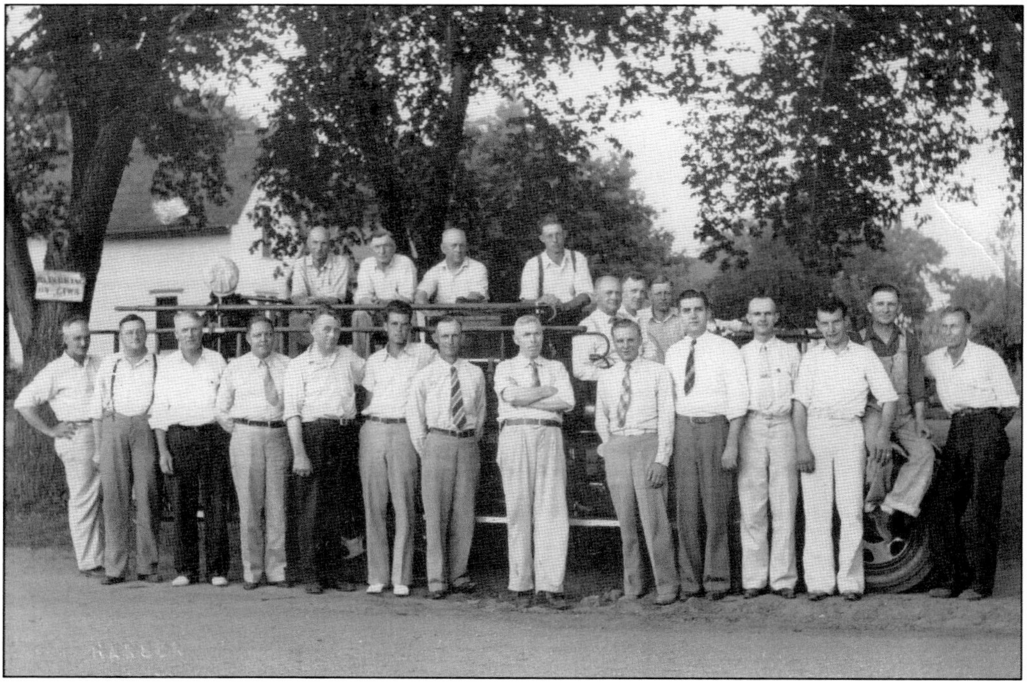

Gathered around a new fire truck in 1929, area residents strike a pose for the camera. Motorized firefighting vehicles were of great benefit in responding quickly to businesses and homes in the community that caught fire. To the far left is a hand-stenciled sign that reads "No Parking On Lawn."

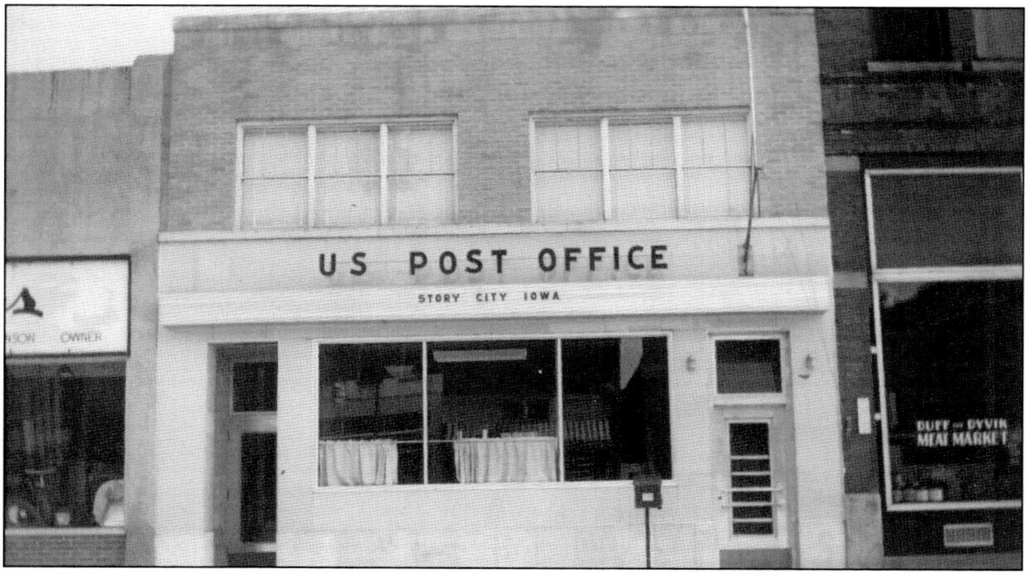

The Story City post office is seen here before it moved to its current location. Throughout the years, the post office has moved around to different buildings in the community. In the lobby of the current post office is a panel showing the past postmasters and the dates they served.

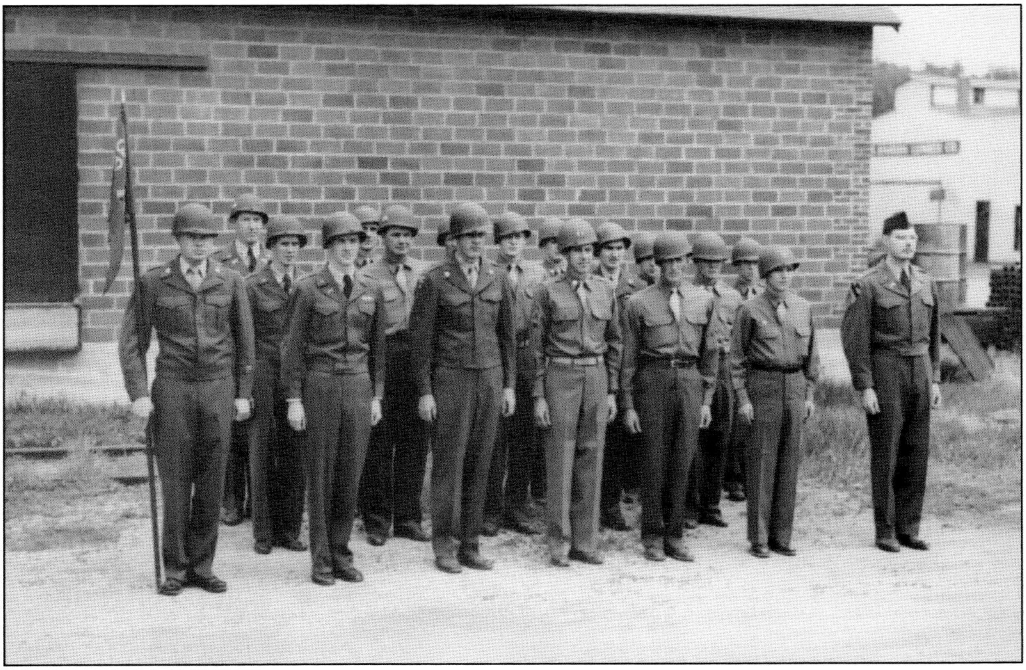

Commanded by Lt. George Burnet, Battery C of the 384th Field Artillery Battalion called Story City home. Made up of local World War II veterans who had served in a number of different divisions, this postwar reserve battery was established to help fund the rent of a legion building. This photograph was taken in 1951 at the Story City Memorial Day parade.

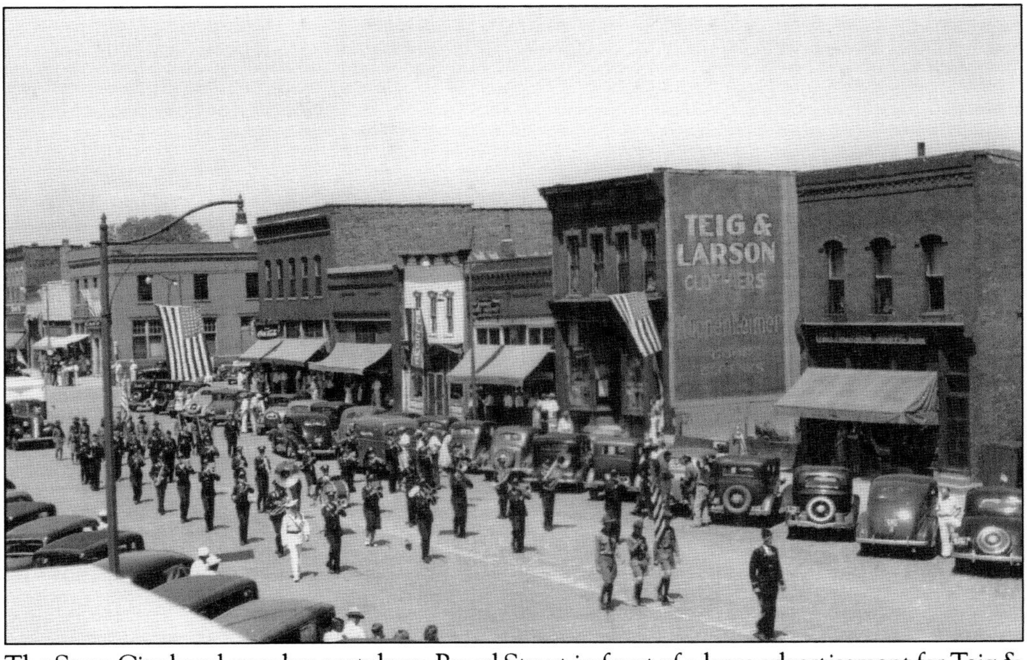

The Story City band marches east down Broad Street in front of a large advertisement for Teig & Larson Clothiers painted on a building. A group of Boy Scouts serves as the color guard with the popular band playing behind them. The architecture of the Main Street district was still dotted with early wood-frame buildings.

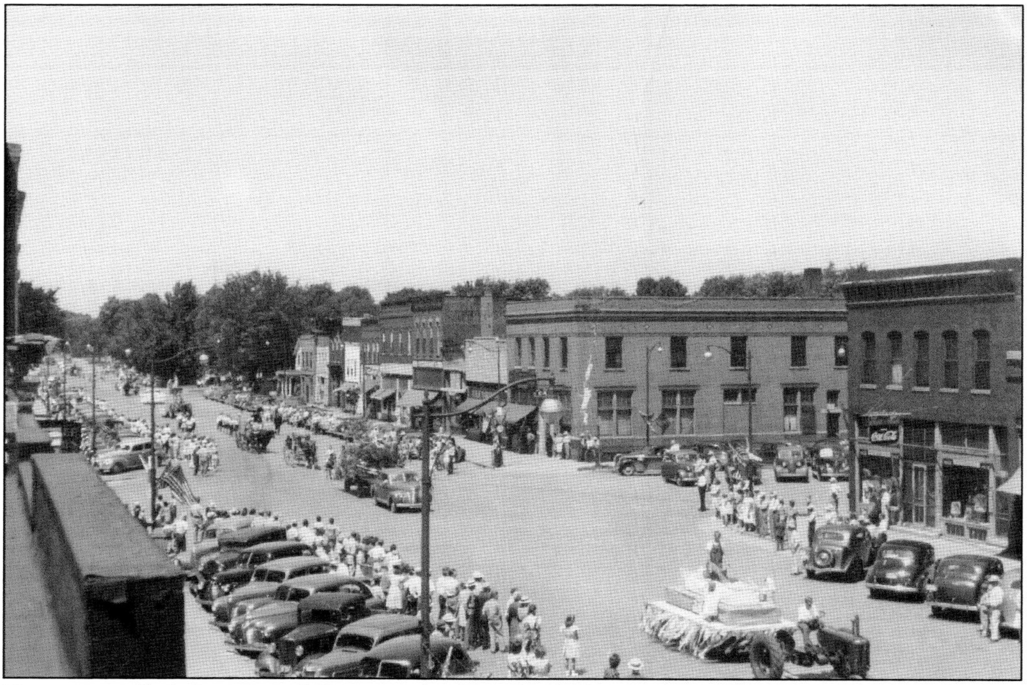

Floats are pulled along Broad Street in this Fourth of July parade. By this time, electric lights had replaced the older streetlights on the curbs. Below the Coca-Cola sign on the restaurant are screen doors, which were a required feature of such businesses in the days before air conditioning.

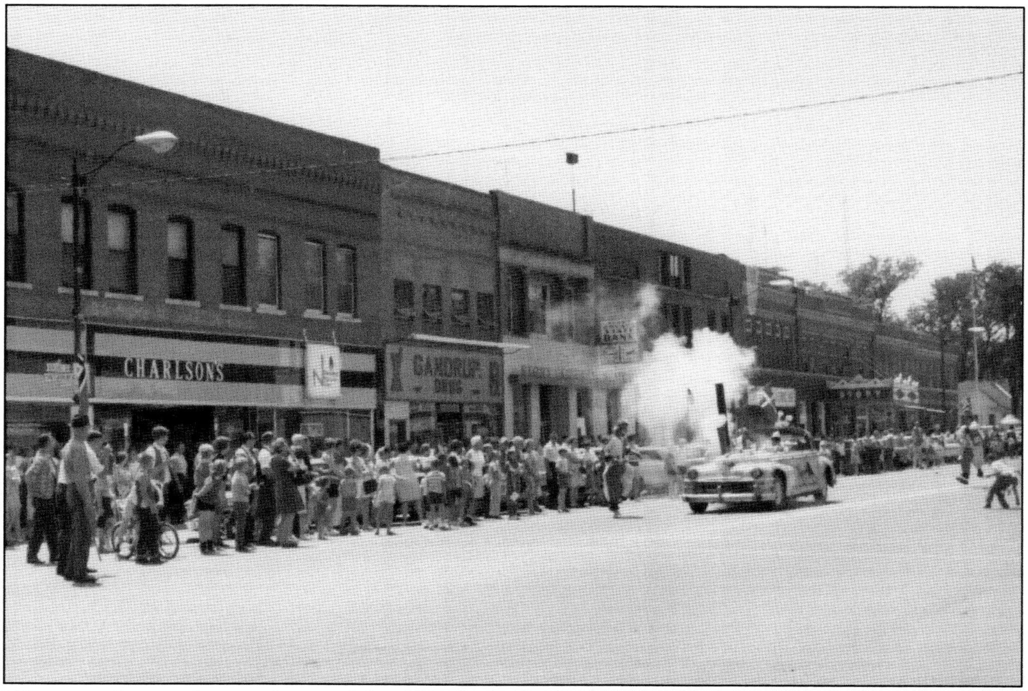

This parade marches in front of the Charlson clothes shop. The 20th-century storefronts and signs differ greatly from those of only a few decades earlier, with the exception of the Story City Theater.

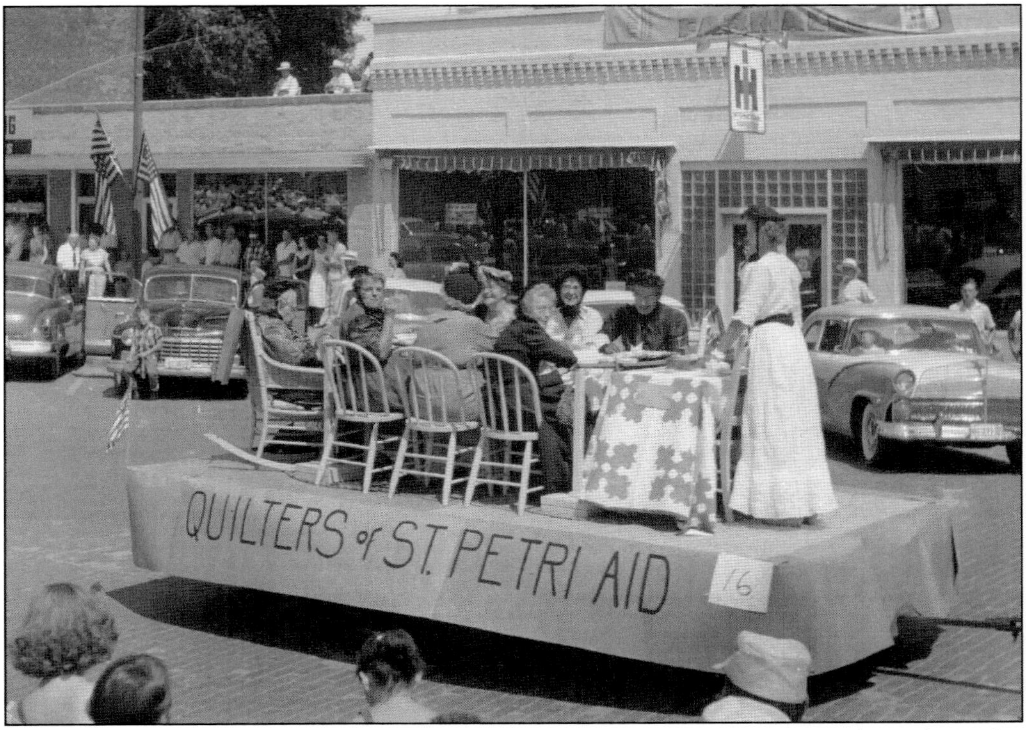

Quilters from St. Petri Lutheran Church ride their float in Story City's centennial parade. In this parade, a number of historically themed floats were entered, offering vignettes of past life and community activities from the previous 100 years.

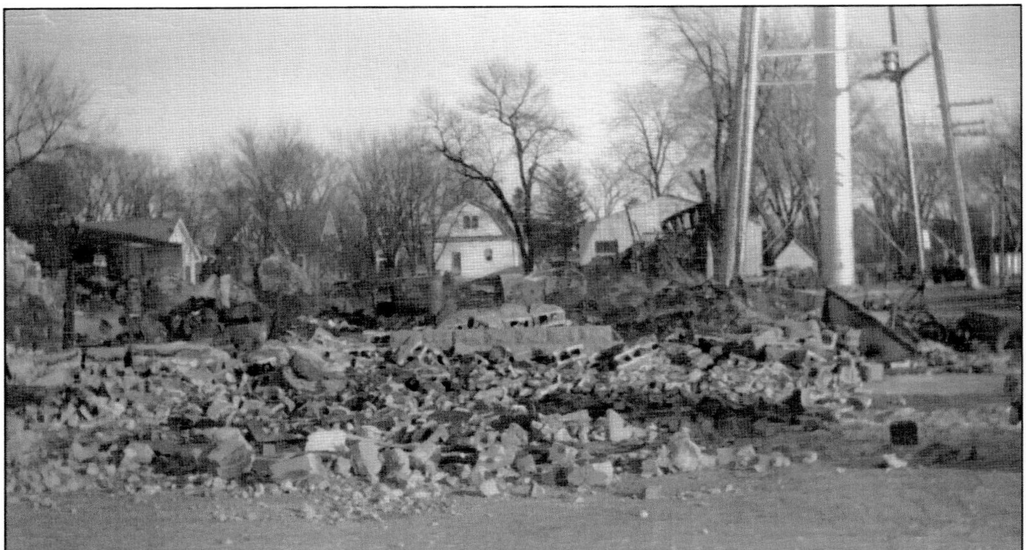

This photograph shows the rubble and debris from the fire that consumed the Baldus hatchery, which was near the base of the water tower.

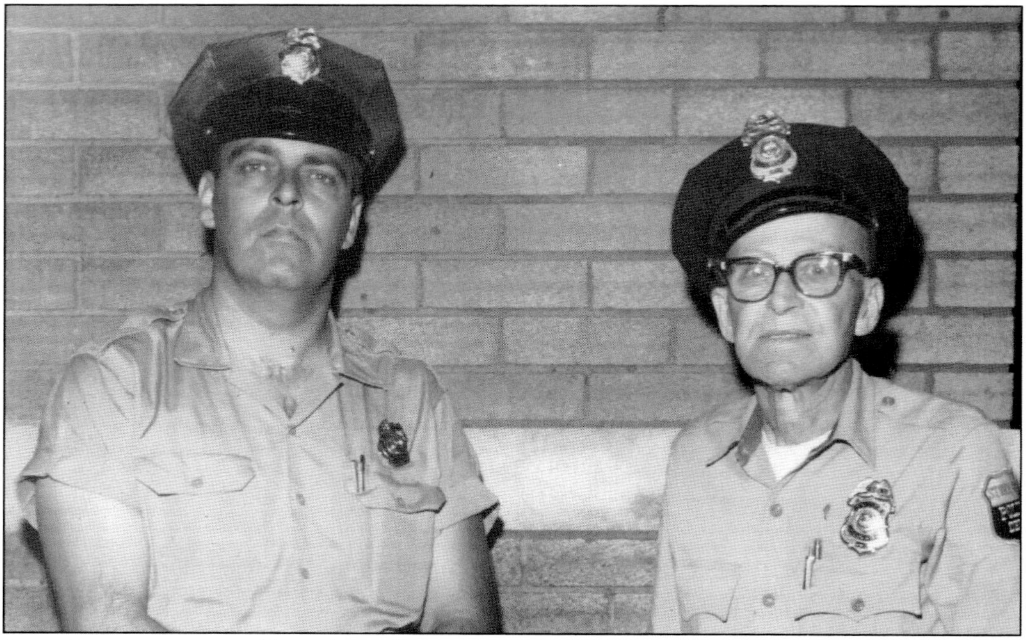

Story City was protected by police officers Homer Larsen and Eastace "Junior" Lake in the early 1960s. For those with an interest in early-20th-century law enforcement, the Story City Historical Society has a historical four-bunk jail cell on exhibit, along with a number of ledger books, which recorded early crime in the community.

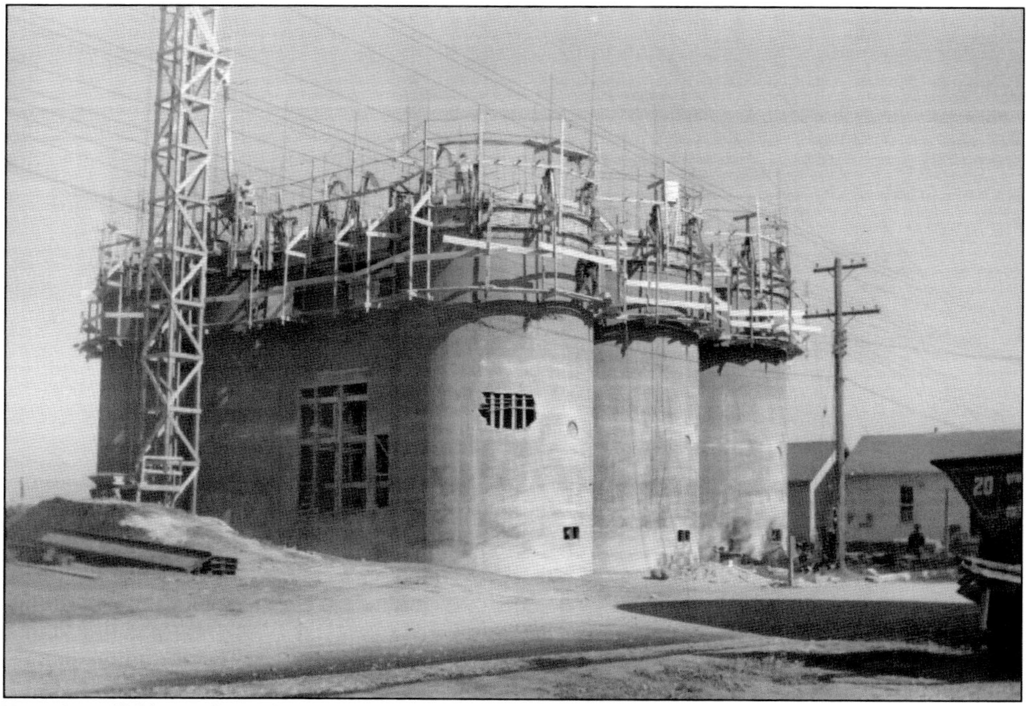

Wood scaffolding allowed workers to gain access to raising the reinforced concrete walls as they built the new grain elevator. Prior to being constructed of concrete, many central Iowa grain elevators were made of wood, often with tin siding on the exterior.

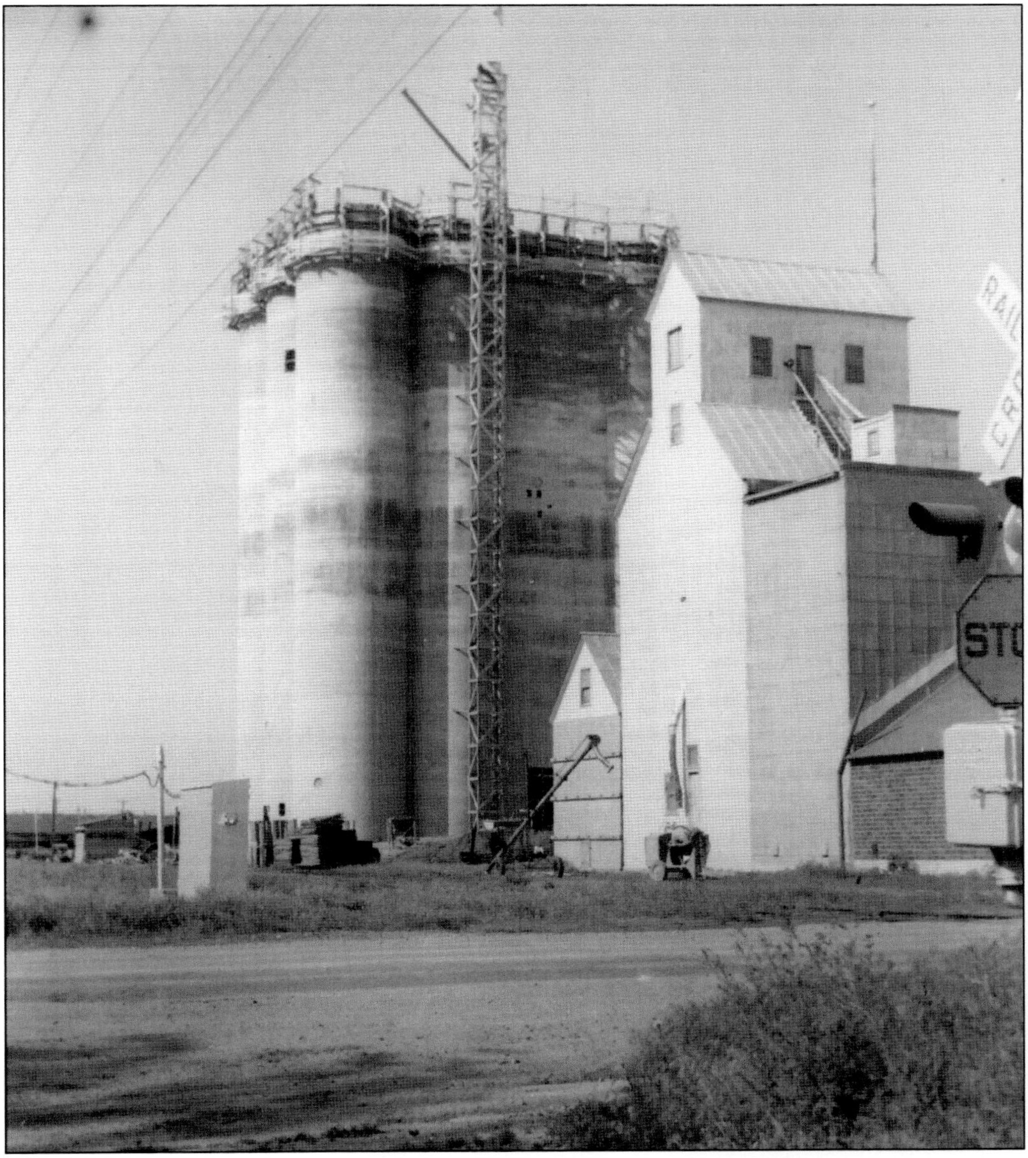

Standing high above the rest of the community, the Story City grain elevator can be seen for several miles. It is from here that area farmers contribute their grain for the feeding of the rest of the world.

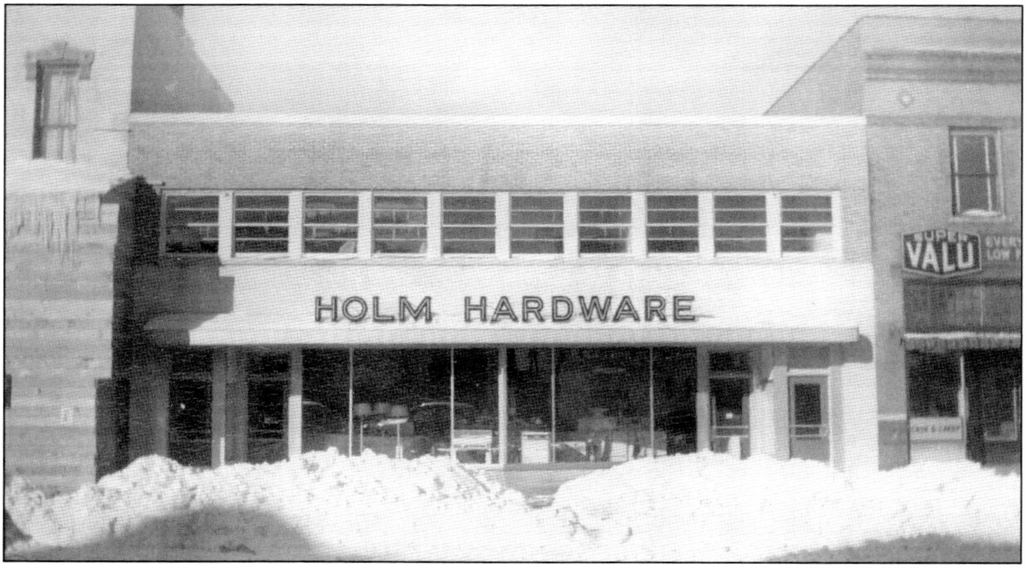

Holm Hardware was a popular store along Main Street. This storefront was next to the Super Value grocery store, which had a sign stating "Cash and Carry," as opposed to the credit or ledger-book system some older grocery establishments had.

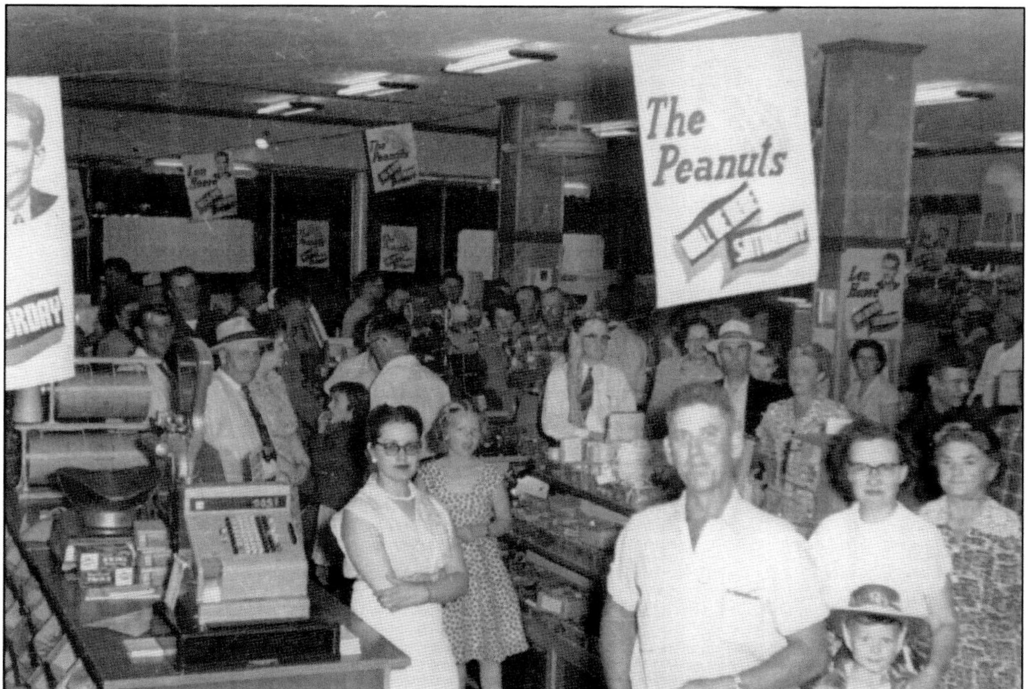

The interior of Holm's Hardware is seen here during their 1949 grand opening as signs hang from the ceiling advertising to customers.

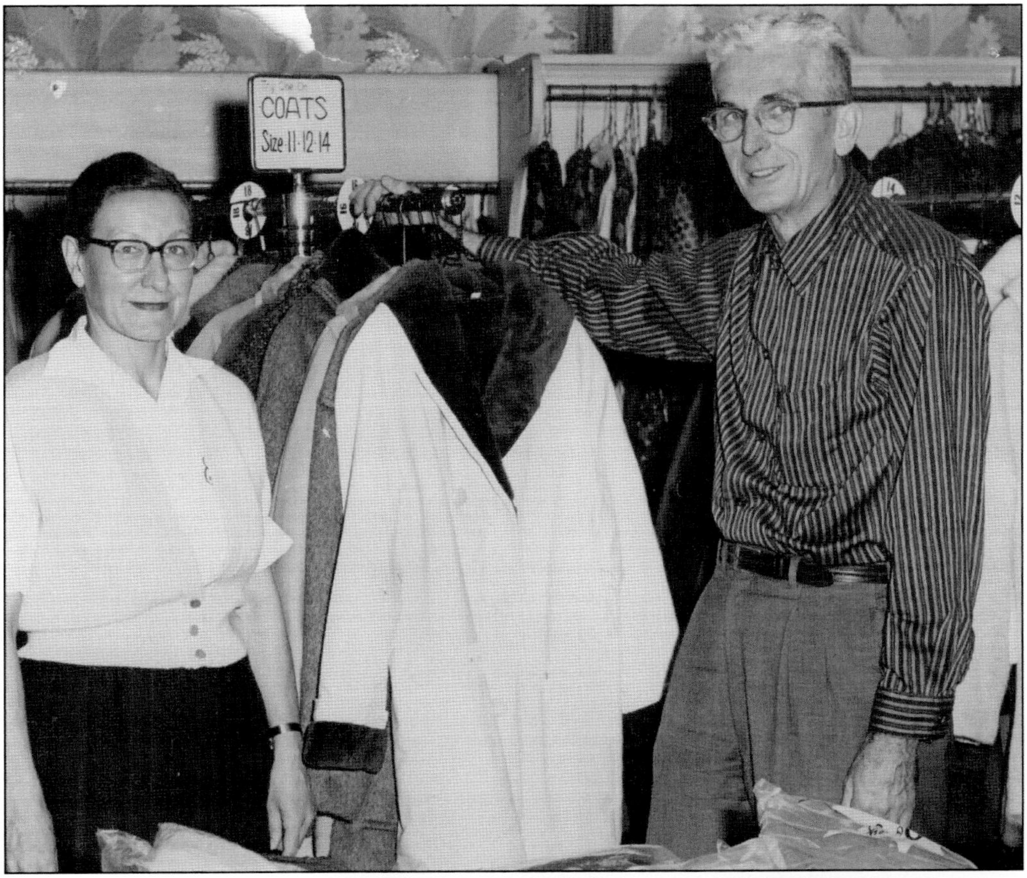

Dick and Edith Lowry pose next to some of the women's clothing they sold at their store at 521 Broad Street, which was previously Lynn's Clothing Store. In those days, Main Street provided much of the fashions in the community.

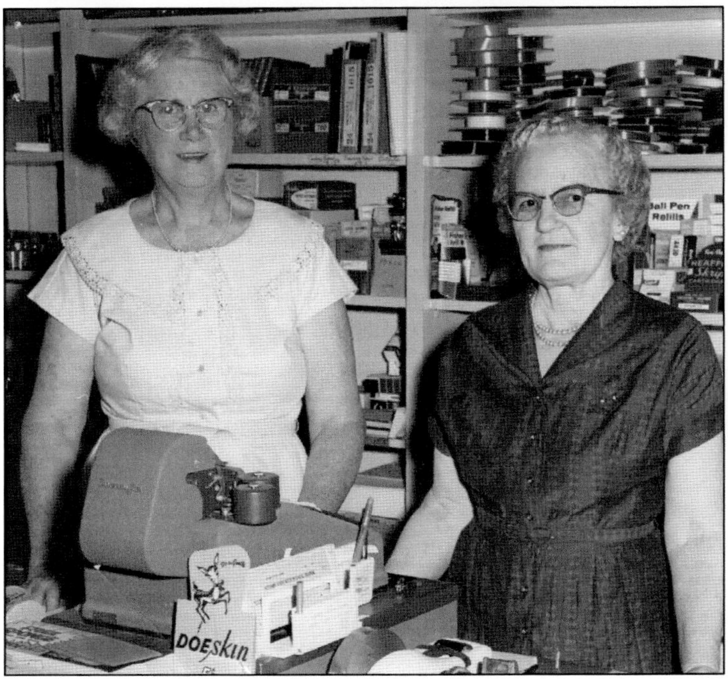

The owners of the Story City bookstore pose in their shop for this photograph. Besides books, this store sold a number of other products to customers, but the influence of local bookstores has waned in recent years.

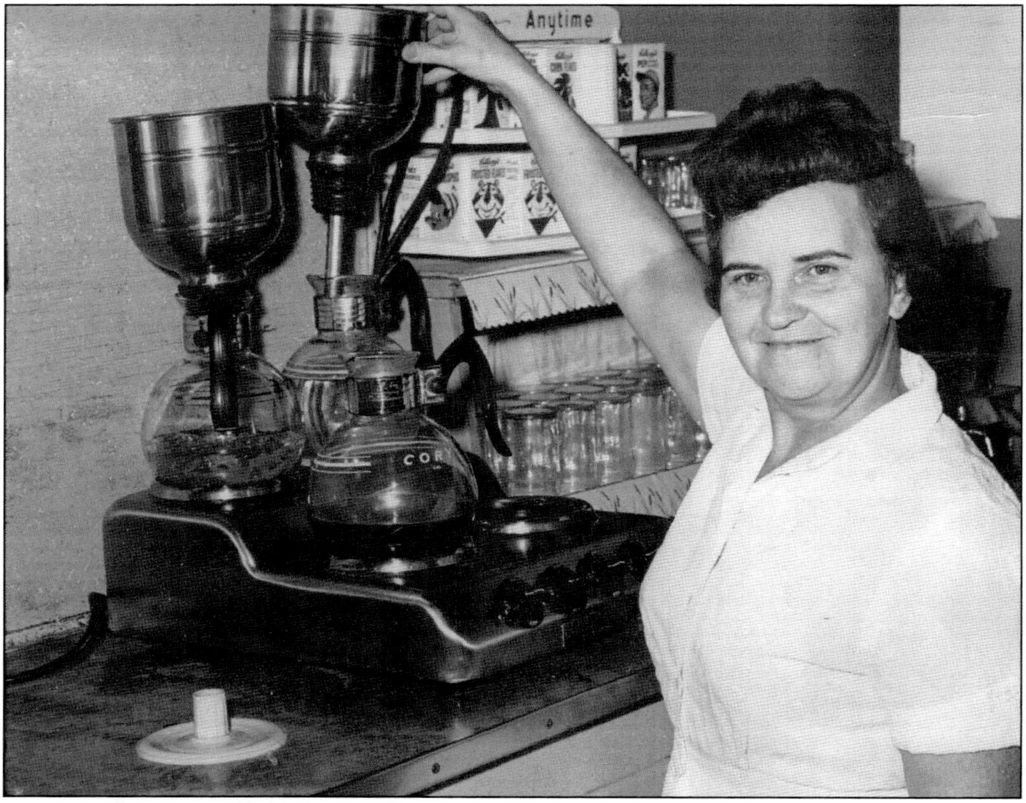

Velda Johnson, the owner of the Story Café at 529 Broad Street, makes coffee with a big smile. On the shelf behind her are small boxes of Kellogs Corn Flakes and Frosted Flakes.

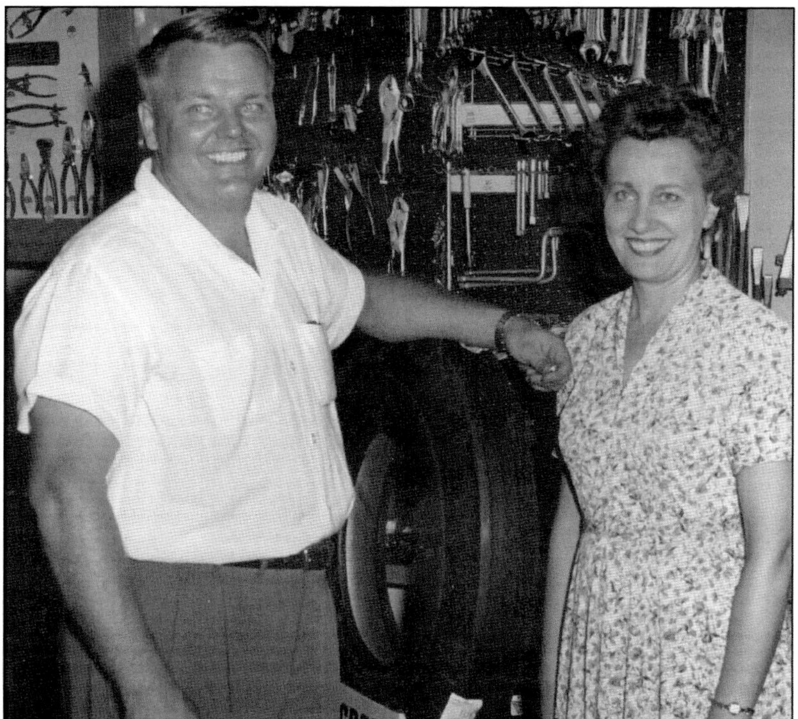

Sterling and Eleanor Anderson owned Gamble's Hardware Store at 525 Broad Street, which sold a variety of merchandise to the community.

As people drove home at night following dances, ballgames, or visits with friends, this scene would have greeted them as they drove down Broad Street. Charlson's clothes shop was a long-standing business in the community and the building is now home to the Story City Welcome Center, an investment office, and an antique store.